Medical Update

The World Book Family Health Annual

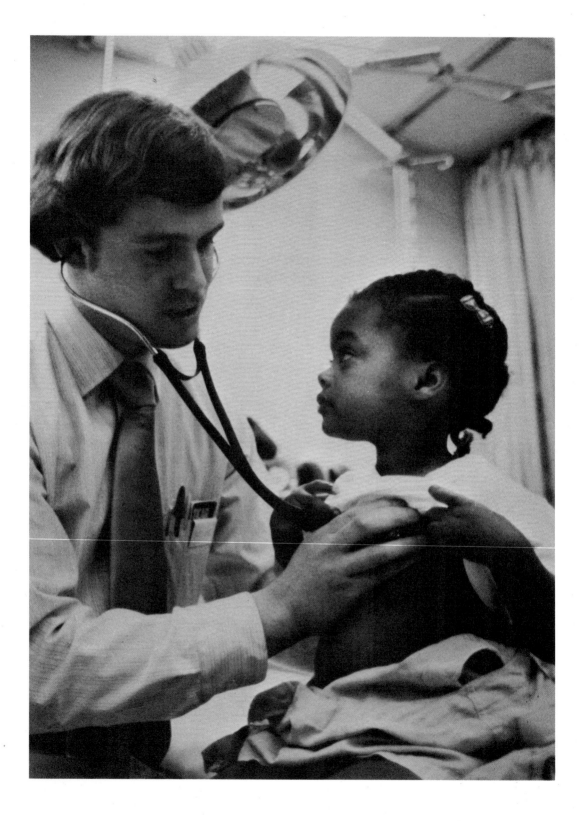

Medical Update 1982

The World Book Family Health Annual

World Book–Childcraft International, Inc.

A subsidiary of The Scott & Fetzer Company

Chicago London Sydney Tokyo Toronto

The publishers of *Medical Update* gratefully
acknowledge the following for permission to use
copyrighted illustrations. A full listing of illustration
acknowledgments appears on pages 261 and 262.

39   © Dan McCoy, Rainbow
43   © Dan McCoy, Rainbow
46   © Peter Simon, Picture Group
49   © Curt Gunther, Camera 5
52   © William C. Pierce, Rainbow
112   © Bill Benoit, Atoz Images
151   © Eli Heller, Picture Group
152   © George Bellerose, Picture Group
154   © Daniel G. Dunn, Picture Group
167   © Christopher Springman, Black Star
178   © Keith E. Jacobson, Brigham and Women's Hospital
189   Joe McNally, *Discover* © 1981 Time, Inc.
193   © 1981 Jack E. Schneider, by Permission of *Saturday Review*
203   © Arthur Grace, Stock, Boston
205   © Tom Campbell, FPG
207   © 1981 Harley L. Schwadron, by Permission of *Saturday Review*
212   © 1980 Sidney Harris, *Discover,* Time, Inc.
217   © Claus Meyer, Black Star
233   © 1981 Rex F. May, by Permission of *Saturday Review*

Preface

Good health and long life may be due, to a large extent, to picking the right parents. Genes notwithstanding, there is a lot you can do to increase your chances of keeping well, or getting well if you fall prey to one of the host of diseases that beset the human race. First, you should know something about how your body works and, second, you should be aware of what medical researchers are finding out about diseases.

Your first line of information, of course, should be your family physician. But a busy doctor usually does not have the time to keep up with all the new drugs, for example, or new surgical techniques. An alternative is to try to become aware of them yourself. To help you, World Book–Childcraft International, Inc., has launched *Medical Update*. It is designed to inform its lay readers of the important work currently going on in the research laboratories. Today, or very shortly, the results of this work may act to cure or prevent many diseases.

For example, did you know that arthritis can strike anyone at any age, and will get most of us eventually? Research is closing in on some of the causes of this crippling disease and finding ways to alleviate the discomfort. In a *Medical Update* Medical Report, Dr. Frederic C. McDuffie of the Arthritis Foundation describes some of this work and warns against quack remedies.

Does everything cause cancer? Sometimes it seems that way. In another Medical Report, Harriet Page, science writer for the National Cancer Institute, quells that notion and suggests that prudent living can help reduce the risks of our getting the disease.

In matters of the teeth, Dr. Paul Goldhaber, dean of Harvard School of Dental Medicine, discusses gum disease, the leading cause of dental troubles, and provides the latest information on its prevention and cure.

Medical Update has a section called Medical File, in which you will find the latest information on a variety of medical subjects listed alphabetically by subject matter.

The editors of *Medical Update* have carefully studied the medical literature, talked with leading medical researchers, and enlisted some of them as contributors. With the help of the *Medical Update* Advisory Board, they have produced a volume that covers the leading edge of medical research. Its contents will be of great interest, and could be of great importance, to the health and welfare of its readers.   [Arthur G. Tressler]

Contents

Staff

9

Contributors

Baxter, Charles R., M.D.
Professor of Surgery and Director
Parkland Regional Burn Center
University of Texas
Medical School at Dallas
Better News About Burns

Caldwell, Frances, B.A.
Managing Editor
*The Physician and Sports
Medicine* Magazine
Sports Medicine

Carmichael, Leland E., Ph.D.
John M. Olin Professor of Virology
Baker Institute for Animal Health
New York State College of
Veterinary Medicine
Cornell University
Veterinary Medicine

Coddon, David R., M.D.
Director, Headache Clinic, The
Mount Sinai Medical Center, and As-
sociate Professor of Neurology, The
Mount Sinai School of Medicine
Help for the Headache

Cowart, Virginia Snodgrass, A.B.
Free-Lance Writer
*Allergy; Birth Defects; Gynecology;
Heart*

Dunn, Eleanor, B.S.
Free-Lance Writer
Fever; Nutrition; Skin; Vision

Finkel, Madelon Lubin, M.P.A., Ph.D.
Assistant Professor
Department of Public Health
Cornell University Medical College
The Second Opinion

Goldhaber, Paul, D.D.S.
Dean and Professor of
Periodontology
Harvard School of Dental Medicine
Dentistry; Grim News About Gums

González, Elizabeth Rasche, B.A.
Associate Editor
Medical News Section
*Journal of the American
Medical Association*
Calling It Quits

Gump, Frank E., M.D.
Professor of Surgery
Columbia University
Surgery

Kempner, Shirlee, B.A.
Science Editor
National Multiple
Sclerosis Society
Multiple Sclerosis

Korcok, Milan
Free-Lance Writer
The Perils of PCP

McBride, Gail, M.S.
Editor
Medical News Section
*Journal of the American
Medical Association*
Blood; Kidney

McCarthy, Eugene G., M.D., M.P.H.
Clinical Professor of
Public Health
Cornell University Medical College
The Second Opinion

McDaniel, Charles-Gene, M.S.
Director, The Journalism Program
Roosevelt University
*Hyperactivity; Mental Health;
Occupational Medicine;
Venereal Disease; Fending Off Fears*

McDuffie, Frederic C., M.D.
Senior Vice-President for
Medical Affairs
Arthritis Foundation
Arthritis is Everyone's Disease

Opp, Marcia J.
Free-Lance Medical Writer
and Editor
*Alcohol; Alcoholism; Birth Control;
Childbirth; Hypertension; Aspirin and
Your Heart*

Page, Harriet Sayles, B.A.
Science Writer
National Cancer Institute
Cancer; Reducing the Risks of Cancer

Phillips, Donald F., M.S.
Free-Lance Medical Science Writer
*Cost of Care; Digestive Disorders;
Neurology; Injury;
Sleeping Disorders*

Reed, Michael, B.S.
Free-Lance Writer and Editor
*Bionics; Bone Disorders;
Virus; Weight Control;
Dealing With Diabetes*

Reidenberg, Marcus M., M.D.
Professor of Pharmacology
and Medicine
Cornell University Medical College
Drugs

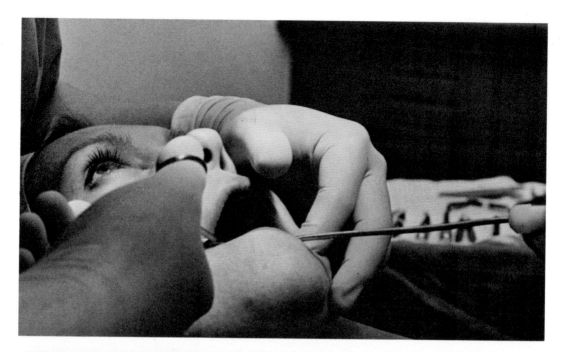

Medical Reports

Medical Reports give in-depth treatment to the major advances in laboratory and clinical medicine.

Dealing with Diabetes

Implantable pumps may replace daily injections

By Michael Reed

Mark Ross scored 30 points for Clifton High School in their final exhausting basketball game of the season. It made him the season's high scorer for the second year in a row. To celebrate, Mark's family went out for dinner at a local restaurant. Mark polished off three cheeseburgers, a mountain of French fries, and his favorite dessert, a double-chocolate, hot fudge sundae. The family arrived home in time for Mark to spend two hours studying for his final exams, which would begin the next morning. Before he went to bed, Mark had some milk and a piece of "victory cake" his mother had baked that afternoon.

Nothing all that unusual for a teen-ager, you might think. But it is unusual, because Mark Ross has diabetes. More precisely, he has insulin-dependent diabetes, a form of the disease that requires its victims to follow a carefully balanced regimen of moderate exercise, strict diet, and periodic injections of insulin. Insulin is a hormone that is produced in the pancreas and normally controls the storage and use of sugar.

So how was Mark able to sail, carefree, through such a day? The answer lies implanted in the wall of his abdomen. It is a tiny electronic device called an insulin pump. The pump continuously monitors Mark's insulin needs and provides precisely the amount he requires to counteract his diabetes and live a normal life.

15

Mark Ross does not exist, but the insulin pump does. In a very short time thousands of diabetics may be living as freely as the imaginary Mark.

Several designs of insulin pumps were in relatively advanced stages of testing in 1981, in animals as well as human beings. Medical researchers are optimistic about the potential of these devices. Dr. Jay S. Skyler of the University of Miami School of Medicine and Dr. George F. Cahill, Jr., of Harvard Medical School reported in the January 1981 issue of *The American Journal of Medicine:* "Five years from now, most patients with insulin-dependent diabetes . . . will likely receive insulin through a portable mechanical continuous delivery system . . . It . . . will be an important step in improving metabolic control of diabetes."

Yet the insulin pump is only one of several recent developments that signal a coming revolution in the treatment of diabetes. With the aid of modern medical science, diabetics are on the brink of a new freedom from the restrictions, complications, and dangers their malady now imposes upon them.

When we speak of diabetes, we usually mean diabetes mellitus. Another, less common form is diabetes insipidus, caused by the lack of another hormone — vasopressin. Diabetes mellitus occurs either when the pancreas, a gland situated behind the stomach, stops producing enough insulin for the body's needs, or the tissues are unable to use insulin properly. Insulin's major role is to stimulate the cells to absorb glucose, a type of sugar from the bloodstream. Your body breaks down much of what you eat into glucose, and your cells use it for the energy they need to keep themselves and you functioning. Insulin also helps your liver to absorb and store glucose for later release and use by your cells.

Without enough insulin, the diabetic becomes weak and apathetic. Even after a good night's sleep, such a person may be excessively tired in the morning. This is because the diabetic's cells, lacking glucose, burn fat, and even muscle, for energy. If this goes on long enough, substances called ketones are formed that can trigger diabetic coma, which can be fatal.

Few people realize what a serious health problem diabetes is. The American Diabetes Association estimates that there are more than 10 million diabetics in the United States and nearly half of them are unaware that they have the disease. Diabetes and its complications account for more than 300,000 deaths in the United States each year,

The author:
Michael Reed is a free-lance writer-editor based in Chicago.

16

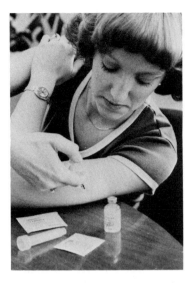

A diabetic injects insulin into her bloodstream at least once a day. This compensates for the lack of the hormone, secreted naturally in nondiabetics, and helps her body regulate its sugar balance.

making it the third leading killer, after cardiovascular disease and cancer. And the number of people who develop diabetes is doubling every 15 years.

There are two forms of diabetes mellitus. The type known as insulin-independent diabetes usually strikes overweight adults. Many of these people can control their diabetes simply by losing weight, thereby making proper use of the available insulin. Others must have their insulin supplemented by injections into a vein in the arm or leg.

Insulin injections are essential for people who have insulin-dependent diabetes, the second and more serious form of the disease. This is also called juvenile-onset diabetes because it usually strikes people under 20 years of age. It is characterized by very little or no natural insulin production.

Those who depend on insulin injections take two or more per day. The amount is based on individual needs. These diabetics use testing kits to measure the amount of sugar in their urine or blood and monitor the effectiveness of the injections.

Insulin injections generally keep diabetics out of imme-diate danger if they also carefully regulate their diet and physical activity. Of course, this regulation seriously crimps the diabetic's life style. And the diabetes poses more serious problems. Some diabetics suffer severe, long-term complications such as blindness, kidney failure, and deadening of nerves in the arms and legs. Other effects are hardening of the arteries and other vascular problems that contribute to possible high blood pressure, stroke, and heart problems.

Doctors who specialize in diabetes feel that most or all of these complications result from the wide swings in the balance of insulin and glucose in the body when injec-tions are its main or only source of insulin. A healthy body monitors its blood sugar and regulates amounts of insulin on a moment-to-moment basis. The diabetic's body must deal with a roller-coaster effect — high levels of insulin right after an injection, decreasing as time passes, particularly overnight. And, blood-sugar levels drop quickly after an insulin shot, and rise slowly until the next one.

The focus of much diabetes research today is on finding a method that will provide insulin to diabetics in a more natural way. The insulin pump may be the answer.

Two types of insulin pumps are under study — open-loop and closed-loop. Open-loop pumps inject a continuous trickle of insulin throughout the day, except at mealtimes when the diabetic adjusts the pump to increase the flow to deal with the food.

Several hundred diabetics in the United States already use open-loop pumps. They wear these battery-powered devices outside the body with a tube delivering the insulin into the body through the abdomen. The pumps are too big to be implanted, ranging in size from 6 by 3 by 2 inches to 5 by 2 by 1½ inches. The most recent designs are a little smaller, about as big as a cigarette pack.

Some of these pumps are little more than syringes powered by batteries, but others are relatively sophisticated. One such device, made by Siemens Company of Erlangen, West Germany, is composed of a control unit and a delivery unit connected by a thin cable. A knob on top of the control unit allows the wearer to adjust the

The Diabetic's Dilemma
In the normal digestive system, the pancreas produces insulin to help regulate the sugar from various foods and permit the liver to process it for storage in body tissues. When a diabetic's pancreas fails to produce insulin, fatty acids are extracted from tissues and processed by the liver into ketone bodies. These, along with sugar, are excreted through the kidneys.

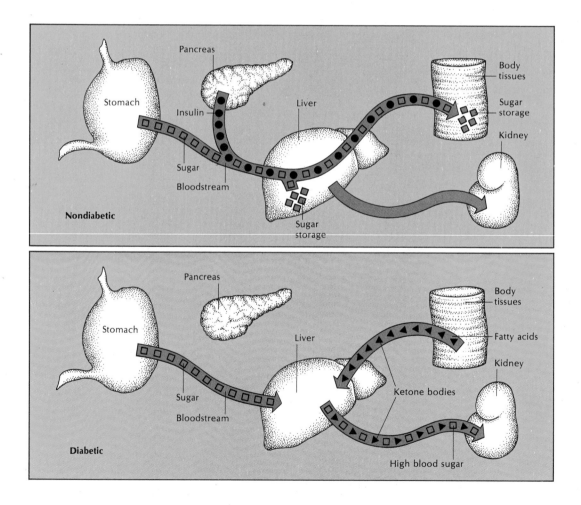

18

insulin-delivery rate. The control unit also has a display readout that indicates the amount of insulin used. An alarm rings if there is a mechanical or power failure.

The delivery unit contains the pump itself, an insulin reservoir, and the connections for the insulin-delivery tube. The reservoir is covered with a special leakproof material that can be punctured with a hypodermic needle for refilling, but reseals itself when the needle is withdrawn.

Open-loop insulin pumps small enough to be implanted are being developed and tested in both industrial and university laboratories. One such device, a product of the Life Sciences Division of Miles Laboratories, Incorporated, in Elkhart, Ind., is about the size of a walnut. Another has been developed by Doctor R. Philip Eaton and Doctor David Schade of the Department of Medicine at the University of New Mexico, Albuquerque, in cooperation with Sandia Laboratories. On Jan. 7, 1981, it was implanted in the abdomen of 41-year-old diabetic Monte Patterson of Albuquerque. After a period in which Patterson's body adapted to the implant, the programmable pump began to deliver insulin on February 10. A report from the University of New Mexico on March 16 revealed that Patterson had not required a single insulin injection during the five-week period.

Success with open-loop devices has increased attempts to develop a closed-loop insulin pump — one regulated by sensing the amount of sugar in the blood. On Dec. 8, 1980, one such pump was approved for use on diabetics by the United States Food and Drug Administration. It is called the Biostator® Glucose Controlled Insulin Infusion System. It had been under development by Miles Laboratories since the early 1970s and has been tested in selected hospitals since 1976.

The key element in this device is its on-line glucose analyzer, which continuously measures the amount of glucose in the diabetic's blood through a tube inserted in a vein in the arm. Blood flows into the analyzer at the rate of 2 milliliters per hour and is sampled every 60 seconds. These measurements are fed to a computer that controls a pump that releases insulin through a tube into a vein in the patient's arm. The amount of insulin is adjusted minute by minute.

The main problem with the Biostator® is its size. The device is as big as a 19-inch television set. So it is not even portable, let alone implantable. Thus its use is restricted to the bedside, where it has performed limited

19

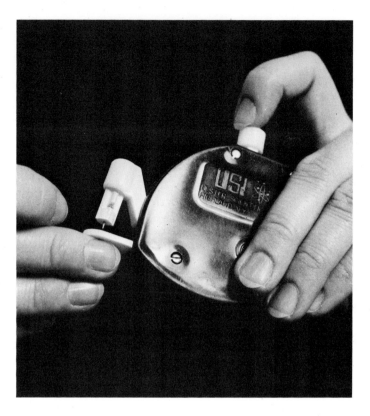

A new device permits diabetics to obtain blood for testing their blood-sugar level quickly and with very little pain.

but valuable duty, such as helping diabetics through the stress of surgery and childbirth, which can play havoc with insulin and glucose blood levels.

Yet an implantable closed-loop pump is probably not too far off. One such device is a glucose analyzer with a diameter of only about three-quarters of an inch and a thickness of about one-tenth of an inch. It was implanted in a diabetic dog in 1977 by researchers at the University of Southern California in Los Angeles and performed successfully.

Although medical researchers are enthusiastic about insulin pumps, they are also cautious. For example, Schade, Eaton, and William Spencer, their co-worker at Sandia, outlined some of the problems that still concern researchers. In an article in the Feb. 20, 1981 issue of *The Journal of the American Medical Association,* they wrote about problems that included finding the best pathway for getting insulin into the body. They are also concerned about the consequences of a high concentration of insulin being distributed to areas of the body that may not be able to process it. And they are not sure how to keep

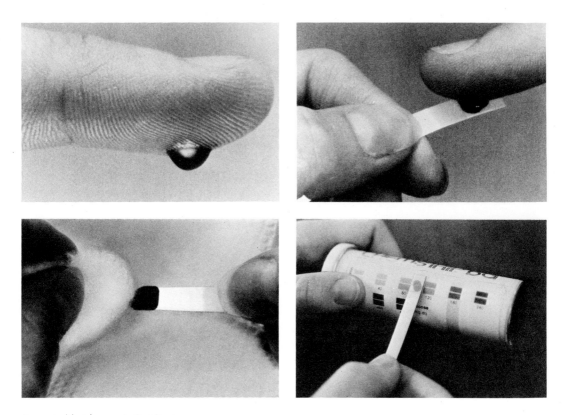

Accurate blood-sugar testing is now possible with a color comparison kit. A drop of blood from a finger, *top,* is transferred to a chemical strip, *top right.* After 60 seconds, the strip is wiped, *above,* and the stain compared to the color chart, *above right,* to determine the blood-sugar level.

insulin from precipitating on the sides of the tube and the reservoir.

Even if insulin pumps become a standard way of dealing with diabetes in the next few years, they may prove to be only a stopgap measure. Medical researchers are investigating the transplantation of islets of Langerhans, cells in the pancreas that produce the body's natural insulin. The idea is to provide diabetics with healthy, naturally functioning cells that will do the job that their own pancreatic cells cannot do. The hope is that ultimately the procedure will permanently reverse all the symptoms of diabetes, and at least in that sense be a "cure."

The major problem with this approach is the one that hinders organ transplants — immunological rejection. The body's immune system attacks and destroys the "foreign" implanted material. There are drugs that can be taken to suppress the immune system, and these would help protect the implanted, insulin-producing cells. But these drugs leave patients vulnerable to infection and disease. In most cases of diabetes, the risk would simply not be worth the gain.

21

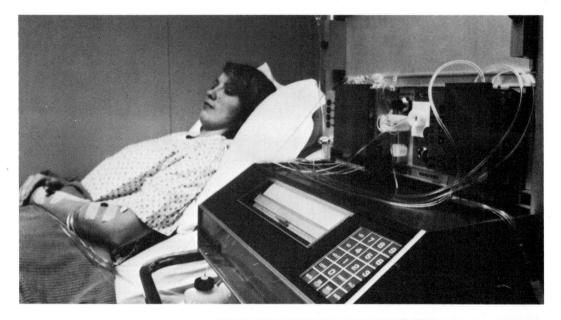

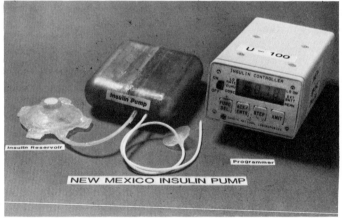

NEW MEXICO INSULIN PUMP

An instrument, *above,* that monitors the blood and releases insulin as necessary is used on diabetics in hospitals during surgery and the delivery of babies. A much smaller insulin pump, *right,* can be implanted in a diabetic and deliver a two-day supply of the hormone.

Recently, researchers have come up with an ingenious solution that is similar in principle to the cage that divers stay inside when they study sharks underwater. The insulin-producing cells are placed inside a miniature "antishark cage." Outside the cage are the body's lymphocytes and antibodies, the elements of the immune system that would normally attack the cells. They stay outside the cage because they are too large to pass between the "bars." But glucose and insulin molecules are small enough to pass between the bars. They move freely in and out, allowing the islet cells to sense and modify glucose and insulin concentrations.

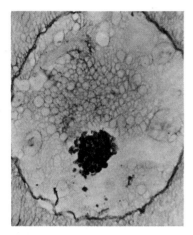

Miniature capsules containing insulin can be implanted in body tissues. The capsules are designed to keep antibodies out while permitting insulin molecules to be released as the body requires the hormone.

Pathologist Franklin Lim of the Medical College of Virginia in Richmond, and physiologist Anthony M. Sun of Connaught Research Institute in Ontario, Canada, reported on this work in the Nov. 21, 1980, issue of *Science*. They described their experiments using insulin-producing cells protected within minuscule hollow capsules composed of a membrane made of a material called cross-linked algin. This material has pores of just the right size for the biological antishark cage.

The researchers implanted the cell-containing capsules into the abdomens of five diabetic rats. They also implanted unencapsulated insulin-producing cells into five other diabetic rats. The unencapsulated cells survived for only six to eight days. But the encapsulated cells not only survived for almost three weeks, but also produced insulin that corrected the rats' diabetes during that period.

A similar experiment was reported in April 1981 by Richard D. Spall and Janice M. Burke of the University of Arizona. They enclosed pancreas cells from fetal rats in hollow tubular chambers made of proteins and a plastic and implanted them in adult rats. They too, observed that the transplanted cells avoided rejection and produced insulin.

With insulin pumps expected to be in common use well within this decade and perfection of a technique for transplanting insulin-producing cells on the not-too-distant horizon, most researchers feel that the outlook for diabetics is bright. Thousands of people like Mark Ross will be living full, active, free lives tomorrow.

Much of medical research is funded by gifts from various sources — the federal government, private foundations, corporations, and individuals. But diabetes research has been aided by a long-eared, pink-nosed, four-footed benefactor — Rabbit 30 K — who has provided the funding for 25 research fellowships.

Until her death, 30 K resided in the laboratories of the Dallas Veterans Administration Medical Center, where she furnished research blood. It contained highly specialized antibodies that are extremely valuable in tests for glucagon — a hormone needed to process sugar in the body.

Samples of the late bunny's blood, which have been frozen, sell for $250 a microliter — about $7.5-million an ounce. Although 30 K is gone, she will not be forgotten. Her stuffed form has been placed on a pedestal in recognition of her distinguished contribution to research.

23

Aspirin and Your Heart

The controversy continues

By Marcia J. Opp

Wouldn't it be wonderful if victory in the battle against cardiovascular disease — the number-one killer in the United States — were to come from a little white pill with which we are all familiar? While even the most optimistic medical researchers do not expect the prescription to be as simple as an aspirin a day to keep heart attacks and strokes away, some physicians are suggesting that a regular intake of aspirin may help prevent death from heart and blood vessel disease in certain cases.

People have become excited about aspirin's possible lifesaving role because it seems like such an easy answer to such a difficult question: How can we help the 40 million heart and blood vessel disease victims in this country to survive? To find out if the solution is as simple as it sounds, we must understand a little more about heart disease and what gave doctors the idea that aspirin might be effective against it.

But don't get your hopes up yet. There is still a lot of controversy surrounding the subject.

Most of the 650,000 persons in the United States who die each year from heart attacks, and the 173,000 who die from strokes, have atherosclerosis, a condition that narrows the arteries through which the blood circulates. Atherosclerosis may begin when the inner layer of an artery wall suffers a tiny wound, perhaps because of a viral infection. In response to the injury, the body's platelets, disk-shaped cells found in the blood, clump together to form a blood clot that stops the bleeding.

If injuries continue to occur in the same location, the lining of the artery gradually thickens with deposits of fat, a clotting material called fibrin, and other debris. Cigarette smoking; high blood cholesterol levels; and high blood pressure may also thicken and roughen artery linings. All these things can narrow the artery, just as the build-up of rust narrows the inside of a pipe. If this build-up blocks an artery leading to the heart, a heart attack occurs. If it blocks an artery leading to the brain, a stroke occurs. Obviously, it would be best to prevent such corrosion.

Researchers have known since 1970 that aspirin can discourage blood-clot formation. It does this by slowing the body's production of two hormonelike substances called prostaglandins that are formed from a fatty acid called arachidonic acid when infections develop. These two substances, prostacyclin and thromboxane, have opposite effects on the body.

Prostacyclin, which is secreted by cells in the blood vessel walls, acts as an anticlotting agent because it not only keeps platelets from clumping together but also expands blood vessels, making it more difficult for a clot to block them. By inhibiting prostacyclin production, aspirin promotes clotting. Thromboxane, on the other hand, causes platelets to clump together and constricts blood vessels, making it easier for a clot to cut off the blood supply. By inhibiting thromboxane production, aspirin works against clotting.

It might seem that aspirin's paradoxical behavior ought to render it virtually useless, but most research data suggest that aspirin blocks thromboxane more effectively than it blocks prostacyclin. Low doses act as clot inhibitors.

Research data from Vanderbilt University School of Medicine in Nashville, Tenn., suggest that doses as low as one-eighth of an aspirin tablet per day inhibit production of both compounds. "But," cautions Garret A. Fitzgerald, assistant professor of pharmacology and medicine at Vanderbilt, "no one knows how much prostacyclin is needed to keep platelets from sticking together, or if complete inhibition of prostacyclin production is harmful. The basic research data just is not in yet."

Instead, results of the major research studies have generated confusion, conflict, and frustration. For example, one study documented an increased death rate for persons taking aspirin, while another showed a reduction in

The author:
Marcia J. Opp is a free-lance medical writer based in Chicago.

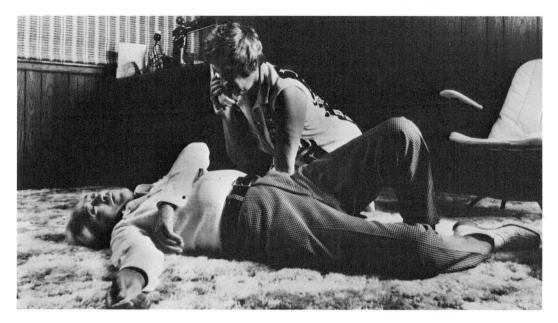

More than a half-million people in
the United States suffer fatal
heart attacks each year. Promptly
summoning emergency aid is vital.

deaths. Enthusiasts and naysayers alike have grumbled
that the studies spawned more questions than answers –
unfortunate endings to efforts involving up to $30 million,
thousands of patients, and hundreds of physicians and
allied health-care workers.

"None of the studies stand out because all have had
design problems," commented Sol Sherry, chairman of
Temple University School of Medicine's Department of
Medicine in Philadelphia. Dr. Sherry reached this conclusion in 1981 after analyzing each study. He considered
the tests' organization, aspirin-dosage patterns, the
amount of time between a person's heart attack and when
they began to take aspirin or a placebo – a substance that
resembles the medication but has no active ingredient –
death rates, and morbidity – the proportion of sickness in
a group or locality.

The earliest hint that aspirin might hold the answer to
the problem of heart attacks came in 1953, when California physician Lawrence L. Craven reported in the *Missis-
sippi Valley Medical Journal* on a study in which 1,465
sedentary, overweight men from ages 45 to 65 took 1 or 2
tablets of aspirin per day for 7 years. Craven said the
aspirin prevented many in the group from having "coronary occlusion or insufficiency." Few physicians took
Craven's conclusions seriously. Perhaps this was because
the study was not controlled – that is, Craven did not

27

compare the aspirin takers with a similar group of men who took no aspirin — or perhaps because the idea was just too new. Then, British researcher J.R. O'Brien reported in 1968 in the British medical journal *The Lancet* on the results of a laboratory study that tested the effects of salicylates, the active ingredient in aspirin, on human platelets. Several similar studies using animals were also published at about the same time. All the studies showed that taking aspirin regularly helped prevent the clotting that can lead to heart attacks.

Results of several more clinical trials conducted during the next 10 years indicated that aspirin prevented blood clots in persons with cerebral ischemia, a condition in which the brain receives an inadequate blood supply. These patients had already suffered at least one transient ischemic attack (TIA), a very slight stroke that is a warning of serious trouble ahead. Physicians prescribed aspirin for them in an effort to avert a recurrence or a more serious stroke, and were fairly successful in doing so.

Also, other studies done during this same period showed that fewer persons in aspirin-treated groups suffered repeat heart attacks, or myocardial infarctions (MIs), compared with persons in control groups who took no aspirin. In three trials, the reduction in death rates among persons taking aspirin amounted to 24 per cent, 30 per cent, and 42 per cent. Although these results sound impressive, they were not considered "statistically significant" according to a rigorous formula devised by statisticians. The formula takes into account the number of patients, the expected number of deaths, risk factors, and statistical variables. Nevertheless, these reductions in death rates prompted large-scale trials to settle the issue of whether aspirin would minimize recurrence of heart attacks and perhaps to hint at whether aspirin should be taken as a matter of course, much as vitamins are, by generally healthy people.

One of the early promising reports on aspirin's effectiveness in preventing death from repeat heart attacks came in 1974 from the Medical Research Council Epidemiology Unit in Cardiff, Wales. Peter C. Elwood, a specialist in epidemic diseases, and his team compared death rates among men who had taken one aspirin daily for two years and men who had taken a placebo. Most of the 1,239 men entered the study within six weeks after surviving a heart attack. Although 25 per cent fewer men in the aspirin-treated group had died at the end of the first year of the study, the figure again was not statistically

How Aspirin Affects Arteries

Platelets produce thromboxane, which influences them to clump together and tends to constrict the arteries they travel in. The blood vessel walls produce prostacyclin, which tends to keep the platelets from clumping and to expand arteries. The substances are in balance in a normal body.

Atherosclerosis, or narrowing of the arteries, begins when platelets responding to an injury form a clot to stop bleeding. Repeated injuries and other agents, such as high cholesterol levels, narrow an artery to a point where a clot may block it completely. Such blockage can lead to a heart attack or stroke.

Aspirin slows production of prostacyclin but slows thromboxane production even more, thereby discouraging blood-clot formation and expanding the arteries.

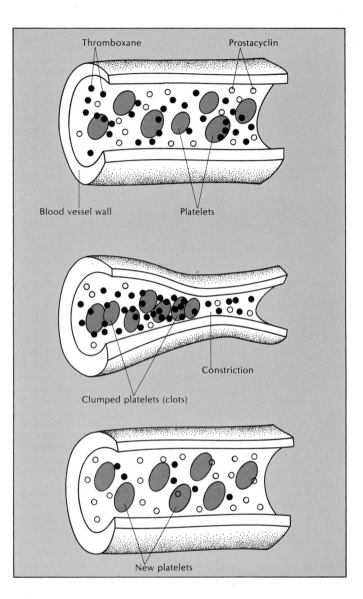

Thromboxane | Prostacyclin

Blood vessel wall | Platelets

Clumped platelets (clots) | Constriction

New platelets

significant because an unknown portion of the reduction in the death rate could have been due to chance rather than to the aspirin treatment.

In 1979, Elwood published the results of a study involving 12 hospitals in Wales. A total of 1,434 men and 248 women took either three aspirin tablets or placebos daily for a year, starting within a week after their heart attack. Although the 17 per cent reduction in the mortality rate in the aspirin group was eight percentage points shy of statistical significance for this trial, the researchers assert-

29

ed that the "difference between the treatments emerges very early, and about three months after infarction little further difference developed."

Philip W. Majerus, professor of medicine and biological chemistry at Washington University School of Medicine in Saint Louis, commented on the trials. He said, "Considering each of the six major coronary artery disease trials between 1971 and 1974, one would conclude that the benefit of aspirin on total or cardiovascular mortality remains unproven." However, Majerus offered another way to look at the statistics. Citing an analysis of the approximately 11,000 survivors of heart attacks in the studies, he said it appears that aspirin reduced the death rate by about 16 per cent. He added that though this reduction is small and difficult to detect, "It is of great importance since in the United States alone, there are approximately 400,000 new survivors of MI each year."

In 1975, researchers began recruiting patients for two major U.S. studies. The studies were not related, but they faced similar problems. The course of research was fraught with friction from the beginning. Chief concerns were which patients were eligible, how much aspirin to give and when to start giving it, and how significant the statistics would have to be to encourage physicians to prescribe aspirin to prevent repeat heart attacks. Finally, researchers in both studies decided to include men and women volunteers ranging in age from the mid-30s to mid-70s who had already suffered at least one heart attack. They were divided into a medicated group and a control group taking a placebo, but only the study administrators knew which group was which. They set aside the question of statistical significance until the end of the studies.

The optimism preceding the launch of the first study, the $17-million Aspirin Myocardial Infarction Study (AMIS) by the National Heart, Lung, and Blood Institute, faded as negative findings began to filter in and ended when results were published in 1980. Because the study was so expensive and so large — 4,021 men and 503 women in 30 U.S. medical centers took part — doctors held high hopes that it would prove once and for all that aspirin could reduce deaths from recurrent heart attacks. However, just the opposite occurred. More people died in the group that took aspirin — 10.8 per cent — than in the group that took placebos — 9.7 per cent.

Researchers were surprised to note, however, that the patients who took three tablets, or 1 gram, of aspirin per day had fewer nonfatal heart attacks, strokes, and incidents of cerebral ischemia than did the controls. The investigators concluded that "aspirin is not recommended for routine use in patients who have survived an MI."

That certainly sounds like a reasonable conclusion, because the statistics indicated that a heart attack patient who took aspirin in an effort to prevent future heart attacks had a higher risk of dying than his counterpart who did not take aspirin. Furthermore, many of the patients given aspirin suffered many unpleasant gastrointestinal side effects, including nausea, heartburn, irritation, bleeding, and stomach pain.

Some physicians who had built up an impressive case for taking aspirin were disturbed by the AMIS results and searched for factors that might have slanted the results. These critics noted that no patient began taking aspirin until at least two months after a heart attack and some did not begin taking aspirin until five years later. Therefore, they said, the study could not assess aspirin's potential beneficial effects during the period right after the heart attack when such effects would be expected and easily documented.

Another key factor that may have accounted for aspirin's poor showing was the way in which the participants were assigned to either the aspirin or control group — a disproportionately large number of high-risk patients fell into the aspirin group. This included persons with a medical history of heart failure, angina pectoris, and arrhythmia, or irregular heartbeat. The net effect of this uneven assignment was that the aspirin group ran a higher risk of dying than the control group before the experiment even started. For the results to be meaningful, both groups should have had the same odds.

The results of the second large and expensive clinical trial differed from those of AMIS. The $8-million Persantine Aspirin Reinfarction Study (PARIS) involved 2,026 patients in 20 U.S. medical centers. It suggested that aspirin can reduce the number of repeat heart attacks if it is given within six months of a person's first attack. Patients in PARIS were separated randomly into three groups: patients in the first group were given three aspirin per day; those in the second group were given three aspirin per day plus dipyridamole (Persantine), a drug that inhibits platelet clumping; and those in a control group were given a placebo. Researchers found the death rate was 16 per cent lower in the group given aspirin plus dipyridamole, and 18 per cent lower in the group given

31

An aspirin a day may keep a second heart attack away, but doctors' opinions on the subject are divided.

aspirin alone, than in the control group.

The total fatal and nonfatal heart attacks were 25 per cent lower in the aspirin plus dipyridamole group and 24 per cent lower in the aspirin group than in the control group. Somewhat paradoxically, patients in the aspirin-treated group had the highest sudden coronary death rate – death within one hour after a heart attack began – but had the lowest incidence of other coronary death.

Very little definitive knowledge has resulted from the cardiovascular (heart and blood vessel) studies completed so far. According to many researchers, the major aspirin and aspirin-plus-other-drug studies have not consistently shown the best time to start and end medication after a heart attack. Although most heart specialists appear to expect greater benefit if aspirin is given early, others have noted subtle reductions in the risk when aspirin is given at later times. Nor has there been a consistent relationship between the amount of aspirin prescribed, which has ranged from one-eighth of a tablet to three tablets per day, and a simultaneous reduction in death rates.

As of 1981, no large-scale studies had been done to determine aspirin's effectiveness as a preventive measure in persons at risk of suffering a first heart attack or stroke. All the studies were secondary-prevention trials, which means that scientists were trying to determine the drug's effectiveness in preventing repeat attacks. Therefore, many doctors hesitate to recommend aspirin usage for anyone at risk, let alone a general population that shows no signs of blood-clotting problems.

According to Dr. Sherry, most physicians who give aspirin to prevent repeat heart attacks do so because it is unlikely to hurt the patient and might even benefit him. But, he adds, "the physicians are not giving it on the basis of any sound data."

"People who are at high risk of developing a TIA — have hypertension, high triglyceride and cholesterol levels in their blood, and who smoke — might very well benefit from taking aspirin," says neurologist William S. Fields of the University of Texas Health Sciences Center in Houston. But unlike some other neurologists and cardiologists, Dr. Fields stops short of recommending it for all high-risk people or everyone over 50 years of age.

In preliminary studies of normal persons taking various amounts of aspirin, "the effect on prostaglandin production is reached at a very low dose — between one-fourth and one-eighth of an aspirin — and doesn't seem to change much thereafter," said Dr. Fitzgerald. However, "the dose-response curve may be very different in people with diseased platelets and blood vessels."

What does all this mean to the person who wants to avoid developing heart trouble? Not very much. A regular dose of aspirin may help, or it may not. Even if it prevents cardiovascular or cerebrovascular ailments, it may upset your stomach. So far, the little white pill has not turned out to be magic. But scientists are continuing to experiment and if you are interested in how their discoveries about aspirin might possibly benefit you, the wisest course is to ask your own doctor.

There is good reason to dread Monday morning, according to medical researchers at the University of Manitoba in Canada. Results of a 29-year study indicate that Monday is the most likely day for a seemingly healthy man to die of a heart attack. The researchers suggested that the psychological stress of returning to work after the weekend may be to blame.

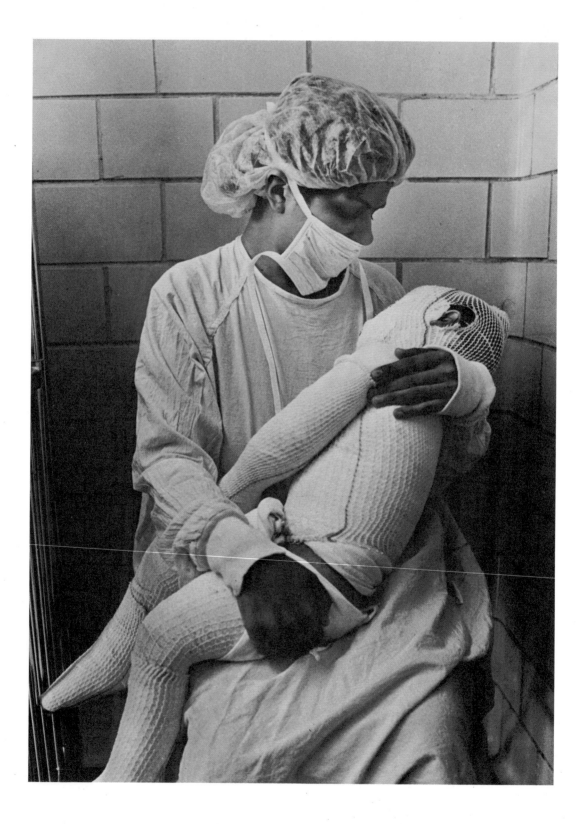

Better News About Burns

Quick action by special teams
saves more lives

By Charles R. Baxter, M.D.

Twelve-year-old Donnie Marlowe was cleaning his dirt-
bike motor parts with gasoline in the garage one fall
evening. His three-year-old brother Timothy stood near
the open door, watching their next-door neighbor burn
leaves in his driveway. A gust of wind blew burning
leaves into the garage, and a glowing leaf came to rest
next to the open gasoline can.

Suddenly, there was a thunderous blast. Flames shot
out from the garage doorway. Timothy ran outside,
screaming and swinging his right arm, his flannel shirt on
fire. The neighbor picked up the boy and rolled him along
the ground until the flames went out. Then he ran to the
garage. Donnie lay writhing in pain on the garage floor.
His face and hands were blackened and his clothes were
smoldering.

This was a tragic accident, but it proved not to be a
fatal one. The boys were lucky to live near the Parkland
Regional Burn Center in Dallas, Texas, the home of a
specially trained burn team. Surgeons and nurses on our
team use the most advanced techniques and equipment to
save the lives of severely burned patients. As the patients
heal, our plastic surgeons, physical therapists, psychologists, and social workers help them to readjust their lives.

Some members of the team even work beyond the walls

of Parkland, as Mrs. Marlowe, the boys' mother, discovered when she called for an ambulance. We had trained the dispatcher to advise people who report burn accidents. After he sent the ambulance to the Marlowes' home, he then told Mrs. Marlowe to watch the boys' breathing and to be sure they were away from all sources of heat. He told her to quickly but gently remove any clothing that might prevent heat from leaving the body. "Do not remove clothing if it sticks to the skin," he said. "Soak it in water at room temperature."

Minutes later, the ambulance crew, also trained at Parkland, arrived and they immediately applied cold, wet compresses to soothe the boys' irritated nerve endings. Burns are extremely sensitive to the touch and even to minor disturbances, such as breezes. The compresses decreased the boys' pain significantly.

The ambulance then rushed the boys to our hospital, where they were immediately wheeled to the burn center. The waiting team of doctors and nurses quickly went into action. First, they checked the boys' throats to make sure that they could breathe properly. Donnie had inhaled hot air and smoke that swelled his vocal cords, narrowing the airway, so a doctor inserted a breathing tube in his throat.

Nurses then bathed the wounds to remove loose skin, bits of clothing, soot, and other debris, and applied antibiotic cream to fight infection. A burn decreases the body's ability to resist infection, and badly burned skin cannot prevent bacteria from reaching underlying tissue. Bacteria had already begun to settle in Donnie's wounds.

The boys were given a special fluid formula intravenously to help them deal with their natural reactions to the burns. A major burn is the most traumatic injury the body can receive. Victims go into *burn shock*. The victim's heartbeat and rate of metabolism — the conversion of food into energy and living tissue — increase while fluids pour into the burned area, dehydrating the rest of the body. Fluids elsewhere behave abnormally, depriving the body of their nutrients, further increasing the need for nutritious liquids.

Accidents such as that of the Marlowe boys account for more than one-third of the 2 million burns that require medical attention in the United States each year. The most common burns in the home are scalds from liquids such as water, grease, and coffee. Others occur when flammable liquids, vapors, and gases such as gasoline, natural gas, paint thinners, and wallpaper glues ignite. About 15,000 persons die of burns each year, while

The author:
Dr. Charles R. Baxter is a professor of surgery and director of the University of Texas Medical School's Parkland Regional Burn Center in Dallas.

36

Depths of Destruction

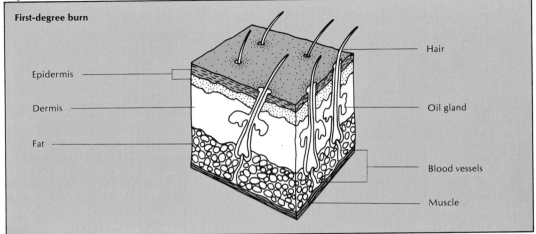

First-degree burn

Hair

Epidermis

Dermis

Fat

Oil gland

Blood vessels

Muscle

A first-degree burn such as sunburn damages the epidermis, or outer layers of skin, but does not affect the underlying layers, known as the dermis.

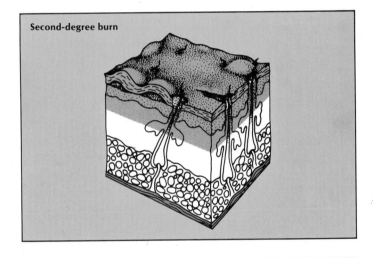

Second-degree burn

A second-degree burn destroys the epidermis and some layers of dermis, but spares the innermost layers that can produce new skin.

Third-degree burn

A third-degree burn kills all layers of skin; destroys hairs, blood vessels, and oil glands; and may even reach layers of fat and muscle tissue.

200,000 burn victims suffer permanent physical or psychological disabilities.

Doctors classify burns according to the number of skin layers damaged or destroyed. A first-degree burn, such as sunburn, is a superficial injury of only the outer layers of the skin. A first-degree burn heals in two to five days. It can be uncomfortable, but is not debilitating.

A second-degree burn is extremely painful, pink to dull-red, and moist. The burn develops fluid-filled blisters within an hour after the injury. The deepest second-degree burns may look waxy and dry, but they are actually soft and elastic. Scalds or burns from hot liquids are much redder and drier, particularly among babies. A second-degree burn may destroy all the outer layers of skin but not the innermost layers that can produce new skin. This kind of burn does not penetrate to a uniform depth throughout the wound. For example, more layers may be burned at the center of the wound than at the edges. Such burns require between 10 and 30 days to heal, depending upon how many layers of skin have been damaged.

Wound depth determines the amount of scarring. For example, if you burn your fingers on a hot skillet, you will probably get a second-degree wound that will heal with normal skin, complete with fingerprints. All your skin has to do is carry out a minor resurfacing project. But when the wound is deep, the body must protect itself by building up many layers of thick, fibrous scar tissue. Burns deep enough to require more than 14 days to heal may scar extensively.

A third-degree burn involves all layers of skin. New tissue will not grow without the aid of an autograft — skin transplanted from another part of the body.

More than half of all burn injuries that require treatment are minor burns — second-degree injuries of less than 15 per cent of the total body surface area in adults or 10 per cent in children and the elderly, and third-degree burns that cover less than 2 per cent of the body. We treat most minor burn victims as outpatients. Medical personnel treating them in an emergency room clean the wounds with a chemical solution and a mild antiseptic, open blisters, trim away loose skin, apply an antibacterial cream to soothe and protect the wounds, and cover them with a dressing. The doctor may also prescribe an injection of tetanus toxoid and antibiotic capsules to prevent infections.

Within 24 hours of the initial injury, the patient will

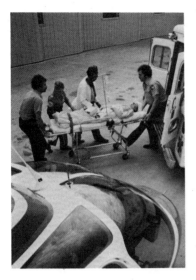

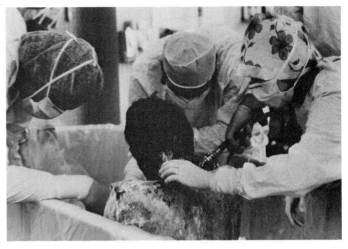

Paramedics transfer a patient from an outlying area, *above,* from a helicopter to a Dallas Mobile Intensive Care Unit that will rush her to the regional burn center. At the center, members of the burn team, *above right,* clean a new patient's wounds and remove dead skin to prevent infection.

return to the center, where the doctor will change the dressing in order to reassess the depth of the injury and the likelihood that it might become infected. After the patient leaves the hospital, the dressing can be changed at home every day. The patient will return every two or three days so that the doctor can examine the burn and be sure that it will heal. After about 10 days, the family physician will take over the care of the patient, consulting with the hospital whenever necessary.

The success of follow-up treatment at home depends upon how well the patient and the family follow the doctor's instructions. The doctor will explain how to clean and dress the wound and how to detect infection. The family must also take simple precautions such as washing their hands and the instruments used to remove the dressing, using chemically treated sponges to clean the wound, and discarding disposable materials. Any sign of infection or inflammation in or around the wound is a signal to call the doctor or hospital immediately. The patient must not expose new skin to sunlight, clothing dyes, strong soap, or cosmetics.

Some second-degree burns are so deep that doctors cover them with a temporary substitute skin that promotes healing and relieves pain. Physicians can use pigskin or human skin for this purpose. The doctors hold the substitute skin against the wound with stitches, surgical staples, or pressure from a dressing. But fluid accumulations under such temporary covers may separate the substitute skin from the wound, giving bacteria a chance to spread. Infection is difficult to recognize in a wound treated in this

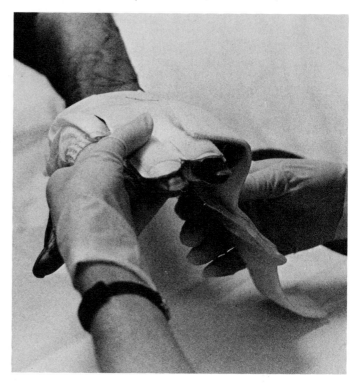

A healing burn patient, *above,*
coats his hand and wrist with
warm paraffin that softens stiff
scar tissue so it can be stretched
to restore flexibility to the
burned area. A therapist puts a
night splint on his other hand,
above right, to prevent scars on
his palm from forming tight
bunches while he sleeps. Such scars
would tend to curl his fingers
when he relaxed his hand and
would limit his finger movements.

way, so patients who receive substitute skin must be
monitored closely.

As the wound heals, the physician determines whether
scar tissue might build up in such a way that it may
disfigure the patient. Scar tissue may also limit motion of
parts of the body, or cause pain with movement. For
example, thick scar tissue forming over the knuckles may
not be flexible enough to allow the fingers to curl properly. In contrast, a scar growing on the underside of a finger
joint may pull skin together, curling the finger permanently. The doctor may prescribe stretching exercises to prevent loss of flexibility and may splint the finger at night so
that the growing scar tissue cannot contract the finger
while the patient sleeps. Special tight clothes called pressure garments keep growing tissues on the body and limbs
flat. Otherwise, scars might form thick, tight masses that
restrict motion. For example, a thick scar behind a knee
might hinder leg movement.

Some second-degree burns may require plastic surgery
after healing — either reconstructive surgery to restore the
function of the body part, or cosmetic surgery to improve
the patient's appearance. The plastic surgeon cuts away

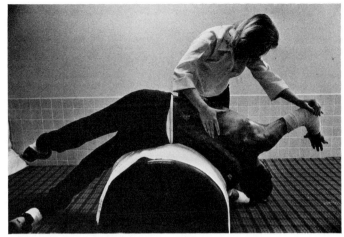

A young patient, *above,* happily stretches healing wounds under his arms to prevent the growing scars from limiting his movement, while a heavily scarred adult, *above right,* must endure a long, painful routine every day to keep his side from stiffening.

scar tissue and applies autografts or homografts – pieces of live skin from donors. If the burn is extremely deep, the surgeon may replace muscle and even bone.

We apply autografts to third-degree burns that cover up to 20 per cent of the body surface as soon as the patient is stabilized. Larger wounds receive autografts and homografts until the body grows more skin that we can use as autograft. We use pigskin on third-degree burns only if a homograft is unavailable.

Some third-degree wounds as they heal require stretching exercises, night splints, and pressure garments to prevent them from forming tight bunches of tissue that would restrict movement. Most third-degree burns require plastic surgery after healing.

While the burn team was stabilizing the injured Donnie and Timothy, it was also determining the extent of the injuries. This would help the doctors decide how to treat the wounds once the boys' metabolism had settled down. Donnie had deep burns over more than 60 per cent of his body. Timothy was burned, but not so deeply, on his right arm, right hand, and face.

Tim's burns were second-degree. Seven days after his injury, we were sure that his wounds would heal, and we released him from the hospital. His care continued at home until his wounds healed 18 days later. Tim follows a regular exercise routine at home to stretch scars on his fingers and arm. He will probably have several small, permanent scars on the inside of his hand, but none on his face or arm. We doubt that he will require plastic surgery.

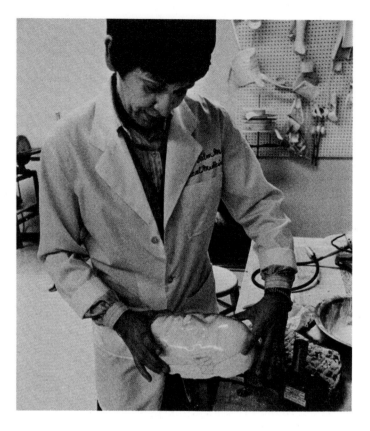

Dr. Phala Helm, head of the burn center's physical therapy and rehabilitation team, examines a facial mold that will be used to make a scar-flattening mask.

However, Donnie's deeper burns required three months of hospitalization, including six operations, and more than two years of care as an outpatient. He will need three more operations on his scars.

Almost all major burns cause extensive scarring and some disability, and if they involve more than 30 per cent of the body, the victim's life is threatened. Even third-degree burns that cover no more than 10 per cent of the body are extremely serious. The care of patients such as Donnie requires special facilities and treatment by specially trained doctors and other medical personnel.

Our ability to treat major burns has greatly increased since the mid-1960s. Until then, a patient who suffered burns over 35 per cent of the body had almost no chance to survive.

Intravenous fluids and antibiotic creams such as those that Donnie received are now our first line of defense against shock and infection. At Parkland, we give major burn patients a formula called lactated Ringer's solution for 24 hours, and then administer blood plasma.

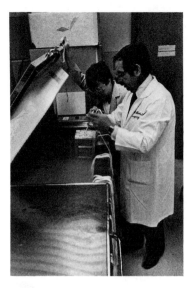

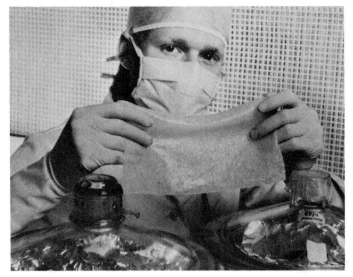

A freezer in the burn center's skin bank, *above,* stores human skin for grafting. The amount of skin in such banks is inadequate, but an experimental artificial skin, *above right,* may ease the shortage.

Patients who survive burn shock and initial infection face further complications stemming from abnormal metabolism. A burn victim's red blood cells live only about one-third as long as normal cells. The patient becomes severely anemic and stays that way for more than two months. We treat these patients with frequent blood transfusions.

Victims of severe burns also require two to three times the nutrition necessary for normal individuals. Burn specialists have successfully met the increased demand by feeding their patients intravenously with nutritive solutions developed for other surgical problems. We use such preparations routinely.

New surgical techniques reduce the danger of infection. Until the mid-1960s, surgeons waited for burned skin to detach itself from healthy tissue before applying temporary skin. Bacteria under the skin spread, killing even more tissue. At the same time, scar tissue began to build up under the dead skin, increasing the risk of disfigurement and loss of mobility.

But then European surgeons began to perform surgery on victims such as Donnie as soon as the patient recovered from burn shock. The doctors removed dead and severely damaged tissue layer by layer until they reached tissue that would accept temporary skin. This technique, which was adopted by doctors in the United States in the early 1970s, reduces the danger of infection, decreases scarring, and lessens the impact of the metabolism chang-

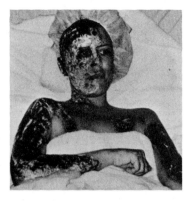

Apartment-fire victim, *above,* begins the slow process of recovery from deep, disfiguring burns. After six years of plastic surgery, she has only light scars, *right.*

es that produce such problems as anemia.

As a result of these biochemical and surgical advances, 85 per cent of the adults and 99 per cent of the children admitted immediately to modern burn centers live. Most patients, if burned over less than 60 per cent of their body, can survive.

After major burns have healed, therapists on the burn team work on the scars that restrict movement. For example, a woman who was burned under her left arm and down her left side must stretch scar tissue until she can raise the arm normally. A physical therapist helps her do this. The patient lies on her right side on a barrel-shaped pad, stretching her body into an arc, left side up. The therapist then helps her raise her elbow in a painful but necessary exercise. Another therapist softens the scars on a man's back with warm paraffin and special creams designed for healed burns. Major burn patients may have to wear pressure garments, do stretching exercises, take paraffin treatments, and wear night splints for one to two years after healing.

During this time, itching and redness, dryness, and thick scars remind the patients constantly of their accidents. And even after the scars assume their final shapes and sizes between two and four years after injury, many

44

patients must face additional years of reconstructive surgery. Months of separation from family, job, and friends, followed by years of surgery and painful treatments place severe psychological stresses on major burn patients. In addition, many such patients must learn to live with disfigurement for years, until the plastic surgeons finish their work.

Psychologists and social workers on the burn team help patients deal with their stresses. At Parkland, a Recovering Burns Group made up of patients and former patients supplements the work of the professionals.

Research chemists have developed special cosmetics that ease the emotional stress of disfigured female patients. Ordinary cosmetics irritate scar tissue, but the new preparations cover sensitive tissue without irritation.

Other researchers are working on temporary coverings. Human skin is better than pigskin for this purpose, so hospitals stock human skin. This skin is removed surgically from corpses of people who indicated before they died that they wanted their bodies to be put to medical use. The skin is frozen in rolls and sheets and can be kept indefinitely.

However, most banks cannot meet the demands for skin, so scientists are experimenting with synthetic skin. One such skin is made up of polymer materials and fibers of a protein substance called collagen. In another approach, scientists take cells from the burn patient and grow them in the laboratory to make a skinlike tissue that they graft onto the patient.

Researchers working on abnormal metabolism may make advances that are even more important to burn patients. Biochemists are studying the abnormal function of white blood cells in burn patients, the abnormal life of their red blood cells, and their dietary deficiencies. Apparently, a severe burn activates abnormal biochemical processes that consume nutrients without normal benefit to the body.

A research breakthrough in any of these areas would greatly increase the body's ability to fight infection, enabling us to save even more patients like Donnie Marlowe.

The population of harmless bacteria that inhabits the surface of human skin varies in density from several thousand residents per square centimeter on the forearm to several million in the armpit.

45

The Perils of PCP

Angel dust is no angel

By Milan Korcok

It is called Angel Dust, Hog, Tic, Superweed, and other strange names. It comes in the form of a powder, tablet, capsule, liquid, crystal, or mixed with leaves so it can be smoked. It can crank you up and let you "float" out of your own body, or plunge you into a depression deep enough to court suicide.

It is the latest in a long line of illicit drugs. Its chemical name is phencyclidine (PCP).

Abuse of drugs is a fundamental fact of American life. The National Institute on Alcohol Abuse and Alcoholism estimates that more than 75 per cent of the people in the United States drink alcohol and that there are perhaps 10 million alcoholics in America.

The National Institute on Drug Abuse estimates that there are between 450,000 and 500,000 heroin addicts throughout the United States. A survey of 17,000 of the nation's 1980 high school seniors prepared by University of Michigan psychologists shows that 6 out of every 10 seniors have tried marijuana and nearly 2 out of 5 have used an illicit drug other than marijuana.

The range of illicit drugs used grows every year. At present these substances include hallucinogenic drugs, such as LSD; "uppers" — stimulants, such as amphetamines and cocaine; "downers" — such as barbiturates, tranquilizers, and methaqualone; solvents and gases; opium products, such as heroin; and cannabis, the dried hemp tops from which hashish and marijuana are made.

There are risks in taking any of these drugs. They all work on the central nervous system, including the brain.

They alter the way the user sees and feels things, and they impair the brain's ability to act as it normally would. But few drugs have raised such concern and anxiety among drug experts, parents, and doctors as has PCP.

PCP, once used as a tranquilizer and general anesthetic for animals, is now one of America's most sought-after street drugs. Experts consider it one of the most dangerous drugs ever to come upon the everchanging drug-abuse scene. And certainly, it is one of the most unpredictable. Federal agencies – the National Institute on Drug Abuse, the Drug Enforcement Administration, and the Food and Drug Administration – estimate that more than 7 million Americans have tried PCP in one form or another. They say that the drug is responsible for more reported medical emergencies than any other drug. Some emergencies include drug poisoning, convulsions, coma, panic, high blood pressure, rapid pulse, irregular heartbeat, heavy sweating, vomiting, impaired breathing, uncoordinated body movements and muscle rigidity.

The Drug Enforcement Administration reports that federal agents shut down 42 illegal laboratories, arrested 315 persons, and confiscated 3.8 million doses of PCP from Oct. 1, 1978, through June 30, 1979. The drug is more widely used now than ever, and various government-sponsored surveys show that 10 to 14 per cent of high school students have tried PCP.

Why do so many teen-agers take a substance that has such a bad reputation, one that has been involved in such gruesome stories? Newspapers, magazines, and television have reported many horror stories – a young man high on PCP gouging out his eyes, another drowning in a shower stall in four inches of water, a young man killing his parents, a mother shoving her baby into a caldron of steaming water, a PCP user pulling out his own teeth with a pair of pliers, a 17-year-old running naked through snowdrifts, a man wandering onto a busy freeway to do pushups.

Many of these stories were sensationalized. Not all the victims had taken PCP and some cases involved combinations of several drugs. But the publicity has created a certain amount of hysteria and has labeled this drug as "a real bummer."

The chemical phencyclidine was first synthesized more than 50 years ago. However, its value as a strong anesthetic and painkiller was not discovered until 1956, when scientists from Parke, Davis and Company were testing its effects on animals.

The author:
Milan Korcok is a free-lance medical writer based in Fort Lauderdale, Florida.

A clandestine laboratory, *above,* is a prime source of illicit phencyclidine (PCP). The pure drug, *top right,* is ground to powder and mixed with tobacco or an herb such as parsley, *above right,* so that it can be smoked.

Pharmacologist Edward F. Domino of the University of Michigan Department of Pharmacology served as a consultant in those early animal experiments and in subsequent human trials. He recalls how cats, given small amounts of PCP, would lapse into catalepsy, or muscular rigidity. One cat sat rock still for 24 hours, only its eyes moving back and forth. An ordinarily wild and vicious rhesus monkey, given low doses of PCP, would sit tranquil and relaxed, eyelids drooping – completely spaced out. A handler could poke his fingers into the monkey's mouth, full of razor-sharp teeth, but the monkey would not bite. It was a perfect demonstration of a drug inducing serenity, tranquility, and peace, said Dr. Domino. As a result of such reaction, the drug was named Sernyl and subsequently Sernylan.

British psychiatrists tried the drug experimentally on human patients in the early 1960s. And in 1963 the U.S. Food and Drug Administration released the drug, known

Too many teenagers seem undaunted by the potential dangers of PCP.

as Sernyl, to Parke, Davis and Company for further testing. But Sernyl soon appeared to produce some serious side effects, including delirium, hallucinations, profound fear, muscle rigidity, and even seizures. In 1965, Parke, Davis and Company requested that further human use be discontinued.

Sernylan continued to be used as an animal anesthetic until 1979, primarily for monkeys. But even that use was stopped for fear that some of the PCP might be diverted to illicit street use. Veterinarians now use a related product called Ketamine.

PCP first showed up as an illicit street drug in San Francisco in 1967 under the name PeaCe Pill (PCP). It then had a reputation of offering a sense of everlasting peace. But that illusion was shattered within a few months. Stories about the drug's bizarre effects and its tendency to provoke violence soon moved it off the streets of San Francisco's Haight-Ashbury district, regarded by many as North America's testing ground for drug trends.

PCP then reappeared as Hog in New York City. However, its bad reputation came along with it, and drug users soon discounted PCP as something to avoid. But the American drug abuse scene demands new fads and trends, and so PCP made a comeback in the mid-1970s. This time, it stayed.

Experimenters found they could control some of PCP's effects by regulating the amount used. They tried different means of using it, and many began to find pleasure in its use. They cited its ability to be at once "an upper and a downer . . . the perfect escape . . . the dream world."

Many felt euphoria. Others just felt tragedy. For example, a young male who was a chronic user left a note before he killed himself. The note, published in the book *PCP: The Devil's Dust* (1981), said:

"My suicide is a must. I am full of anxiety. Depression is too much. My love to Mom, Dad, Brother, and Sister. Thanks to Jane to whom I owe my availability to PCP . . . At last I will be at peace . . . I pray I go to heaven and be at peace forever."

PCP is unique among street drugs because it has so many faces. It does not fall neatly into any one known drug category. It may act as a depressant, a stimulant, or a hallucinogen, depending upon dosage, the way the drug is taken, and the frame of mind of the person taking it.

PCP can be snorted, or sniffed, when it is in powdered form, smoked in combination with other drugs such as tobacco or marijuana, or with such herbs as parsley, mint, catnip, and oregano, swallowed in the form of pills and capsules, and occasionally injected. It is smoked about 70 per cent of the time. PCP acts more gradually when smoked than when it is swallowed or injected.

PCP tablets sold on the street average about 5 milligrams (0.077 grain) and may be almost any color. PCP in powdered or crystalline form is white, yellow, green, gray, or pink.

It is impossible to say precisely how PCP will affect a given individual. It may strike one user as enjoyable, it may cause panic in another. Surveys of chronic PCP users show that more than 70 per cent rated their first experience with PCP as pleasant. But as they continued to use it, most of them reported feeling unpleasant and disturbing effects.

When PCP is injected or snorted, most users report feeling its effect almost immediately. When swallowed or smoked, its effects begin in about 15 minutes and they may last for several hours or days.

Low doses may generate a feeling of "floating" or numbness, or being separated from one's own body. They may also bring on visual or auditory illusions. Often, things seem to slow down for the PCP user. Heavier doses often produce agitation, anxiety, and confusion, and sometimes talkativeness. This may go on to *catatonia* (mental stupor and muscle rigidity), loss of concentration and memory, delirium, and feelings of isolation.

One of the more common hallucinations associated with PCP is a vague sense of death in which the user seems to leave his own body. Some users have described this as a pleasant sensation, others have been plunged

51

into periods of intense crying because of it.

Even small to moderate doses of PCP can cause a very wide range of physiological and psychological reactions. Phencyclidine can produce mental disturbances that mimic schizophrenia, an experience that can be intensely frightening to the user. The drug can also raise blood pressure enough to be fatal and cause rapid pulse and rapid eye movements. Sweating, flushing, drooling, dizziness, and difficulty in controlling body movements are other symptoms.

Psychiatrist Sidney M. Cohen of the Neuropsychiatric Institute at the University of California, Los Angeles (UCLA) reports that repeated use of PCP may result in the destruction of brain tissue and that long-term chronic users may suffer memory gaps, some disorientation, visual disturbances, and difficulty with speech during sober intervals.

Several researchers, among them psychiatrist Paul V. Luisada, medical director at Mount Vernon Center for Community Mental Health in Virginia, have also described a full-blown PCP-induced psychosis — a major mental disorder that impairs an individual's ability to think, communicate, and behave normally. Dr. Luisada has reported such psychoses lasting an average of two weeks in patients with no previous history of psychiatric

The PCP-laced weed can drive its user into states ranging from euphoria to despair, but always a great distance from reality.

illness. Symptoms similar to those of schizophrenia characterize the psychoses — unpredictable violence; withdrawal; feelings of persecution; delusions, users felt they had superhuman strength; and unpredictable feelings toward their families and friends.

Psychiatrist David Smith, medical director of San Francisco's Haight-Ashbury Free Medical Clinic has also seen many cases of PCP psychosis. The doctors, nurses, and counselors at this well-known outpatient clinic and crisis center have been treating drug-abuse victims since the mid-1960's. Dr. Smith says that after the acute psychosis, which lasts about two weeks, some patients remain in a prolonged psychosis, complaining of impaired thinking and depression, for up to 12 weeks.

Witnessing acute PCP intoxication can be a very frightening experience for family members or friends who might have to deal with agitated and often violent behavior. This tendency to violence and to make people behave in a way they ordinarily would not behave may be the most dangerous effect of PCP. In fact, most of the deaths and accidents attributed to PCP are caused by drownings, burns, falls from high places, car accidents, and erratic behavior, not by drug poisoning. Many users become so violent that they strike out at innocent bystanders, or friends, or themselves.

For example, a 38-year-old black man who had smoked marijuana regularly for more than 20 years but had no psychiatric problems began smoking what was described to him as a new "superweed." He found himself becoming paranoid, delusional, and hostile, which was totally unlike him. He stopped using the substance for a day, but his symptoms persisted. He resumed smoking the "superweed," and in a sudden burst of unexplained hostility, he cut off the head of his dog and assaulted a stranger in the street with a razor. When the man went to the Haight-Ashbury Free Medical Clinic for examination and help, attendants found that the "superweed" was marijuana laced with PCP.

PCP appears to have more undesirable reactions than any other commonly used drug, and the more often it is used the greater the chance that negative reactions will set in. Obviously, high-risk groups such as pregnant women should avoid using PCP, because the drug is absorbed directly by the fetus. They should also stay away from those who use the drug. One study has shown that small babies and young children who were in rooms where PCP was being smoked showed up in hospital emergency

53

rooms later with all of the classic PCP effects – breathing difficulties, drooling, rapid eye movements, and alternating stages of agitation and lethargy.

The heaviest concentration of PCP use is in the Los Angeles area, although recent surveys have shown that virtually every state has now recorded some illicit PCP use. No part of the country can now be considered free of this drug.

Though it is impossible to indicate precisely who is likely to use PCP, there are a few general guidelines to suggest who these high-risk groups are. The National Institute on Drug Abuse, after studying a sample of young PCP users in Chicago; Miami, Fla; Philadelphia; Seattle; and Tacoma, Wash., came to these conclusions: The typical PCP user is a young person who identifies strongly with other drug users, many of whom think they understand about drugs and are also willing to take the risks that are part of PCP use. In fact, the challenge of taking these risks and perhaps talking about them later seems to be one of the major reasons for taking PCP. Certainly, this may explain why so many young people continue to take a drug that has such a bad reputation.

Most of the users in this survey came from stable homes; 75 per cent of the fathers and 50 per cent of the mothers held full-time jobs. In 67 per cent of the cases, the users lived with one or both of their parents, and 46 per cent of them were still in school. A stunning 68 per cent of the users were 19 years old or under, and more than half of these ranged from 14 to 16. In a national sample of 2,750 youthful PCP users representing 97 drug-treatment programs, the median age of the PCP users receiving treatment was 16; 61 per cent were male, and 90.5 per cent were white. Parents have a role in trying to determine if their children are using drugs, and doing something about it if drugs are a problem. Neglecting the obvious, hoping it will go away, is one of the worst things any parent can do.

Spotting drug use in a child is often extremely difficult, but there are many signs, short of seeing a child intoxicated, that should raise a parent's suspicion of drug use. The child may act unpredictably, may be unlike himself and become withdrawn and secretive. He may drop long-standing friends and take up with new ones who are drug users. He may become disruptive in school or just let normally good grades slide.

Most experts believe that if a parent suspects a son or daughter of using PCP, it is time to talk to the child

A person in the grip of PCP can become so violent that tear gas and a strong net may be needed to bring him under control.

directly and honestly. They emphasize that the most important step is for the user and those closest to him to be open and honest in discussing the drug problem and determining what is to be done about it. If the parents cannot convince their child that PCP is hazardous and will not be tolerated, then they should seek help. Many schools now have counseling programs that can help both parents and students, and there are various community agencies that deal with drug abuse.

The community also has a deep stake in dealing with PCP. In *PCP: The Devil's Dust*, authors Ronald L. Linder, Steven E. Lerner, and R. Stanley Burns estimate that it takes from $10 to $100 per week to support a chronic PCP user. The authors spent most of the 1970s in research on how to recognize, manage, and prevent PCP abuse. Linder is assistant director of the Department of Continuing Education in Health Sciences at UCLA. He also directs California's PCP Abuse Training and Prevention Project. Lerner, a clinical researcher in drug abuse, is project coordinator for the California PCP Abuse Training and Prevention Project. He has consulted or testified in more than 80 PCP-related homicide cases. Dr. Burns, a specialist in neurology and pharmacology, is staff neurologist with the National Institute of Mental Health. He has had extensive clinical experience in treating drug abuse.

Linder, Lerner and Dr. Burns note that many chronic PCP users end up in hospital emergency rooms at an average cost of $45 a visit. Acute PCP poisoning can require as much as six weeks of hospitalization, with the total bill "not uncommonly hitting $40,000." There is also the cost that nobody can really estimate but everyone knows is there — the community's and the family's

A poster used in a Los Angeles campaign to proclaim the dangers of PCP was drawn by a 12-year-old.

loss of a productive and loved person.

The first order of business in caring for a hospitalized PCP user is to manage the acute effects of the drug such as coma and high blood pressure, to maintain sound respiration and heart function; and to manage psychiatric problems such as fear, anxiety, or panic. This is often done with medications, and it may be helpful to have the patient in a quiet room that shuts out extraneous sounds and sights.

Dr. Luisada says that the immediate treatment goals should be to prevent injury to the patient and to others, assure continued treatment, reduce agitation, and avoid external sensations such as loud and disturbing sounds. After emergency treatment, the patient may have to un-

dergo more extensive treatment of other forms of psychosis. Treatment is often necessary for depression, which is
one of the most serious consequences of PCP abuse.

Says Haight-Ashbury's Dr. Smith: "All clinicians experienced in PCP-induced psychotic reactions agree that the
recovery phase can be quite prolonged and should be
managed on an inpatient basis."

The federal government classified phencyclidine under
Schedule 11 of the Comprehensive Drug Abuse Prevention Act in 1978, subjecting it to very tight controls. It is
illegal to possess PCP for personal use or to sell it to
others. But phencyclidine is a compound that is relatively
easy to make out of chemicals that are readily available.
Consequently, the manufacturing of Angel Dust is widespread; very few of the PCP users surveyed complained
that the drug was hard to get. As a result, many experts
believe that it will take much more than just cracking
down on basement chemists and street-corner vendors to
get PCP off the streets. So long as there are as many
buyers as we have today, there are likely to be sellers.

The answer seems to lie in prevention. Somehow,
potential PCP buyers must get the message – the honest,
unadorned facts about this drug and how it can suddenly
turn peaceful, loving human beings into brooding, violent
creatures capable of murder; how it can warp healthy
minds and destroy happy families. Potential PCP buyers
may then make up their own minds that they do not want
to use this dangerous drug.

Drug abuse is not a recent social phenomenon – opium addic-
tion was already a fact of American life in 1840, when 24,000
pounds of the drug were imported into the country. By 1900,
the annual importation rate had risen to 500,000 pounds, and
200,000 Americans had become opium addicts.

Physicians were largely to blame for this epidemic. They used
opium to treat many different ailments – intestinal disorders,
sprains, inflammation, coughs, colds, menstrual cramps, and
insomnia. Those who became addicted to "the cure" could feed
their habits easily. Until 1914, opium was available without
prescription in a wide array of tonics.

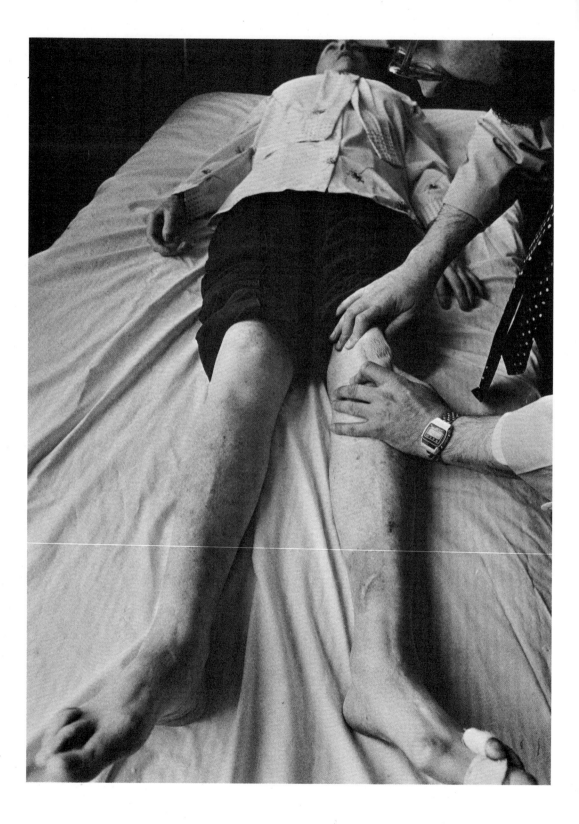

Arthritis is Everyone's Disease

Most of us will have some form of it
by the time we are 60,
but new treatments
may spare us the crippling pain

By Frederic C. McDuffie, M.D.

Elmer G., a pipe fitter, looked forward to his retirement.
He planned to garden and to take long walks through the
woods near his Connecticut home. But soon after he quit
working, in the winter of 1979, he broke his hip in a fall
on the ice. Although the bone mended, he was troubled
by stiffness that became steadily worse. When X rays
indicated that the cartilage of his hip socket was ragged
and enlarged, his doctors diagnosed his condition as
osteoarthritis and began daily physical therapy and heat
treatments, which were largely ineffective. His pain increased and he was confined to a wheelchair. His doctors
tried cortisone injections, but they provided only a few
hours of relief from the pain. Finally, only one option
seemed suitable for Elmer — joint replacement.

The technique for replacing a damaged hip joint with a
plastic-and-metal prosthesis, or artificial part, was developed in the early 1960s by Sir John Charnley, a British
orthopedic surgeon. The first total hip replacement in the
United States was performed in 1968. An estimated
75,000 to 80,000 hip-replacement operations were performed in the U.S. in 1981.

Normal Knee

Knee Replacement

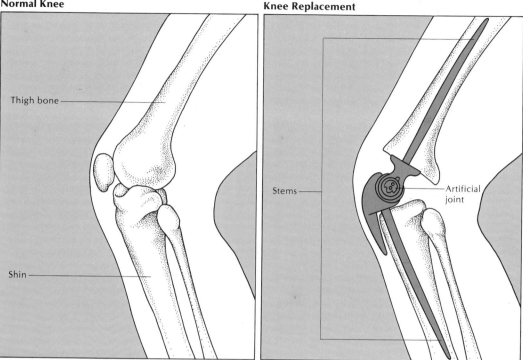

Thigh bone

Shin

Stems

Artificial joint

Artificial joints that effectively duplicate natural sockets can replace knees ravaged by arthritis. A socket made of a cobalt-chromium alloy that does not react with body tissues substitutes for the heads of the thigh and shin bones. It is anchored by stems cemented into shafts drilled into the bones. Protected by the natural kneecap, the new joint is as flexible as a natural healthy knee.

The author:
Frederic C. McDuffie, M.D., is Senior Vice President for Medical Affairs of the Arthritis Foundation in Atlanta, Ga.

Elmer felt that his operation was miraculous. His pain was gone, he could move about normally, and he was able to resume his daily walk. However, Elmer's recovery was not unusual — hip-replacement surgery has a remarkable rate of success, relieving pain and restoring the ability to move in 90 to 95 per cent of those who undergo the operation. Doctors have also begun to replace smaller joints, such as knees, elbows, shoulders, and fingers, although not quite as successfully.

Joint-replacement surgery is only the latest in a long succession of attempts to alleviate or cure one of humanity's oldest known afflictions. Archaeologists unearthed evidence of arthritis in Egyptian mummies dating back to 8000 B.C. The disease drove a Roman general to suicide, forced the bedridden King Henry VI of England to cancel his wedding, and impeded the productivity of French impressionist painter Pierre Auguste Renoir.

By 1776, medical science had identified only two major classifications of arthritis: gout, which is characterized by swelling of the big toe; and "rheumatism," a vaguely defined ailment. By 1935, doctors had recog-

60

Shoulder Socket Replacement

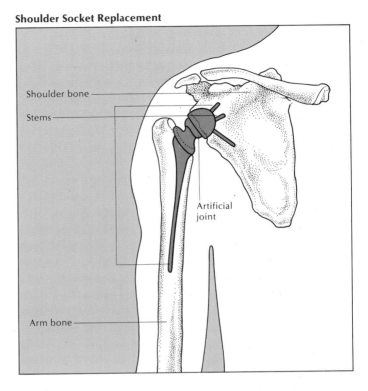

Shoulder bone

Stems

Artificial joint

Arm bone

An artificial shoulder enables the arthritis sufferer to resume normal activities such as lifting, reaching and throwing, that were once impossible because of excruciating pain. The joint is held in place by three short pins embedded in the shoulder bone and a longer stem anchored to the upper arm bone.

nized 12 categories of arthritis; today, there are more than 100 known forms of the disease.

Because it affects so many people, arthritis has been called "everybody's disease." According to the Arthritis Foundation in Atlanta, Ga., 1 in 7 people in the United States — more than 31 million Americans — currently has some form of arthritis and almost everyone can expect to develop some form of arthritis after the age of 60.

Elmer suffered from arthritis in its most common form, *osteoarthritis*. It has become known as a disease of old age because 97 per cent of X rays taken of persons over 60 show some evidence of osteoarthritis. However, only about 33 per cent of these people have troublesome symptoms.

In osteoarthritis, the joints gradually wear out due to simple use and injury as the body ages. First, cracks develop in the cartilage — the fibrous material covering the ends of the bones. When new cartilage grows during the healing process, it does so in an irregular pattern, over the original smooth surface. Sometimes the cartilage may wear out completely. When the cartilage between two

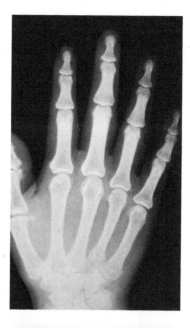

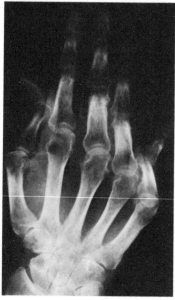

In an X ray, the bones of a normal hand, *top,* appear straight and uniform; the finger joints are well defined. In a hand gnarled by arthritis, *above,* the heads of the bones are misshapen. Ghostlike images at the joints are cartilage deposits that have distorted and immobilized the hand.

bones is lost, the bones no longer slide smoothly over each other. Instead, they rub against each other, causing friction. Moving these joints then becomes painful, and sometimes even impossible.

Scientists do not know exactly what causes osteoarthritis, but they suspect that heredity plays an important role. One form of osteoarthritis, Heberden's nodes, in which the bone and cartilage in the finger joints become enlarged, appears to run in families. Heredity may also determine at what age osteoarthritis first occurs.

Osteoarthritis can also strike young people, especially when there is excessive wear and tear on certain joints. Athletes, ballet dancers, and others in physically demanding occupations often develop this form of arthritis. Many professional football players have been sidelined permanently by osteoarthritis in their knees, and coal miners and construction workers often develop osteoarthritis in the shoulder.

Osteoarthritis is limited to the joints and thus does not cause general illness. However, other forms of arthritis, such as rheumatoid arthritis, have much more complex and serious symptoms.

Rheumatoid arthritis is often a chronic, or long-lasting, disease accompanied by inflammation – a reaction of various body tissues characterized by swelling, redness, pain, and heat. The disease affects more than 1 million people in the United States, and usually strikes people between the ages of 20 and 50, although it can start at any age. And, for some unexplained reason, 3 of every 4 rheumatoid arthritis victims are women.

Allison M., a college freshman, had been feeling run-down for a week. She was exhausted, had a low fever, and her joints felt stiff and sore. She attributed her symptoms to a virus that had been going around campus and the pressures of final exams. However, when she went home at the end of the term, still feeling under the weather, the family doctor diagnosed her condition as rheumatoid arthritis. As in Allison's case, rheumatoid arthritis may masquerade as the flu or a viral infection. Its symptoms – fatigue, fever, and stiff, sore joints – last a few days and then go away, only to return later. Physical and emotional stresses like those of finals' week may make the condition worse. Rheumatoid arthritis most often affects the joints of the hands, arms, feet, and legs, but internal organs – particularly the heart, lungs, eyes, and blood vessels – can also become inflamed.

As with other forms of the disease, rheumatoid arthritis

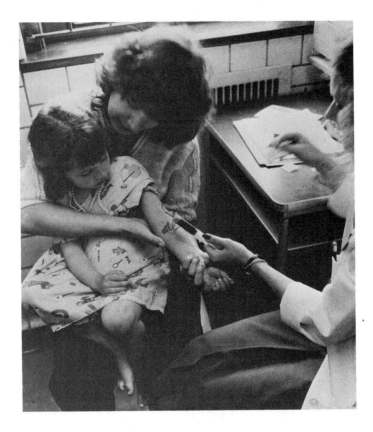

A blood sample drawn from a little girl's arm can reveal whether she is one of some 250,000 children who suffer from arthritis.

can be very mild or it can be a severely crippling condition. The disease may run three different courses. Thirty-five per cent of rheumatoid arthritis victims have a mono-cyclic (single-cycle) form of the disease. These people have severe attacks lasting for up to two years, and then the illness disappears, usually not to return. For about 15 per cent of rheumatoid arthritis sufferers, the disease gets progressively worse and may eventually destroy vital organs, such as the heart and lungs. In the remaining 50 per cent, the disease comes and goes for the rest of their lives. These people have a polycyclic (many-cycle) form of the disease.

Autoimmunity, a condition in which the body's immune system malfunctions and begins attacking its own healthy cells, also plays a role in rheumatoid arthritis. However, it is even more of a factor in one of the most complex and mysterious diseases in the arthritis family — *systemic lupus erythematosus*.

Lupus strikes nine times as many women as it does men, usually during the childbearing years. Lupus has no

63

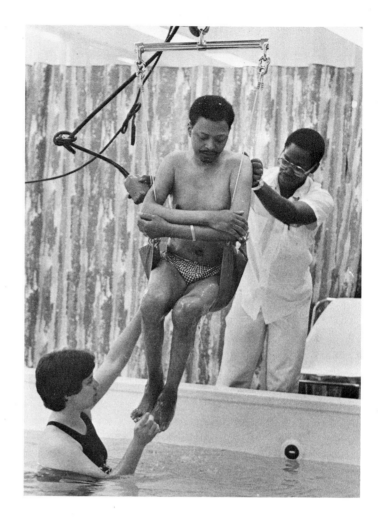

An arthritis sufferer is lowered into a tub for hydrotherapy — actually two treatments in one. His inflamed joints will be soothed by the heat of the water and his limbs exercised as his therapist guides him through a series of maneuvers to improve flexibility.

single pattern or set of symptoms. Because of this, it is sometimes extremely difficult to diagnose, requiring months of observation and many laboratory tests. Lupus affects each person differently. It can be a mild condition, or it can be very serious — involving joints and skin, kidneys, blood, heart, brain, and other internal organs. Thirty years ago, lupus in its severe form was nearly always fatal, but improved diagnostic methods and drugs that keep the immune system from running amuck have made lupus deaths much less common.

Scleroderma is another arthritic disease that discriminates against women — primarily those in their 40s and 50s. Literally, "hard skin," it is a disorder of the body's connective tissue — especially of collagen, a protein that forms a major part of cartilage, bone, and skin. In sclero-

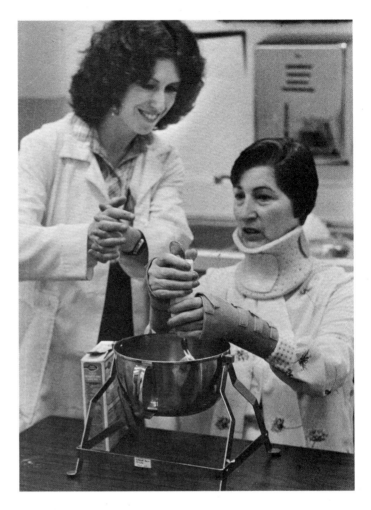

Everyday chores such as mixing cake batter can provide valuable therapy for arthritis victims. Wrist supports and a stand to raise and steady the bowl help a woman to perform this once-impossible task.

derma, excess collagen builds up. This causes the skin, especially that over the fingers, arms, and face, to become hard and thick. In some cases, collagen build-up or scarring extends to the internal organs, and this may severely damage the lungs, heart, kidneys, and digestive system.

Unlike most other forms of arthritis, *ankylosing spondylitis* — an inflammatory arthritis of the spine — affects more men than women. It usually begins in the teens or early 20s with pain and stiffness in the lower back. In its worst form, the joints of the spine fuse progressively until the spine is completely rigid. It may also affect other joints, especially the hips and shoulders. People who have a certain type of molecule on the surface of body cells, called HLA B27, have a greater

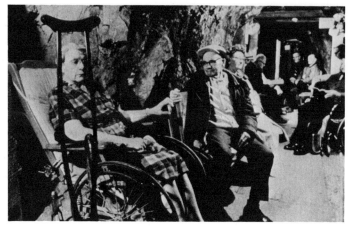

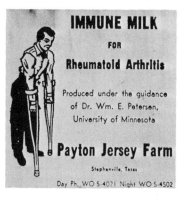

Historically, arthritis sufferers
have invested great hope and millions
of dollars in quack cures. Arabs of
the Middle Ages received a hot iron
wielded by the local barber as a
treatment for rheumatism, *top*.
The mysterious, yet ineffective
properties of "immune milk" were
touted in the mid-1900s, *above*. Some
arthritics received dangerous doses
of radiation by "taking the cure" in
uranium mines, *top right*. Although
the copper bracelet will not harm its
wearer, it will not cure her of
arthritis, either, *opposite page*.

tendency than others to develop this disease.

Gout, another inherited, but less serious form of arthritis, was once considered a wealthy man's disease because it seemed to strike those who ate too much rich food and drank too much alcohol. However, rich food and alcohol do not cause the condition, although they can make it worse. Most cases of gout are caused by a genetic defect in which the body contains too much uric acid. Because the kidneys cannot get rid of the extra uric acid fast enough, it forms needlelike crystals in the joints, causing inflammation and acute pain. The big toe is usually the first joint to be affected.

Although gout cannot be cured, most cases can be effectively controlled through diet and medications. People who suffer from gout should avoid foods such as liver, kidney, sweetbreads, beans, and peas, that are high in purine, a substance that breaks down into uric acid. Gout patients may be treated with a variety of drugs that limit the average attack to from three to five days.

Juvenile arthritis is a catchall term for several kinds of arthritis that may begin as early as infancy. With treatment, most children either outgrow the disease or suffer only minor effects. However, some children are forced to live with some disability for the rest of their lives.

What doctors can do for any case of arthritis depends on the form and severity of the disease. For the majority of patients with mild to moderate disease, treatment begins with aspirin, the single most important drug for arthritis. Aspirin is both an *analgesic,* or painkiller, and an anti-inflammatory agent that reduces the redness and swelling that accompany inflammation.

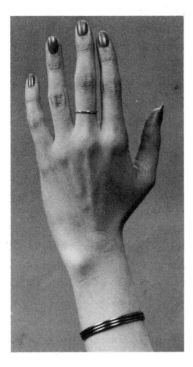

However, the dosage of aspirin determines its effectiveness. To take full advantage of the anti-inflammatory powers of aspirin, a physician may prescribe as many as 24 tablets per day for several weeks. Although aspirin is by far the safest anti-inflammatory drug available, the high dosages can cause upset stomachs and other side effects.

For those who cannot tolerate aspirin, the physician will prescribe other, more expensive, anti-inflammatory drugs. These may be drugs that work much like aspirin, such as Andomethacin; or steroids, such as cortisone. But such drugs also may have many serious side effects. For example, cortisone may keep the immune system from fighting infections, and cause diabetes.

To relieve pain temporarily, doctors may inject cortisone directly into the joints rather than prescribe it in pill form. Because it is directed precisely at the trouble spot, the drug has fewer side effects when injected.

One of the most important new anti-arthritis drugs is penicillamine, which can suppress inflammation for longer periods of time than analgesics. Other powerful drugs are currently being tested by the U.S. Food and Drug Administration. All of them have serious side effects, and some may make the patient more uncomfortable than the disease itself.

One drug awaiting FDA approval is Auranofin, a form of gold that is taken orally. Although rheumatoid arthritis patients have been helped by gold injections for more than 50 years, a preparation that could be given by mouth would make the drug easier to administer.

Physicians usually prescribe rest as well as medication to keep the joints from being damaged. This may be bed rest to allow the entire body to recover, or rest for individual joints, which usually means using splints to keep them immobile.

This rest may be alternated with exercise or other forms of physical therapy to keep joints from becoming permanently stiff. Such exercise usually involves gentle movements designed to put the joints through their full range of motion, rather than strenuous workouts. Heat is also a valuable therapy for arthritis. Warm baths, heating pads, and melted paraffin may be used to soothe stiff and aching joints.

In many cases, medication, rest, and exercise are not sufficient to allay the ravages of arthritis' most serious forms. Then the disease can damage the joints so badly that the victim suffers excruciating pain and finds it difficult, and at times impossible, to move. Then joint replacement therapy, like the type Elmer G. underwent, becomes the best form of treatment.

Unfortunately, the treatments prescribed by physicians – rest, exercise, medication, and surgery – are not the only therapies sought by arthritis patients. Many turn to unorthodox treatments or unproved drugs and devices, which have become a huge business – grossing an estimated $1 billion annually. Since arthritis cannot yet be cured, victims are sometimes willing to try anything. If they try drinking a mineral water, or wearing a copper bracelet, and their condition improves, they are likely to think that they are feeling better because of the treatment. However, more often than not, this improvement is due to the cyclic nature of the disease – the symptoms are disappearing as the disease goes into remission. The disease might improve temporarily without any type of treatment whatsoever.

Also, any new treatment may appear to work because of the *placebo effect*. Placebos are inactive substances such as sugar tablets that are sometimes given to patients, who are told that they are getting some form of medicine. The patients' belief that they are receiving a cure may trigger the release of powerful painkilling substances in the brain.

According to Arthritis Foundation estimates, 25 times the amount that goes for scientific arthritis research is spent on such unorthodox treatments. These treatments may be harmless, hurting only the arthritis sufferer's pocketbook. Or, they can be extremely dangerous – like the radioactive jewelry advertised as an arthritis cure a few years ago, which was eventually found to increase the chances of getting skin cancer. Experimentation with quack remedies, in place of proper medical care, can lead to needless crippling and permanent, unnecessary damage to the joints.

Arthritis research has produced many successful treatments, and current areas of investigation hold great promise for the future. One of the most exciting avenues of research has evolved from the recent discovery that certain types of genetic markers – proteins that serve as identification tags for the body's cells – are found in many people who develop such diseases as spondylitis and rheumatoid arthritis. Although some people who have a given marker do not develop the corresponding form of arthritis, and some who have these diseases do not have any of the markers, scientists suspect that the markers signal a susceptibility to the particular disease, which is triggered by an outside agent such as a virus.

Scientists at Yale University in New Haven, Conn., discovered that viruses transmitted by the bite of a wood tick are responsible for *Lyme arthritis,* a recently identified disease. This leads researchers to think that other forms of arthritis may be caused by bacteria and viruses.

Although arthritis cannot yet be cured, modern forms of treatment offer the assurance that no case of arthritis is hopeless. Early detection and prompt, proper medical care can minimize pain and prevent deformity. But, for medical science, the task remains to pinpoint the causes of these diseases, so that they — and the misery they cause — can be eliminated.

It has long been known that such strenuous activities as football and ballet dancing cause great wear and tear to the body's joints — often resulting in arthritis. However, in 1980 and 1981 a series of reports to *The New England Medical Journal* made it apparent that even sedentary pastimes may carry the same risks.

A medical student reported developing a baffling stiffness and pain in his right wrist. He had no history of disease and could not recall injuring the joint. However, the ailment had appeared after he had become addicted to a video game that required the player to guide a spacecraft through a field of attack by operating a lever on a remote-control box. As he became more skilled at the game, his wrist maneuvers became quite elaborate, taxing the ligaments in his lower arm. When he abandoned the game for final exams, the ailment disappeared.

A Northern California physician reported two cases of severe right-shoulder pain. Like the medical student, neither patient could recall a recent injury to the joint. Subsequent questioning revealed, however, that both patients had paid recent visits to casinos at Lake Tahoe, Nevada, and that both had spent many hours playing the slot machines there — producing excessive strain on the right shoulders.

These two afflictions, suitably recorded in the annals of medicine as "Space-Invaders Wrist" and "Slot-Machine Tendinitis," may be only the first in a series of new disabilities — exertion ailments that can be contracted without leaving one's chair.

69

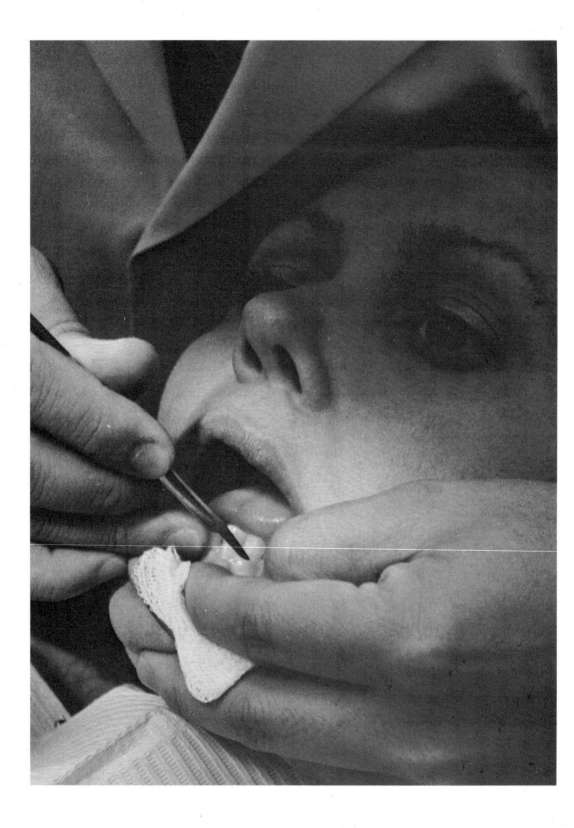

Grim News About Gums

Millions of healthy teeth each year are lost to periodontal disease

By Paul Goldhaber, D.D.S

As a dentist, I have often heard the old joke, "Your teeth are OK, but your gums will have to go." As a periodontist — a specialist in gum disease — I do not view this as a joke. For many people, this situation is a sad reality.

Many dental patients over the age of 30, with few cavities and teeth in good condition, lose their teeth to gum disease. In fact, gum disease is the leading cause of tooth loss among adults throughout the world today.

Although the serious effects of gum disease usually do not appear until persons are in their 30s or early 40s, the disease often begins in adolescence. Researchers estimate that most adolescents have gingivitis, an inflammation of the gums, and that 75 per cent of all American adults have periodontitis, or pyorrhea, a more serious form of gum disease that affects the underlying bone.

Modern dental care and hygiene, along with fluoridated water supplies, have cut the percentage of tooth loss due to decay. People therefore have the potential to keep their teeth far longer than they did even 25 years ago. Yet it is this very fact that has made gum disease a major dental problem.

Dental caries, or cavities, have received a great deal of attention from dentists and the public, perhaps because this disease mainly afflicts younger people. In forming caries, bacteria attack the tooth, dissolving the protective enamel cover, the hardest material in the human body. If the decay is not treated, it can destroy the inner pulp, commonly called the "nerve," and eventually cause an abscess to form at the tip of the tooth's root. Dentists treat caries by removing the decay and replacing the missing tooth structure with a filling or crown. Even infected pulps can be removed and treated by root-canal procedures. Thus, caries can advance pretty far, and yet the tooth can be saved by modern dental techniques. But if the tissues that hold a tooth in place are destroyed by *periodontal disease,* even a healthy tooth may be lost.

The roots of a healthy tooth are anchored deep in the underlying bone by tissue fibers that make up the periodontal ligament. The bone is covered by the gingivae, or gums, up to the neck of the tooth, where the root and the exposed portion, or crown, meet.

Like caries, periodontal disease is caused by bacteria, although of different types. The bacteria adhere to the teeth and form plaque. Even with fairly good dental hygiene, some plaque forms and with time becomes calcified or hardened into material called tartar or calculus. Dentists once thought that mechanical irritation from the tartar was the principal cause of gum disease, but the bacteria in and on the calculus are now thought to be the main problem. Housed in and supported by the tartar they have made around the crown of the tooth, they give off chemical products that attack the gum tissue.

As periodontal disease begins, inflammation caused by the bacterial infection causes little spaces to form between the gum and the affected teeth. This, the gingivitis stage of gum disease, is not necessarily painful. Gingivitis may linger on for many years without growing worse, but as a rule it develops into the more serious stage.

In periodontitis, the inflammation leads to destruction of the underlying bone. This destruction begins at the surface of the root closest to the crown and progresses slowly down through the bone along the root. As the bone is destroyed, the periodontal ligament detaches from the root surface, creating a space, or pocket, between the gum and the root. This pocket harbors masses of bone-destroying bacteria, setting up a vicious cycle of deepening pockets and further bone loss. If this cycle continues unchecked, the teeth will loosen and eventually have to be pulled out.

The symptoms of periodontal disease vary from person to person. Common symptoms of gingivitis include swelling, redness of gums, and bleeding gums after brushing.

The author:
Paul Goldhaber is a periodontist and dean of the Harvard School of Dental Medicine.

72

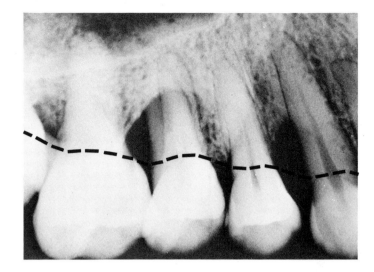

Healthy gums, *below,* fit snugly against the crown of a tooth. But when gum disease develops, *below right,* deep pockets of bacteria form between the tooth and gum, destroying bone and the periodontal ligament that anchors the root. When bone has been eroded from its normal level, *right* (dotted line), almost to the root tip, the tooth cannot be saved.

How Periodontal Disease Develops

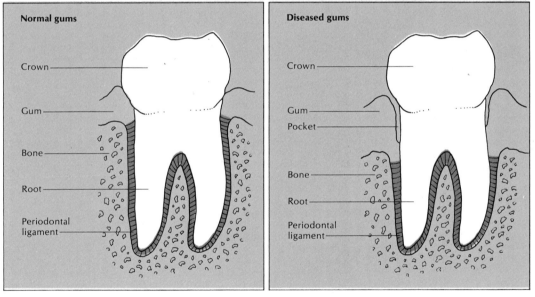

Normal gums

Crown
Gum
Bone
Root
Periodontal ligament

Diseased gums

Crown
Gum
Pocket
Bone
Root
Periodontal ligament

Patients with advanced periodontitis may have receding gums and exposed roots; loose teeth; abscesses on the gums, which may be painful; pus around the teeth; and bad breath. However, persons with early periodontal disease may have only a few of these symptoms, which they might fail to recognize or choose to ignore.

Dentists are trained to recognize the onset of periodontal disease, even in the absence of obvious symptoms.

73

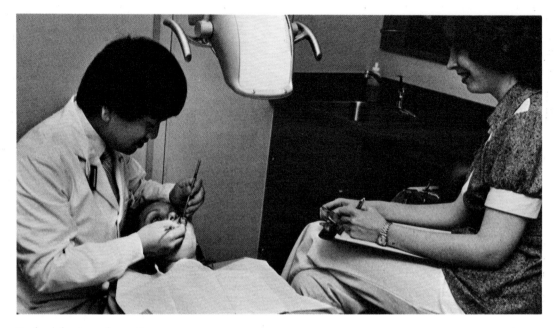

To check for signs of gum disease, a periodontist inserts a special probe between a patient's teeth and gums, while his assistant records how far the probe enters.

They check for pocket formation by examining the areas around the teeth with a periodontal probe, a thin instrument marked off in millimeters. The dentist inserts the probe between the patient's teeth and gums and measures how far in it will go. If it enters more than three millimeters, the dentist knows a pocket has formed. Dentists also use X rays to check for bone loss around the tooth.

The leading cause of periodontal disease is poor or inadequate dental hygiene — allowing plaque to build up around and between the teeth. However, certain diseases and other bodily conditions may also affect the periodontal tissues. These include diabetes, infectious mononucleosis, leukemia, nutritional deficiencies, stress, white blood cell disorders, and normal changes during pregnancy or puberty. Excessive biting force, such as teeth clenching or grinding, can also aggravate any breakdown of periodontal tissues.

Gingivitis, the milder form of gum disease, is fairly easy to treat. The dentist usually cleans the teeth thoroughly, scrapes off the calculus that has formed on the tooth surface, and prescribes a routine of home care that includes frequent brushing and use of dental floss.

But there is no simple remedy once periodontitis, with its pockets of infection, is established and areas of supporting bone are lost. No amount of brushing or flossing can reach the calculus and bacteria in the deep pockets.

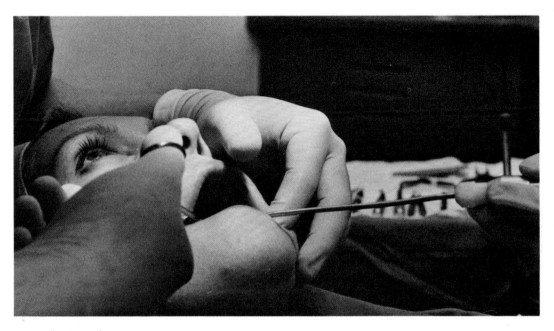

A periodontist performs surgery on a patient's diseased gums as part of an effort to prevent the teeth from eventually falling out or having to be extracted.

Periodontitis must be professionally treated.

Periodontists can treat the disease in several ways. Sometimes they use a technique known as deep scaling. At frequent intervals — perhaps as often as every two to three months — the root surfaces within the pockets must be curetted, or scraped. It is important for the dentist or periodontist to make sure that the deepest areas have been properly cleaned. This procedure works well if the pockets are not too deep and if the procedure is done frequently enough. But even the most experienced periodontists may have difficulty cleaning out deep pockets of infection.

Surgery combined with scrupulous hygiene is more likely to provide a long-term solution to most periodontal problems. When the periodontal disease is located around the front teeth, surgery is likely to expose the roots of the teeth. So the periodontist may want to avoid this for cosmetic reasons. Deep scaling, done skillfully and frequently enough may then be an acceptable alternative to surgery.

Periodontists use several surgical techniques. One of the most common is the gingivectomy. In this operation, the periodontist removes a small amount of gum tissue to eliminate shallow pockets. The periodontist can also clean the root surfaces without exposing bone. The cut area is then covered with a surgical pack, a plasticlike

75

material that fits over the gum like a cast, during the first week or two of the healing period.

In open-flap curettage, the periodontist flaps back a section of the gum to gain access to the root surface and the underlying bone defects. When the disease has caused irregular defects on the bone surface, it is difficult to prevent pockets from re-forming, so the periodontist may reshape the bony topography during this surgical procedure. However, a minimal amount of gum is surgically removed. The gum tissue is sutured back into position, exposing little of the cut surfaces. This procedure is used in patients with advanced periodontal disease where a gingivectomy to eliminate deep pockets would expose too much root surface.

The apically positioned flap combines the open-flap curettage technique and the gingivectomy. The flap of gum, instead of being replaced at its original level, is cut back and sutured down close to the bone.

Sometimes the periodontist will use a bone graft to restore lost bone around teeth having deep, narrow pockets or craterlike sites within the bone. The graft material frequently comes from the patient's own jawbone or hip, but sometimes bone from another individual is used. Evidence indicates that these procedures arrest the disease and help the damaged bone to repair itself. However, more long-term studies on patients who have undergone these procedures are needed.

Following surgery, the patient must keep the disease under control by brushing and flossing after each meal and massaging the gums with a rubber tip. Some periodontists also require their patients to have their teeth professionally cleaned three or four times a year. Studies have shown that effective plaque removal is essential for control of this disease, regardless of what surgical technique the periodontist used.

But sometimes problems persist. Very deep pockets cannot always be completely eliminated, and they may develop again. Thus, the area may need deep scaling at fairly frequent intervals, and surgery may again be required, even though the procedure was expertly done the first time.

The primary method of preventing gum disease is scrupulous oral hygiene. Having teeth periodically cleaned by a dental hygienist is very important. Dentists recommend six months between cleanings, on the average. But some people may need to have their teeth cleaned more frequently. Unfortunately, many people find it time-consuming to keep up adequate care, so periodontal researchers must look for other approaches that could serve as prevention as well as treatment.

Because bacteria are the cause of gum disease, a good deal of attention has been focused on ways to deal with the disease-causing organisms. One area of research involves trying to develop a vaccine that would prevent gum disease from developing in inoculated persons.

However, it seems unlikely that a vaccine can be developed soon for periodontal disease, because about 50 to 100 species of bacteria appear in the pockets during various stages of periodontal disease. A vaccine effective against one species of bacteria would not be effective against another. Researchers believe there is more hope of developing a vaccine for caries because just one species of bacteria is thought to be the major culprit.

Since the early 1970s, periodontal researchers have tried mouthwashes and gels containing antimicrobials, or substances that kill bacteria, and these show some promise in the treatment of gingivitis. In principle, the mouthwash approach is a good one, but there are some problems. For example, chlorhexidine, one of the more effective germ-killing agents, stains teeth if it is used for long periods of time. Despite this drawback, studies conducted in Great Britian and Scandinavia on the short-term use of chlorhexidine to control gingivitis have been encouraging. As yet, chlorhexidine is not available for patient use in the United States.

Mouthwashes are useless in combating periodontitis. Once periodontitis has set in, mouthwashes are ineffective because they cannot reach the bacteria deep in the pockets of infection. But scientists at Forsyth Dental Center in Boston are pursuing another promising line of research in this area. They are studying a timed-release material that could be filled with an antimicrobial drug and then stuffed into the pocket. Unlike mouthwashes, these antimicrobials would be delivered directly to the site of infection and be released over a period of time, in much the same way as some popular cold-remedy capsules release decongestant drugs. If the material packed in the periodontal pocket released the drug very slowly, patients could go to the dentist from time to time to have the pack replaced.

In general, though, it is more practical for the dentist to prescribe antibiotics in pills. The antibiotic is absorbed into the bloodstream and circulates to the deep pockets, entering through the tiny blood vessels on the pocket

To guard against the onset of gum disease, teeth must be kept very clean. This calls for regular brushing. Use a soft toothbrush and brush away from the gumline.

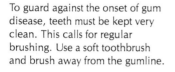

Dental floss removes trapped food and accumulated plaque between teeth. Use unwaxed floss, moving it up and down between the teeth.

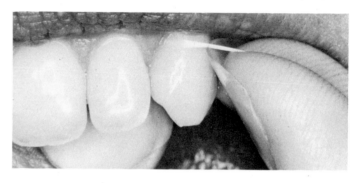

A rubber gum massager helps stimulate gum tissue. Insert the rubber tip between the teeth and wiggle it around.

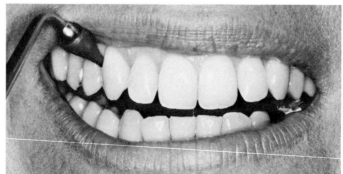

A special disclosing dye stains plaque red, revealing areas where plaque adheres to the teeth and must be removed by more brushing and flossing.

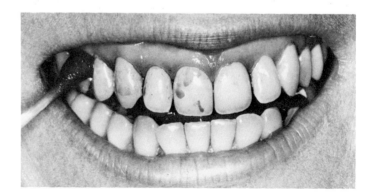

walls. The drug can then attack the bacteria on the bottom and sides of the pocket, rather than simply making a head-on assault through the pocket opening.

Here again, dental scientists run into problems. If antibiotics must be taken for long periods, as they probably would be in cases of periodontitis, the scientists must conduct long trials to answer questions about the dosage, possible side effects, and the possibility of the bacteria becoming resistant to the drug. So far, the most promising drug is the antibiotic tetracycline. In studies on the treatment of acne, scientists have found tetracycline to be safe for long-term use. But many questions must be resolved before it can be accepted as a standard therapy for periodontitis.

Scientists at the Harvard School of Dental Medicine are studying the effects of daily doses of tetracycline on the progression of periodontal disease in beagle dogs. We have found that after 18 months of treatment, dogs receiving tetracycline had a significantly slower rate of bone destruction than untreated dogs. Although the rate of bone loss increased between the 18th and 24th months of treatment, the overall rate of bone loss during the two-year test period was still significantly less in the treated animals than in the untreated ones.

Improved treatments for periodontitis appear to be on the research horizon. But for the time being, the best defense against this tooth-threatening disease is a toothbrush, a good supply of dental floss, and frequent professional cleanings.

Dental problems, rather than a lack of good humor, may be responsible for George Washington's grim visage on the dollar bill. His biographers report that Washington kept his lips closed to conceal a set of bad teeth, which he lost, one by one, as he grew older.

At the time of his inauguration as President, he was wearing the first in a long succession of ill-fitting dentures. Although his dentist, Dr. John Greenwood, tried crafting false teeth out of a variety of materials — from wood to hippopotamus tusk — Washington was never satisfied with the results. He complained that: "they bulge my lips out in such a manner as to make them appear considerably swelled." Many historians attribute Washington's legendary aloofness to his discomfort and self-consciousness as a denture-wearer.

Fending off Fears

Clinics for people with phobias
have had substantial success

By Charles-Gene McDaniel

Jean was a prisoner in her own home. An attractive,
active, and outgoing mother of three young children in
her late 30s, she suddenly found it impossible to leave
home, even for routine trips to buy the family's groceries.
One day, she had been suddenly overcome by panic in a
supermarket aisle. Her heart raced, her knees trembled,
and waves of dizziness engulfed her. She clutched the
handle on her shopping cart in a sweaty, white-knuckled
grip. Faces around her blurred as she suddenly abandoned the cart, ran from the store, and drove home.

After that, Jean could not bring herself to leave her
house or yard, unless her husband was with her. But that
was not easy, because he is a manufacturer's representative whose job takes him out of town frequently. Jean and
her husband began buying the family groceries once a
month, on weekends. They continued this unusual routine for months, until Jean heard about the therapy program at the Glenview Family Guidance Center in a suburb
north of Chicago. Treatment there cured her and enabled
her to resume a normal life.

Jean was a phobic, one of millions of people whose
fears have overwhelmed them. Authorities estimate that
from 7.5 to 10 per cent of persons in the United States
alone suffer so intensely from fear that their lives are
limited, often severely, in some way.

81

Everybody is afraid of something sometime. That is nature's way, a built-in mechanism designed to help us avoid danger. But some people become so afraid of certain things or situations that they become ill. These people are suffering from phobias. To those who do not have the problem, a phobia may seem like a trivial matter to be laughed at. But for the phobic whose life is handicapped, it is no laughing matter.

The word *phobia* is derived from the Greek word *phóbos*, which means panic or fear. In Greek mythology, the god Phobos could provoke fear and panic in one's enemies. The prefix before phobia is usually derived from Greek, though some are Latin. They designate the type of fear. For example, apiphobia means fear of bees; pyrophobia, fear of fire; hydrophobia, fear of water; and phobophobia, fear of fear. Science writer Fraser Kent lists more than 300 phobias in his book *Nothing to Fear: Coping With Phobias* (1977).

Agoraphobia is the most complicated and most common of the phobias. This term originally was used to indicate fear of open space, but agoraphobia is now recognized as a cluster of related fears.

Researchers say that other phobias that occur with some frequency include animal phobias; sexual phobias; social phobias, such as fear of eating, drinking, or speaking in public; illness phobias, such as fear of cancer; and phobias of being trapped. Pterygophobia, the fear of flying, is well known now and constitutes about 10 per cent of all phobias. Epistemophobia, the fear of schools, which afflicted Spanish artist Pablo Picasso among others, is also well known but does not occur often now.

The incidence of phobia has no relationship to the degree of real danger posed by an object or phenomenon. For example, few people are exposed to snakes and even fewer are actually bitten by them. Yet ophidophobia, fear of snakes, is far more common than fear of automobiles, which are involved in thousands of deaths each year. Similarly, riding in an airplane is far safer statistically than riding in an automobile.

Human beings are not alone in their fear of snakes. This fear is shared by most other primates, which suggests that some fears may be innate, or inborn. Other phobias are directly related to physical or psychological trauma, such as a fear of dogs that develops after a dog bite. British psychiatrist Isaac M. Marks says in his book *Fears and Phobias* (1969), "Many phobias begin after more general stress in the life situation, while yet other phobias start

The author:
Charles-Gene McDaniel is a free-lance writer based in Chicago. He is the Director of the Journalism Program at Roosevelt University.

82

spontaneously without an obvious trigger."

In addition to being the most common and complex phobia, agoraphobia is the most debilitating. Its victims may be afraid of being in open places or crowds — *agora* is a Greek word meaning *market place.* Paradoxically, many agoraphobics are also claustrophobic. That is, they fear enclosed or confined places. People in more normal situations may avoid the objects they fear — snakes, insects, dogs, or horses, for example — without affecting their life style. But agoraphobics, in avoiding the things they fear, must deny themselves a real part in the life that goes on around them.

Psychologist Larry J. Kroll, supervising therapist at the Glenview Family Guidance Center, one of only a handful of treatment centers for phobics in the United States, estimates that about 2.5 million Americans suffer from agoraphobia. An estimated 85 to 90 per cent of these agoraphobics are women, and Kroll blames cultural factors for this. Women have been taught from an early age to be submissive and dependent, while men learn that they must be aggressive and independent. Kroll points out that many parents protect girls more than boys; most parents are more careful about what they allow their daughters to do.

Scientists do not know what causes agoraphobia. But Kroll says that agoraphobics tend to come from families in which the parents are highly critical or overprotective, which generates self-doubt and creates insecurity; or from families in which a parent is phobic, so that the behavior is learned from childhood.

Gail, a 24-year-old secretary who underwent therapy at the Glenview center, is a typical agoraphobic patient. She had been suffering from the problem for about 18 months. She recalls that her illness started after a friend died. She experienced a *blaster,* an intense attack of panic, at the funeral, but she had no idea then what it was. As the condition grew worse, she thought she was losing her sanity.

"I was not going out, not going to work. I really thought I was going insane," Gail said. Her physician sent her to a psychiatrist, who put her on tranquilizers. Within a month, she could hardly get out of bed, and she had given up her job.

"The doctor had me so doped up on drugs that for about three months I almost didn't get out of bed." Her mother had to stay home to care for her. Then she was sent to the Mayo Clinic in Rochester, Minn., for a brain

Fear of closed places, *right,* or high places, *opposite page,* often severely limits the lives of people who experience them.

scan and neurological treatment. Gail finally found help after her sister brought home a magazine article about a phobic woman who had received treatment at the Glenview center. Gail's illness is typical. Attacks of agoraphobia usually occur in persons between the ages of 18 and 35, and they usually follow an illness or some other traumatic event.

Don, a middle-aged Chicago executive who has finished his therapy, is not a typical phobic. He is male and his agoraphobia did not appear until late in life. However, his description of a phobic attack is typical.

"I feel like I'm going to have a heart attack," he said. "My palms sweat, I have flashes, my knees grow weak, my heart beats rapidly, I experience butterflies in my stomach, I'm dizzy, and severely depressed."

And how does it feel to have a blaster? "You feel like you're out of control," Don said. "You feel that something terrible is going to happen to you." He told about fleeing a country club brunch and leaving his irate fiancée stranded. The depression that Don spoke of is two-pronged, according to Glenview therapists. One part stems from the condition itself; the other comes from the agoraphobic's restricted life style, loss of self-esteem, and feelings of helplessness and dependency.

Some people have to pass up promotions because they cannot face traveling; they must live and work in the same area because of their agoraphobia, according to Arthur Hyams, executive director of the Glenview center. And the problem is not confined to any particular race, level of education, or social or economic class.

Not surprisingly, agoraphobia causes family problems and destroys friendships with people who cannot understand how someone could be afraid to leave the house. Maria, another Glenview patient, recalls that she used to plead with her husband over the telephone to come home from work because she was afraid to be alone. Her husband, like the spouses of many other agoraphobics,

had to act as family chauffeur and do most of the family errands because of her fear of driving.

Denise, another agoraphobic, suffered a social stigma. Two of her friends rejected her after she told them about her problem.

"They told people I was crazy, I was mental, and things like that," she said. Worse yet, she even began to believe that herself. "I'm crazy, I'm going crazy," she thought. Most agoraphobics are sensitive, warm, and outgoing human beings. Because of these qualities, they are good listeners, and many have helped their friends with problems. But when the tables are turned, their friends will not or cannot return the favor.

Until recently, there have been few effective therapeutic techniques to help phobics cope with their fears, even though the problem dates back to the time of Hippocrates, the father of modern medicine, who referred to this illness more than 2,300 years ago. Many techniques have been tried, including those of Sigmund Freud, the father of psychoanalysis. Freud suggested that phobias are related to sexual repression, but this belief is generally discounted by contemporary therapists.

Some therapists use tranquilizing drugs to treat phobics, but this technique has become highly controversial. Behaviorist psychologists, who believe that observable behavior is the only reliable source of information, argue that drugs are not effective. They contend that drugs in effect anesthetize the patient, who then is unable to learn a more adaptive kind of behavior. They acknowledge that tranquilizers and other prescribed medications may help a person to function. But the drugs do not cure anxiety or phobias. As a patient workbook distributed by Glenview Family Guidance Center says, "Once the medication is withdrawn, your anxiety returns, your phobia remains."

Like other behaviorists, Richard R. Bootzin, chairman of the Northwestern University Psychology Department in Evanston, Ill., is critical of the use of medication in treating phobias. "I do feel strongly that for phobics what is important is for a person to learn a set of skills, and the patient is not learning those skills with medication," he said. Medication, Bootzin points out, "undermines the learning process." Some of the drugs used may also have serious side effects.

"Psychiatry has come to rely on pills," Bootzin said, because of phenothiazine and the beneficial effect it has on schizophrenia and because of Valium and other tranquilizers used for less severe disorders.

Desensitization therapy ranks among the most effective therapeutic techniques recognized in the last 20 years. Developed by psychiatrist Joseph Wolpe of Temple University School of Medicine in Philadelphia in the late 1950s, desensitization involves systematically exposing the victim in his or her imagination to the phobia while relaxing the tension. These techniques also include elements of Gestalt psychology in which the therapist, unlike psychoanalysts and other "insight" therapists, treats the fear rather than looking for the cause by probing the subconscious. Behaviorists hold that fears are learned reactions and can be "unlearned," that they are a kind of habit that can be broken.

Other treatment methods include implosion, or "flooding," therapy. This is almost the opposite of desensitization in that the patient is suddenly thrust into the fearful situation, rather than approaching it gradually. For example, implosion therapy might call for throwing a child afflicted with hydrophobia into a swimming pool. This method has proved effective in some cases, but most therapists seem to prefer the slower, more deliberate method of desensitization.

Fantasy desensitization can effectively cure some individual phobias. Such phobics help themselves by imagining varying degrees of contact with the feared object — for example, envisioning bees from afar, then looking at pictures of them, seeing dead bees in a jar, and finally looking at live bees close at hand.

Desensitization requires far less time than traditional psychoanalysis or other insight psychotherapy. Dr. Wolpe found that an average of about 23 sessions were required for this technique, and it was a high degree of success. Psychoanalysis can take hundreds of hours spanning many years, and the results are not so consistent.

Hyams says that 75 to 85 per cent of the agoraphobics who come to the Glenview center for treatment have already had "some form of treatment that hasn't been successful because many of the practitioners use insight or traditional therapy in terms of approach to phobia." Some have been hospitalized because they were diagnosed originally as suffering from a neurological or psychiatric disorder. One young man spent about $14,000 on psychotherapy before coming to the Glenview center for the treatment that cured his phobia.

Behavioral psychologists emphasize that agoraphobia is a stress-management problem, not a mental illness, and that overcoming it is a problem-solving process. The

A way to overcome an incapacitating fear is to face it head on with the advice and encouragement of someone who is trained to help.

comments of some Glenview patients offer insights into the program. For example, Maria was afraid to leave her house, to be alone, and to drive the family car. After entering therapy, she said, "In four weeks, it was unbelievable how my life was turned around. I finally did it!" she exulted. "I took my kids to the baseball game."

Gabrielle, an agoraphobic patient who completed the 20-week therapy program at Glenview and now acts as a paraprofessional to help others there, had advised Maria to write on the bathroom mirror in lipstick, "I love myself. I think I'm great. I am important." Doing this raised her confidence, Maria says. This is one step in the therapy program — re-establishing self-esteem. Maria's therapy has also given her husband the feeling of "a noose letting up," she added. Her agoraphobia had put a strain on their marriage, even though he was extremely supportive.

Gail is also optimistic now. After four months in therapy, she had not yet completely overcome her phobia. However, she has been able to leave her house alone and, "on good days, I can drive a little bit.

"The good thing about coming here is that I can see the light at the end of the tunnel," Gail said, "and I know I am not going crazy." Others in her group repeated the reassurance that they, too, felt upon learning, once they entered therapy, that they were not going crazy and that there were others like themselves.

While being reassured that they are not crazy and having their self-confidence restored, the agoraphobics gradually take on assignments. They venture forth on little trips that they would earlier have found overwhelming, until gradually they can drive on the expressways and go into the city. They share their triumphs during therapy sessions, and they receive encouragement from others in the group. At first, they may go only to the mailbox on the corner. If they find that they cannot complete their assignment, they are told there is nothing to be ashamed of or to feel defeated over. They tell themselves, "I was not ready," rather than, "I failed," and continue to practice until they eventually complete the assignment.

Agoraphobics are also taught the "defocusing" technique. When they begin to feel overwhelmed by panic, they immediately start to think about something else or do something to distract themselves, such as snapping a rubber band on their wrist. Agoraphobics tend to focus on the negative aspects of their lives, to dwell on the things that they cannot do, according to Kroll. The therapists reinforce the positive aspects of their patients' lives, the things they can do.

Agoraphobics also tend to engage in "what-if" thinking, imagining the worst possible consequences of their feelings — what if they faint, what if they collapse with a heart attack, what if they have to run from church in a state of panic? They learn in therapy that the dreadful things they imagine probably will not happen. And even if they have to flee a social situation, they are assured that there is nothing dreadful about that.

Gordon Paul, a University of Houston psychologist and a behaviorist specialist, said that there is virtually no recidivism among patients who complete desensitization therapy for agoraphobia. That is, these patients do not again become restricted by their fear. In fact, Paul said, the training is generalized to lesser anxieties — that is, smaller problems become less bothersome.

Group therapy sessions are useful to phobics because they can share their problems with each other.

The effectiveness of behavioral therapy was confirmed in a study conducted at Oxford University in England and published in 1980. In the study, agoraphobic patients were monitored for five to nine years after treatment. The study found that agoraphobia had not returned and that the former patients had not developed other disorders as substitutes for the fears they had suffered.

Being afraid is a perfectly normal part of growing up, if it is not allowed to become pathological – that is, develop into an unhealthy trait. Typically, children are afraid of the dark and of imaginary monsters. Sudden, unexpected noise or movement frightens them. Dr. Marks points out that children fear different things at different stages, and that these fears are related to their maturation, perceptual growth, and learning experiences. "For these reasons," Marks said, "fears occur in children for little or no apparent reason and die down as mysteriously, without further contact."

Girls have been found to have more fears than boys, especially after puberty. Perhaps this is rooted in the same cultural reasons cited by Kroll for the disproportionate frequency of agoraphobia among women.

Marks offers advice on how to help children overcome their fears and to prevent childhood fears from developing into full-blown phobias. "Perhaps the most important measure to prevent the development of phobias is also the most difficult to put into practice," he wrote. "This measure is the provision of a milieu [environment] from infancy onwards in which the accepted mode of behavior is that of readiness to face difficulties and overcome frightening situations, and to reward a similar attitude in the child himself.

"When the child is sufficiently confident, gentle encouragement should be given to enter mildly frightening situations until the child has lost all his fear," Dr. Marks said. But he cautioned that children should not be forced into frightening situations, "except under special circumstances where additional support is given until the fear has been overcome.

"Whatever happens," Dr. Marks warned, "the child should feel accepted and should not be rejected for appearing frightened. Praise and other rewards should be given freely for brave behavior." This is particularly important with a timid child, he said, but it might be necessary to caution a tougher child against excessive bravery when it amounts to foolhardiness. Dr. Marks cautions against trying to help a child face fear when the child is tired, depressed, or not feeling well.

The same advice applies to adults, Dr. Marks said. Kroll pointed out that adults should be aware of the symptoms of developing phobias. Remember, he counseled, that there is a big difference between realistic fear, the proper regard for dangerous situations, and unrealistic fear, the unhealthy, unreasoning kind that can render you helpless and afraid to join in life. Facing life's challenges with respect and a sensible amount of caution can help you enjoy a full, active life.

I believe that anyone can conquer fear by doing the things he fears to do, provided he keeps doing them until he gets a record of successful experiences behind him.

Eleanor Roosevelt

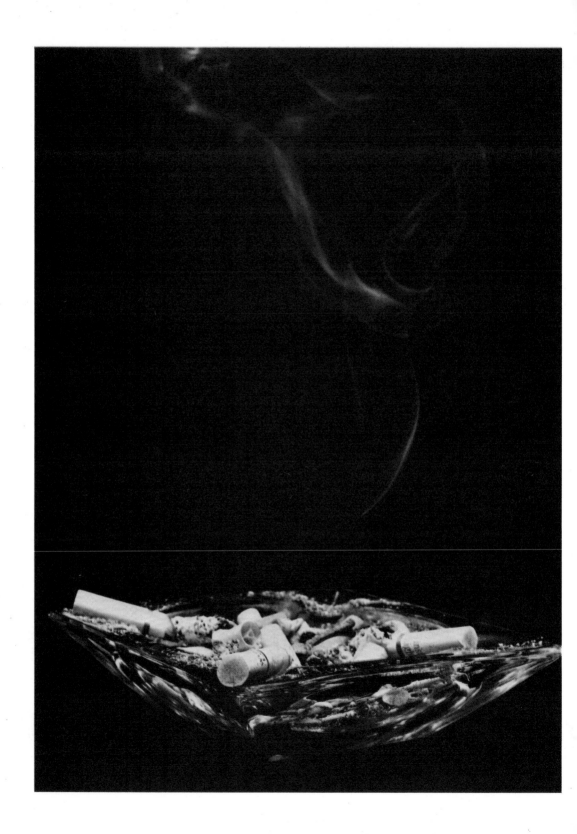

Calling It Quits

Whether you taper off or go "cold turkey,"
you can find help
when you want to stop smoking

By Elizabeth González

If you are going to stop smoking cigarettes you must prepare yourself for a difficult time. Your body, accustomed to nicotine, may rebel at the loss of its drug "fix." Your mind, conditioned to link smoking with numerous daily habits and social patterns, may try to trick you into forgetting your vow when sipping your morning cup of coffee or evening cocktail, or talking on the telephone.

For many smokers, cigarettes are like old friends — customary and welcome companions in times of stress or of relaxation. It is not easy to give up old friends. Yet every year, 40 million Americans try to stop smoking cigarettes. Why do so many people put themselves through the misery that ensues?

The brutal truth comes from a hypnotist instructing a client who wants to stop smoking. "Every time you want a puff," he says, "just repeat to yourself, 'Smoking cigarettes is sucking death . . . Smoking cigarettes is sucking death. . . .'"

Cigarette smoking is indeed a slow, seductive form of suicide. It causes debilitating disease and painful, often lingering death. It has harmful effects on almost every organ and system in the body. One way or another — sooner or later — it is going to get you.

In fact, if you smoke, the habit is already getting you, perhaps in subtle ways you have not really noticed. According to the United States Surgeon General's 1979 report on smoking and health, smokers spend considerably more days — including workdays — in bed because of illness than their nonsmoking friends. They have more chronic sinusitis and more peptic ulcers than nonsmokers. They and the children who share their smoke-filled homes have more upper respiratory infections than people not chronically exposed to cigarette smoke.

Smokers get winded more readily than nonsmokers; this breathlessness is a forerunner of emphysema, an incurable chronic disease that progressively destroys lung function. Eventually, the lungs can no longer keep oxygen circulating through the body, and the victim must be assisted with respirators and other devices. Every year, 30,000 such victims are killed by emphysema in a protracted process that Chicago physician Alan Blum likens to "being slowly smothered to death by a cellophane bag." Emphysema often goes hand in hand with another lung ailment, chronic bronchitis.

Heart experts agree that smoking is one of the major risk factors for the number-one U.S. killer — coronary heart disease. Smoking helps promote the build-up of a sludgy deposit called atherosclerotic plaque on the inner walls of the heart's arteries. Ultimately, plaque can completely block an artery, causing a heart attack.

But arteries do not have to be blocked by plaque for the blood supply to be interrupted; sometimes a coronary artery with little or no plaque will suddenly constrict, becoming so narrow that blood cannot get through. Such a coronary artery spasm can cause severe attacks of chest pain, or angina pectoris, and may contribute to many heart attacks and sudden deaths. Heart specialists noted at a 1979 conference of the American Heart Association in Anaheim, Calif., that some patients who have stopped smoking cigarettes no longer have coronary artery spasms.

Smoking may also interfere with the flow of blood to the brain, and this may cause strokes. Moreover, women who smoke and also take oral contraceptives run a greater risk of heart attack and a certain type of brain hemorrhage, according to the Surgeon General's report.

The evidence is overwhelming that smoking causes lung cancer, and the cancer often spreads to other organs, such as the brain and liver. Moreover, there is a ghastly irony to the slogan aimed at women smokers, "You've come a long way, baby," in view of a recent American Cancer Society report that lung cancer is now second only to breast cancer in causing cancer deaths among women. The habit is also linked to cancer of the throat,

The author:
Elizabeth González is an associate editor, Medical News Section of the *Journal of the American Medical Association*, in Chicago.

mouth, esophagus, bladder, kidney, and pancreas.

Overall, smokers have a much higher rate of death from all diseases combined than do nonsmokers. Smoking is a major factor in 354,000 deaths in the United States each year, the Surgeon General's report points out. The life expectancy of a 30-year-old person who smokes 15 cigarettes a day is reduced by five years, according to *The Merck Manual of Diagnosis and Therapy*.

And smoking does more than shorten the smoker's life. It can harm the unborn and the newborn. Female smokers run a higher risk of spontaneous abortion or miscarriage, death of the fetus, and sudden death of the newborn baby, says the Surgeon General's report, as well as a higher risk of premature delivery, hemorrhage, and prolonged rupture of the amniotic membrane. On the average, the babies of women who smoke weigh 6 ounces less than infants born to nonsmokers. And there is growing evidence that smoking during pregnancy has repercussions well beyond birth, retarding the physical and mental development of children and contributing to behavioral problems and learning disabilities.

And if all this is not enough to persuade you to quit, consider your own vanity. Smoking stinks. "My mother and I," says one former smoker, "both quit because we like pretty scents — perfumes and colognes. What was the use if we both reeked of tobacco?" Smoking also stains the teeth and skin. And a smoker's cough hardly enhances a conversation.

Or, consider your bank account. Smoking is expensive, and likely to become more so. In many places, the cost of a pack of cigarettes is nearing $1. That price makes it easy to figure the annual cost for a pack-a-day smoker. Moreover, a burning cigarette is a fire hazard. It is a rare and impeccable puffer who has never singed a couch, or burned a hole in a favorite garment.

There are positive reasons for quitting. Not all the harm done by smoking can be undone, but the Surgeon General reports that the death rate among smokers 15 years after they quit is very close to the death rate for those who have never smoked. Even after only 10 years, former smokers have death rates for coronary heart disease and lung cancer approximating those of nonsmokers. Quitting does not repair the damage done by emphysema, but it preserves whatever healthy lung tissue remains.

For those who are not ready to quit, it helps to smoke as little as possible. The risk of disease and death increases in direct proportion to the number of cigarettes smoked.

At a pack a day, a young smoker can expect to puff away 365,000 cigarettes before he retires at 65 — assuming he lives that long.

Some diseases are related to the tar in cigarettes, so lower-tar brands theoretically offer a certain amount of protection. But American Cancer Society researchers and other scientists suggest many smokers who switch to "light" brands actually smoke a greater number of cigarettes. They may also puff more often or inhale more deeply without realizing it.

With such an inventory of horrors directly attributable to cigarette smoking, your one remaining question may be, "How do I get off cigarettes?"

There are almost as many ways to stop smoking as there are former smokers, but there are some basic considerations that apply to everybody. For example, it is usually easier to stop smoking during a peaceful time in your life. Marital discord, job problems, and financial difficulties exert the kind of personal stress that makes it all too easy to begin smoking again. Also, you should eat and exercise sensibly while you are breaking the smoking habit.

Most importantly, do not give up hope if you weaken and start smoking again. It may take several tries, perhaps over a period of several years, but any former smoker will tell you it is worth the effort.

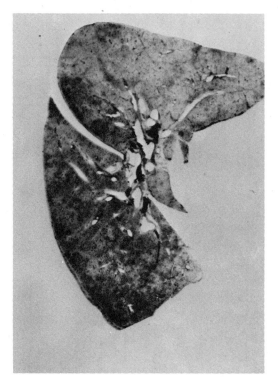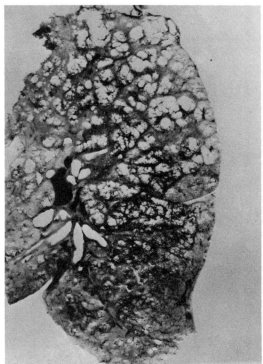

The lung of a nonsmoker, *above,* appears normal, while a smoker's lung, *above right,* shows distended air sacs that impair breathing. So far, the lung appears to be unaffected by emphysema or cancer.

Should you go "cold turkey" and immediately stop all smoking, or should you taper off — gradually reducing your cigarette and nicotine consumption? Each method works for some people but not for others. This is a personal decision.

Should you go it alone, or join a group trying to break the habit? Again, each method will work for some people.

Many reformed tobacco junkies attribute their success to groups — either commercial enterprises that charge up to several hundred dollars for a course of treatment, or not-for-profit groups run by the American Cancer Society, the American Lung Association, and other organizations. These groups may use various techniques. They include "aversive smoking" methods, for example, rapid puffing without inhaling while viewing vivid color slides of body organs that have been damaged by smoking; group discussion and support; specific instructions for gradual weaning or abrupt withdrawal; special diets; and relaxation techniques, such as meditation. In addition, many therapists offer to help smokers break the habit through techniques ranging from hypnosis to acupuncture.

If you decide to seek outside help, a good person to

Rauchen verboten!

Thank you for not smoking
American Cancer Society

Robert Blend

With varying degrees of wit and politeness, signs now appear in stores, offices, and public places all over the world, urging — or ordering — people not to smoke.

SMOKING POLLUTES
YOU AND EVERYTHING ELSE

American Cancer Society

consult is your personal physician. Some former smokers say that they finally quit on their doctor's advice, and many physicians believe that doctors may be able to make a crucial difference in American smoking habits.

Dr. Blum, co-founder of Doctors Ought to Care (DOC), a group of physicians involved in educating the public about smoking, takes a dim view of group programs. He believes most of them are unsuccessful.

On the other hand, some physicians, such as psychiatrist Robert B. Millman of Cornell University Medical College in New York City, think groups can be effective. Millman, who specializes in drug addictions, believes that some tobacco addicts can benefit from group programs in much the same way that some alcoholics benefit from Alcoholics Anonymous. He feels that the dynamics of this kind of group support could be helpful to many would-be ex-smokers.

Betty Gilson, professor of health services and adjunct professor of family medicine at the University of Washington in Seattle, points out that we still do not know much about effective group programs. She says, "I think the evidence is that there's not much that does help, except something we have not been able to put our finger on yet. Some people do quit and stay quit, but I don't think anyone's been able to identify what it is that does that." Dr. Gilson thinks that physicians can provide help and encouragement for smokers who want to stop.

If you elect to go it alone, you should be well informed about your smoking behavior. Psychologist Nina G. Schneider, research psychologist of psychiatry and biobehavioral sciences at the University of California, Los Angeles, has spent 10 years in smoking research and advises, "Know your habit. Why do you smoke? When? How often? The key is to be armed with knowledge. If you know what triggers the cues, you're in a better position — even months after you quit — when the urge comes back again."

The next important step, Dr. Schneider says, "is to find the right tool for the job. You as the individual smoker must determine whether you need a life change, an American Cancer Society program, hypnosis, acupuncture, or whatever." She adds, "Bear in mind that smoking perfectly [combines] all the physiological, psychological, and social factors — all of them operating simultaneously. What this means is that while you're getting the effects of nicotine, you're simultaneously getting the oral, handling, and social benefits of the habit."

For many years, cigarette smoke was an accepted part of the social scene, the workplace, and the home. Recent research, however, has shown that "second-hand" smoke can adversely affect those around smokers. The closer the relationship, the greater the potential harm.

At a smoking clinic, a therapist uses hypnotic suggestion to help a group of people quit smoking.

A number of publications may help you to evaluate and understand your smoking habit. For information on free materials and smoking programs, get in touch with the local heart association and local chapters of the American Lung Association and the American Cancer Society. You may also want to browse through the array of how-to-quit-smoking books on display at your local bookstore. Some former smokers regard these books as a waste of money, but others have found them useful.

Current publications may not include one particular tip: Substitute sources of nicotine sometimes make the first few months of withdrawal easier. One readily available source is chewing tobacco or snuff, which you can park in your cheek so that you absorb the nicotine through the membranes of your mouth. If you continue this unpleasant habit for long, however, you will increase your chances of developing benign or cancerous growths in the mouth. But if you are a true nicotine addict, you may find it helpful temporarily.

A handful of researchers are now testing a nicotine chewing gum called Nicorette in the United States. The gum must be chewed slowly and intermittently over a half-hour period. It is manufactured in Sweden, and distributed for research purposes only by Dow Chemical

101

Company in the United States. The gum is available by doctor's prescription in Great Britain, Canada, and other countries, but the U.S. Food and Drug Administration has not yet approved it for prescription.

Dr. Schneider is one of the American investigators testing Nicorette. "I'm not quite sure yet if the gum can help everybody or just a selected few," she says. "But when it's compared with placebo gum [gum that does not contain nicotine], it looks like it's more successful in keeping people off cigarettes and reducing withdrawal symptoms."

When you are finally free of cigarettes — and, ideally, all sources of nicotine — what next? According to psychologist Saul Schiffman of the University of South Florida in Tampa, "People should consider that at least half the battle occurs after they quit. They must be vigilant for three to six months. Specifically, they must develop some coping mechanisms for situations that make them want to smoke."

These might include simple relaxation exercises when stress develops, leaving the scene of temptation for a few minutes, or drinking coffee. "People are often unprepared for a common experience — having a slip," Dr. Schiffman says. "They smoke one cigarette," he explains, "and think they've blown it. They go back to smoking regularly. Instead, they need to use this as an opportunity to discover what triggered the slip and to ask themselves how they might better handle such a situation in the future. One slip does not a relapse make," he emphasizes.

Weight gain is a potential problem, but most smokers gain only a few pounds when they quit. Some people actually lose weight, and some experience no change. If you maintain a nutritious but relatively low-calorie diet from the start, you may be able to avoid those dreaded bulges. Munching raw vegetables will keep your mouth busy as well as keeping down the calorie count. Sugarless gum and candy also may help, and exercise will combat flab as well as aid your lungs and circulatory system.

A final consideration, and one that stop-smoking programs stress increasingly, is the force of cigarette advertising. Some groups require participants to clip cigarette ads from magazines and bring them to group meetings, where they can be discussed and debunked. The tobacco industry spends enormous sums to persuade potential customers that smoking is masculine, feminine, "liberated," sophisticated, outdoorsy — in general, desirable. Anyone who intends to stay off cigarettes permanently must re-

Whether you put out your last cigarette with fear or hope, regret or relief, that final butt can mark the beginning of a new, healthier – and longer – life.

main constantly and consciously aware that these messages are destructive lies.

If you have decided to stop smoking, congratulations! You are choosing health and life over anguish and premature death. But let no one tell you that quitting is a breeze. It may become easier as doctors and therapists develop new ways to help smokers stop. In the meantime, 70 per cent of those smokers who try to quit, succeed, but three-fourths of that 70 per cent resume smoking within six months.

If you fail in your first attempt to quit – or even your 10th – do not despair. Some former smokers report that they made it only after repeated tries spanning a period as long as 10 years. But remember that the earlier you can stop smoking, the less damage you will have inflicted on your body.

You will quickly notice changes in your body when you quit. If you cough up mucus in the beginning, this is temporary and completely normal. It simply means that the cilia, small hairlike structures in your lungs, have come out of their cigarette-induced paralysis and are doing their natural job of clearing your lungs.

You will smell fresh air again, and enjoy the subtle flavors of your favorite foods. Your mind will be clearer, a direct result of increasing the oxygen and decreasing the carbon monoxide flowing into your brain. You will have cleaner, healthier teeth and gums.

In addition, you will no longer be polluting your environment and endangering the health of those who live and work with you. You will no longer be enslaved by an addictive and toxic drug. You will have many extra dollars to save or spend as you desire. Most importantly, you will have something of incalculable value – precious additional years in which to live your life.

Smoking is in a way a greater curse than drink, inasmuch as the victim does not realize its evil in time. It is not regarded as a sign of barbarism; it is even acclaimed by civilized people. I can only say – let those who can, give it up and set the example.
Mahatma Gandhi

Smoking is a shocking thing – blowing smoke out of our mouths into other people's mouths, eyes, and noses, and having the same thing done to us.
Samuel Johnson

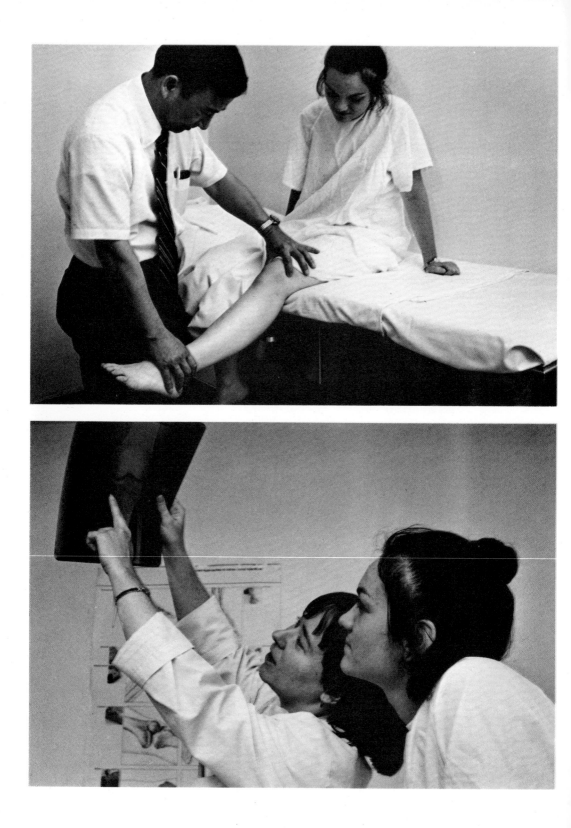

The Second Opinion

Why you should get one for non-emergency surgery

By Madelon L. Finkel, Ph.D. and
Eugene G. McCarthy, M.D.

Your doctor has just told you that you need an operation. Your first reaction is probably fear; you are uncertain and a little doubtful. Much as you may rely on the judgment of your physician, many questions may race through your mind: "Is the operation dangerous? How much pain will there be? How much will it cost? How long will I be unable to work? Is there another way?"

There are several things about having surgery that you should bear in mind. One is the risk. While operations such as tonsillectomies, hernia repairs, and knee operations present few problems, others — major intestinal, brain, or heart surgery, for example — have a high rate of serious complications, even death. In addition to the dangers of the surgical procedure itself, the anesthesia carries a degree of risk. It has been estimated that 2 of every 10,000 persons undergoing surgery die because of a reaction to the anesthesia. A person's general medical condition can present additional problems. People who are overweight and persons suffering from diabetes, heart ailments, or high blood pressure are more likely to suffer complications and have a higher death rate.

Surgery can also be very expensive. Americans spent $65 billion for surgical services alone in 1978. Many operations end up costing thousands of dollars and require a period of convalescence during which the patient is unable to work.

Also, the evidence of the need for surgery is not always precise. There may, indeed, be "another alternative." Obviously, an operation is a serious event in anyone's life and there may be an alternative treatment for your condition that would be more attractive and convenient for you. It is in your best interest to learn all you can about your condition and to be aware of all your options so that you can make a wise and informed decision.

Unfortunately, some doctors do not discuss all the alternatives freely with their patients. So how can you find out all you need to know? Where can you get the information? It may surprise you to learn that second opinion consultation programs have been set up in several parts of the United States. These programs are designed to help you get a second opinion if your doctor has recommended elective surgery.

The referral of a patient by one doctor to another is a long-established practice. The basic difference between such referrals and second opinion programs is that the latter are offered by the institutions that pay for medical care and services, such as health insurance companies, corporations, unions, and most recently, state and federal governments.

The amount of surgery performed in the United States has risen dramatically during the last decade, particularly among women. In general, the north-central region of the United States has the highest rate of surgery, although it has been found that certain procedures are performed more frequently in specific regions. For example, there was a 28.3 per cent increase in hysterectomies in the South from 1971 to 1978, but the number of hysterectomies declined 22 per cent during that period in the Northeast. Many factors account for these differences, including the number of surgeons in an area and the type of insurance coverage available.

Statistics also show that the number of persons undergoing surgery has increased consistently with advancing age. Children under 15 years of age were the only group that did not show an increase in surgery from 1971 to 1978. Knee surgery increased 70 per cent during that period, cataract surgery increased 46 per cent, and prostate surgery increased 43.5 per cent. Conversely, tonsillectomies declined 43 per cent.

The basic problem underlying the effort to document unnecessary surgery is the lack of an acceptable definition for each surgical procedure. Medicine is not an exact

The authors:
Eugene C. McCarthy is clinical professor of public health at Cornell University Medical College. Madelon L. Finkel is assistant professor in the Department of Public Health at Cornell University Medical College.

106

science and when doctors disagree on the recommendation for surgery, it is hard to say that one surgeon is right and another wrong. However, a congressional subcommittee report issued in 1978 conservatively estimated that in 1977 between 1.9 million and 2.4 million operations were performed unnecessarily at a cost of $4 billion and resulted in more than 10,000 deaths.

The New England Journal of Medicine reported on March 12, 1980, that 11 patients of a group of 36 admitted to Boston's Peter Bent Brigham Hospital died of complications caused by surgeons' mistakes. According to the study, "90 per cent of the errors were those of unnecessary contraindicated surgery or technically defective surgical activity." Other problems included wrong diagnoses and delays of needed surgery. Many medical authorities believe the study's findings accurately reflect conditions in hospitals throughout the United States.

Peer review committees are set up by doctors to ensure that incompetent surgeons not be allowed to perform surgery. However, these organizations are often hesitant to censure "one of their own," and it is of little use to the patient to find out after the operation that the surgery was unnecessary and the surgeon was incompetent. Second opinion programs can serve as a form of physician peer review.

Most second opinion programs are voluntary, but some are mandatory, such as the Massachusetts Medicaid Program. In a mandatory program, each person facing surgery *must* consult another doctor for a second opinion in order to have their basic hospitalization and physician coverage paid for. Only the consultation is required, however; the person is free to decide for himself whether or not to have the surgery. He will not lose benefits, regardless of the consultant's recommendation.

In voluntary programs, people may question the need for surgery, or perhaps they may have decided to have the operation and want a second opinion to provide reassurance that their decision was the right one. In voluntary programs, only 2 to 5 per cent of those eligible for a second opinion take advantage of that benefit.

Cornell University Medical College-The New York Hospital, in cooperation with several Taft Hartley Welfare funds, established the first second opinion program. This program has been in continuous operation since 1972. Findings from the Cornell-New York Hospital program indicate that a second opinion program can help to control the sky-rocketing medical costs by cutting down on

107

questionable surgery. Sixty per cent of those who were not recommended for surgery by the second opinion consultant had not undergone surgery one year after the consultation. Of these individuals, 41.6 per cent of those in voluntary programs and 51.3 per cent of those in mandatory programs had received no medical treatment since the consultation.

This group represents potential surplus surgery. Since no surgery was performed, no further medical treatment was received, and their health was not impaired, we can legitimately question why surgery was recommended in the first place. Getting a second opinion spared these individuals the pain and risk of surgery and the discomfort and time lost during convalescence — not to mention the cost.

Second opinion programs allow you to take an active role in your health care. They are intended to educate you about your condition and explain the risks and benefits of an operation. A second opinion consultation enables you to make a more informed decision about the proposed surgery. Each of us has the right — as well as the responsibility — to take an active, informed part in caring for our own health and well-being.

Most people want to make their own decisions, as far as possible, about what happens to their body. We have become better educated about alternatives to medical and surgical treatments as we have grown less inclined to let others call the shots. We are also becoming more conscious of the high cost of health care. Second opinion programs are a logical expression of this new awareness.

One American in 10 will probably have surgery in 1982. A small percentage of these people will be faced with a life-threatening condition requiring emergency surgery. For example, immediate surgery may be required to treat a patient who is experiencing breathing problems or for injuries suffered in an accident. Emergency operations were performed in 1981 on President Ronald Reagan and Pope John Paul II to remove bullets after assassination attempts, for example. A person whose life is in imminent danger is hardly in a position to ask for a second opinion.

The second opinion programs are set up to deal with elective surgical procedures only. Many elective surgical procedures involve the partial or complete removal of a part of the body. These are the "ectomies" from the Greek *ektome,* meaning *excision.* These operations include *hysterectomy* (removal of the uterus); *cholecystectomy* (removal of the gall bladder); *prostatectomy; tonsil-*

lectomy; *bunionectomy*; and *mastectomy* (removal of part or all of a breast). Some operations involve repair or replacement of a body part as in knee or hip surgery. In an elective surgical procedure, the individual is usually not in danger of dying from the condition and will probably have an uneventful recovery from the surgery.

Depending on a person's condition, however, it may well be that another procedure might be equally effective. Rather than a hysterectomy, for example, the consultant may advise a *dilatation and curettage* (a scraping of the uterine wall), or hormone therapy, or simply frequent examinations to watch the progress of the condition. Instead of a mastectomy, the physician may recommend radiation therapy or removal of just the lump, followed by hormone therapy. Instead of a knee operation, the consultant may advise physical therapy or a special exercise program.

The ultimate decision on whether to have surgery should always be made by the patient. Even if the consultant says that surgery is not necessary or that the operation can be deferred, you can elect to proceed with the surgery if *you* think you should.

While most elective procedures are included in a second opinion program, there are some exceptions. For example, Caesarean sections are not included because of the urgent nature of this procedure; breast and skin biopsies are not included because they are performed to provide diagnostic information.

When you have decided that you want a second opinion, there are several options open to you. If your employer or your medical insurance policy provides for a second opinion, a telephone call will begin the process. If not, you can call 800-638-6833 — a nationwide toll-free "hot line" — that gives advice on getting a second opinion. Also, state and county medical societies can provide you with the names of qualified physicians and surgeons from whom an opinion can be sought. In some states, such as Massachusetts, New York, and Michigan, Medicaid and Medicare recipients are eligible for second opinion consultations.

After you have made the initial phone call, most second opinion programs will arrange an appointment with the consultant for you. Other programs, such as Blue Cross Blue Shield of Greater New York, will give you the names of surgeons willing to act as consultants and you can make the appointment yourself. However, in all current second opinion programs, the cost of the consultation and

Surgical Advice: How Patients Responded

	Consultant said yes	Operation done (%)	Consultant didn't say yes	Operation done (%)
Colorectal	40	20 (50)	11	1 (9)
Diagnostic	36	19 (53)	10	0 (0)
Orthopedics	165	91 (55)	84	23 (27)
Ophthalmology	67	37 (55)	25	8 (32)
Otorhinolaryngology	163	100 (61)	61	16 (26)
Vascular and cardiac	44	29 (66)	10	0 (0)
Other	101	69 (68)	36	9 (25)
Breast	45	32 (71)	18	2 (11)
Urology	76	54 (71)	36	12 (33)
Gynecology	242	174 (72)	98	37 (38)
Abdominal	122	99 (81)	22	7 (32)
Total	**1,101**	**724 (66)**	**411**	**115 (28)**

The number of operations in most categories was substantially reduced during the 12-year period from 1966 to 1977.

any tests ordered by the consultant are paid for by the sponsoring organization. There is no charge to the patient.

The consultants in second opinion programs are certified surgeons, specialists who have passed rigorous examinations sponsored by each specialty's college – for example, the American College of Surgeons. Each individual seeking a second opinion consultation will be examined by a specialist whose expertise qualifies him or her to perform surgery. A woman recommended for a hysterectomy, for example, would be examined by a specialist who is certified in obstetrics.

A second opinion consultant will give you an unbiased objective evaluation of your medical and surgical condition. He is not concerned with what other doctors might think and, since he is not permitted to perform the surgery, he has no financial incentive to confirm the need for surgery. His only interest is the patient's well-being.

The consultant will examine you to determine whether surgery is indeed warranted and appropriate. You should bring all X rays, laboratory tests, and diagnostic test results to the consultation so that the consultant can review them. If the test results are not available, he may request that specific tests be performed. You should also take a list of questions you want to ask and make a note of important points so that you can consider them later at your leisure.

On the basis of the examination and the test results, the

The Increase in Surgery			
Procedure	1965	1977	Per Cent Change
Appendectomy	379	342	−9.8
Cardiac catheterization	44	278	531.8
Cesarean section	174	455	161.5
Cholecystectomy (Removal of Gall Bladder)	355	446	25.6
Dilation and curettage diagnostic	775	995	28.4
Dilation of urethra	96	247	157.3
Extraction of lens	142	350	146.5
Herniorrhaphy (Hernia repair)	517	749	44.9
Hysterectomy	505	706	39.8
Ligation and division of fallopian tubes, bilateral	69	346	401.4
Oophorectomy; salpingo-oophorectomy (Removal of ovaries)	291	458	57.4
Prostatectomy	191	299	56.5
Surgery of the back	78	166	112.8
Surgery of the knee	71	166	133.8
Tonsillectomy and adenoidectomy	1215	617	−49.2

Figures are in thousands.

Patients who seek a second opinion on prospective surgery do not hesitate to avoid the operation if it is suggested that they do.

consultant either confirms or does not confirm the proposed surgery. He confirms the surgery when he feels that it is in the best interest of the patient and is the most effective means of correcting a medical condition – and that no alternative forms of treatment should be tried first. In short, the consultant agrees with the initial diagnosing, or first, doctor.

A second opinion confirming surgery reassures the pa-

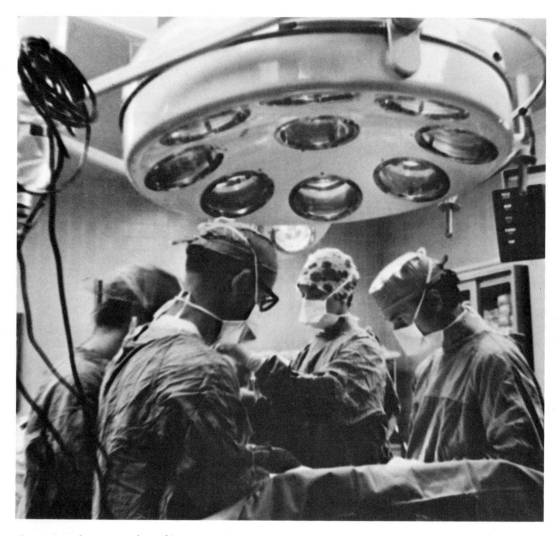

The amount of surgery performed in the United States has risen dramatically during the last decade.

tient and helps to bolster his confidence in the operation. For example, Robert Jones, a 50-year-old carpenter, decided to get a second opinion after his dermatologist suggested that the lump on Jones's arm be surgically removed. The consultant ordered a biopsy, which showed cancerous tissue, and then confirmed the recommendation for surgery. Jones later said that he would never have had the surgery without the information and reassurance he got from the second opinion consultation.

The consultant does not confirm the need for surgery if he feels that there are other means of correcting the condition. There may be no medical justification for

112

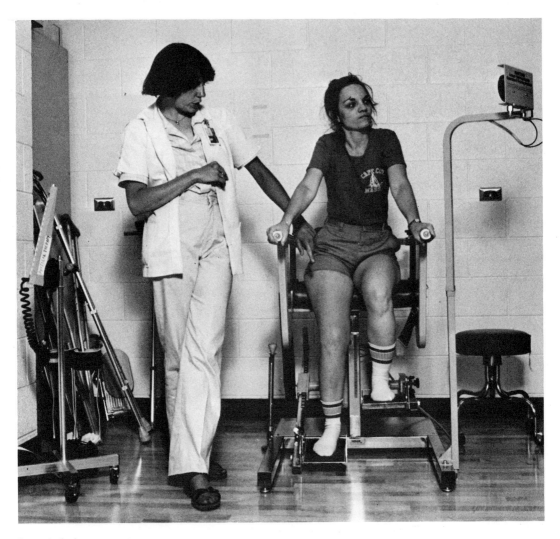

Instead of a knee operation, a consultant may advise physical therapy or an exercise program.

surgery; medical treatment, such as medication or physical therapy, may be preferable to surgery; or the consultant may believe that the first doctor's diagnosis is incorrect. In some cases, the consultant may suggest that the patient wait to see if the condition clears up by itself. For whatever reason, the consultant does not confirm the surgery when he feels that surgery should not be performed at that time.

The experience of Margaret Kelly, a 35-year-old salesperson, is a case in point. Kelly was informed that a biopsy indicated the presence of a localized cancer on her breast. Kelly wanted the surgery done immediately and refused to have a second opinion consultation. After a lengthy discussion with her union health benefit representative, she finally agreed to see a consultant.

The consultant found that the cancerous breast tissue was the type that would respond to hormones. He did not confirm the need for surgery, but suggested a course of chemotherapy with anticancer drugs and hormones. Kelly decided to defer the surgery and follow the suggested medical treatment. Twelve months after the treatments began, she seemed to be doing very well. For now, there seems to be no need for surgery to treat her condition.

In some cases, the consultant may advise an alternative surgical procedure. For example, Ruth Rubin, a 50-year-old woman who was experiencing irregular bleeding, was told by her doctor that she needed a hysterectomy. Rubin sought a second opinion and the consultant confirmed the need for surgery. But he suggested that the uterus be removed by opening the abdomen, rather than by extracting the uterus through the vagina, as was suggested by the first doctor. The abdominal hysterectomy was performed and early cancer of an ovary was discovered and removed. Had the vaginal procedure been performed, the cancer would probably not have been found until it was too late.

If the consultant does not confirm the surgery, a "tie-breaker" third opinion may help the patient to make a decision. Most second opinion programs will also pay for a third opinion.

Acceptance of second opinion programs by the medical community has increased in recent years, and many surgeons who once refused to participate are now submitting credentials for review. The American College of Surgeons and the American Medical Association have accepted the concept of voluntary second opinion programs as a desirable part of good surgical practice.

Some people hesitate to ask for a second opinion. In most cases, such patients are afraid of losing their doctor's good will. The patient may be afraid that he will not get the doctor's prompt attention the next time he is ill. Actually, most doctors welcome another professional opinion — 75 per cent of the surgeons surveyed by the American College of Surgeons think a second opinion is good for both the patient and the doctor.

However, there are some doctors who feel that second opinion programs interfere with the doctor-patient relationship and cause disagreement between physicians. If you go to such a doctor and do not want him to know that

114

a second opinion is being sought, the consultation will be kept confidential.

Increasing medical costs mean higher insurance premiums for all of us, and it would seem that consulting two or more doctors would be expensive. Analysis has shown, however, that such programs are economically sound. The Cornell-New York Hospital program reports that for every dollar spent, $2.63 is saved.

Second opinion consultations also help by emphasizing the need or appropriateness of surgery. Cornell-New York Hospital records show that the overwhelming majority of those who were confirmed for surgery proceeded to have the operation, usually within three months.

Of 7,000 persons who participated in the mandatory program, the Cornell researchers found that 19 per cent were not confirmed for surgery. Of the 5,000 individuals in the voluntary program who sought a second opinion, 33 per cent were not confirmed for surgery. The large difference in the results is due to the structure of the two programs.

Until more precise criteria for surgery can be developed, it is our personal right and responsibility to make sure that any proposed surgery is really in our best interest. So if your doctor tells you that you need an operation, give yourself the benefit of a second opinion. It will provide you with a better understanding of your condition and it may allay your fears; you will be a better informed and more confident patient.

A Point to Ponder

If one doctor doctors another, does the doctor who doctors the doctor doctor the doctor the way the doctor he is doctoring doctors? Or does he doctor the doctor the way the doctor who doctors doctors doctors? (Anon.)

Reducing the Risks of Cancer

We cannot avoid all of the carcinogens that surround us but there are things we can do to minimize their effects.

By Harriet S. Page

In the last several years, we have seen and heard so many reports about cancer-causing agents — in newspapers and magazines, on television and radio — that it seems *everything* causes cancer. Reports of the latest discovery of a carcinogen, or cancer-causing agent, make a lot of people want to throw up their hands in frustration and say, "What's the use!"

For instance, during two weeks early in 1981, there were two press reports of carcinogens. First, on March 12, a scientific study at Harvard University linking cancer of the pancreas with coffee drinking was publicized. Then, on March 26 another study was reported that links the use of snuff to cancer of the cheek and gums. Of course, a lot more people drink coffee than use snuff, but both join a seemingly endless list of substances that may cause cancer — saccharin, hair dyes, X rays, cigarettes, sleeping pills, bacon, a flame retardant used in children's pajamas, sunlight, asbestos, and vinyl chloride are just the beginning of the list.

Can we live in this "sea of carcinogens"? Is there a way we can assess the dangers? Let us first look at some facts. Each year the American Cancer Society (ACS) publishes a booklet, *Cancer Facts & Figures*. From the 1981 edition, we learn that in 1977 (the latest data available in 1981)

117

386,686 people died from cancer — accounting for 20 per cent of the 1.8 million deaths in the United States that year. Heart disease — chiefly heart attack and stroke — killed 718,850 people, almost 38 per cent. And, from the World Health Organization, we learn that the United States ranks 20th in cancer mortality in a list of 40 countries.

The ACS publication also shows that over the last 45 years, the death rate from most cancers, except for lung cancer, has remained steady or has fallen slightly in both men and women. Lung cancer has been increasing sharply for men since 1930 and for women since 1965. The ACS has estimated that in 1981, some 34 per cent of men and 15 per cent of women who have lung cancer would die of it.

What other kinds of cancer contribute to the overall cancer death rate? For women, breast cancer is the most lethal, accounting for 19 per cent of all cancer deaths. Cancer of the lung is second with 15 per cent, and cancer of the colon and rectum (colorectal cancer) is third with 15 per cent. In men, colorectal cancer, second after lung cancer, accounts for 12 per cent of all cancer deaths, and cancer of the prostate gland is third with 10 per cent.

Now, how do we relate these major cancer killers to the agents that may cause them? First, we must understand the different kinds of evidence used to relate a carcinogen to a particular type of cancer.

The strongest sort of evidence, of course, is direct cause and effect in humans. But we cannot expose a human being to a carcinogen deliberately, so we have to study the life style of people who have cancer and try to find out what might have caused the disease. This is usually done through case-control studies, in which people with cancer are compared with people who are similar in most respects but do not have cancer.

We can also compare large populations of people with cancer to other large populations who do not have cancer in what are called epidemiological studies. We can test a suspected substance in animals. But we cannot say for sure that an agent that causes a cancer in animals will cause that cancer, or any cancer, in humans. We have only a strong reason to suspect that it can.

Smoking, particularly cigarette smoking, seems to be the largest single cause of lung cancer in both men and women. According to the ACS, smoking is associated with about 83 per cent of lung-cancer cases among men and about 43 per cent among women. The ACS also estimates

The author:
Harriet S. Page is a science writer for the National Cancer Institute in Bethesda, Maryland.

"Is cancer any reason to give up cigarettes?"

The strongest link statistically between a cancer and its cause is between lung cancer and smoking.

that at least 100,000 cancer deaths each year are due to smoking. Smoking is also linked to cancers of the mouth, pharynx, larynx, esophagus, pancreas, and bladder, and further linked to heart disease, ulcers, chronic bronchitis, and emphysema. For people who work at jobs where other carcinogens are present, smoking seems to increase the risk of getting lung cancer.

Smoking, Tobacco, and Health, a book issued by the United States Public Health Service's Office on Smoking and Health, reported that people in the United States would smoke some 600 billion cigarettes in 1981, a steady increase from about 200 billion per year during the 1940s. So it is not surprising that the death rate from lung cancer among men has followed an upward curve since 1945. In the 1940s, increasing numbers of women began to smoke cigarettes. Because of the latency period – the time between the first contact with a carcinogen and the development of cancer – the lung-cancer death rate for women did not swing sharply upward until the middle of the 1960s. The cigarette advertisement, "You've come a long way, baby," would seem to describe aptly the death rate of women from lung cancer as it rises to catch up with that of men.

Sir Richard Doll, a British physician, was among the first to suspect a link between cigarette smoking and lung cancer. In a 10-year study begun in the 1950s, Doll collected the observations of British physicians on thou-

119

sands of their colleagues who did or did not smoke cigarettes. He published the results of the survey in the *British Journal of Medicine*. The survey showed a definite link between smoking and lung cancer.

There have been numerous other studies. One was conducted for the ACS by statisticians E. Cuyler Hammond and Daniel Horr. They surveyed about 188,000 men for more than 44 months and found evidence that the mortality rate from cancer and heart disease rose with the number of cigarettes smoked. The rate ranged from 3.4 to 217.3 per 100,000 persons.

So if you want to avoid lung cancer, it would seem smart to stop smoking, and certainly to discourage your youngsters from taking up the habit.

At present, we know of no other habit that is linked so strongly to a particular cancer death rate as is smoking to lung cancer. We do not know what causes breast cancer in women, for example. There is some evidence that breast cancer is linked to levels of the production of estrogen — the chief female hormone. In some cases, it may be linked to heredity; there has been some indication that breast cancer runs in families. In addition to this, women who have never had children, or those who had their children late in life, have a high risk of contracting this disease.

Some intriguing observations about breast cancer and

Self examination that helps assure early detection is the best defense against breast cancer.

SACCHARIN NOTICE

This store sells food including diet beverages and dietetic foods that contain saccharin. You will find saccharin listed in the ingredient statement on most foods which contain it. All foods which contain saccharin will soon bear the following warning:

USE OF THIS PRODUCT MAY BE HAZARDOUS TO YOUR HEALTH. THIS PRODUCT CONTAINS SACCHARIN WHICH HAS BEEN DETERMINED TO CAUSE CANCER IN LABORATORY ANIMALS.

THIS STORE IS REQUIRED BY LAW TO DISPLAY THIS NOTICE PROMINENTLY

Eating habits have been implicated in several cancers of the internal organs. The Japanese diet, *above,* seems to be connected with stomach cancer, as do charcoal-broiled dishes, *above right.* Artificial sweeteners, *top,* have been proven to cause cancer in laboratory animals.

other cancers have been made on large groups of people who move from one country to another. If a particular cancer had a genetic cause, we would expect the cancer rates among an ethnic group to remain constant, regardless of where its members lived. But statistician William Haenszel of the National Cancer Institute (NCI) found different evidence. He published a report in 1972 on extensive studies of Japanese immigrants, showing that when they move to the United States their high rate of stomach cancer goes down in subsequent generations and becomes similar to that of native U.S. residents. Furthermore, the breast-cancer rate among women, which is low in Japan, rises to U.S. levels in subsequent generations.

This leads researchers to suspect diet as a cause. The average U.S. diet has much more fat, particularly animal fat from such foods as fatty meats and butter, than the usual Japanese diet. This dietary fat might contribute to the breast-cancer rate, perhaps by increasing the amount of estrogen-producing tissue in a woman's body. The lower rate of stomach cancer might be connected to the quantities of vinegar and salt generally used in foods in Japan, but given up when the Japanese come to the United States.

For the time being, our chief efforts in the prevention of breast-cancer deaths must be confined to its early detection, which seems to improve the rate of cure. Doctors are making considerable progress, meanwhile, in treating the disease. They are using less radical surgery, in many cases turning instead to precise radiation therapy and new combinations of anticancer drugs.

Colorectal cancer does have some genetic links. NCI scientists Ernest L. Winder and Bamduru Reddy published data in 1973 showing that a family history of colorectal cancer or of polyps — small growths — in the colon or rectum is linked to a higher risk of this cancer. There is increasing evidence that this cancer, too, may be related to the American diet with its high fat and low fiber content.

Scientist Dennis T. Burkett published a report in the *Journal of the NCI* in 1975 on his observations of other countries where colorectal cancer rates are low and diet, by comparison with ours, contains a greater proportion of high-fiber foods. Fecal matter contains mutagens, substances that cause changes in genes, and these may cause cancer. A high-fiber diet moves through the bowels relatively quickly compared with low-fiber, high-fat diets. Thus, any mutagens in what we eat are in contact with the bowel wall for a shorter period of time when the diet is high in fiber.

We do not know what causes prostate cancer. There is some evidence, however, that some occupational carcinogens — those encountered in the work place — may play a role. Here, too, efforts to prevent death from prostate cancer must rest with early detection and improvements in treatment. X-ray therapy or chemotherapy, or a combination of both, seems to be the most effective treatment.

Leukemia and lymphoma — cancers of the blood and lymph systems — account for about 10 per cent of cancer deaths in both men and women. As yet, we do not know what causes them, although we do know that industrial chemicals, such as benzene, for example, and excess radiation are linked to these diseases. There also may be a link with mononucleosis, the "kissing disease" of college students, but this link is tenuous.

Except for cigarette smoking, we have not yet been able

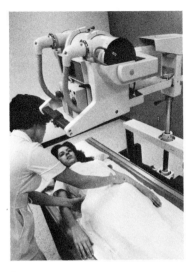

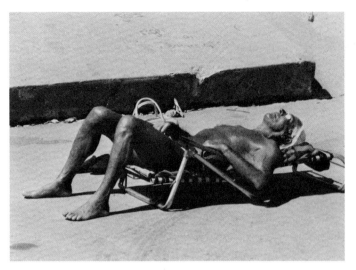

Too many diagnostic X rays, *above,* and over-exposure to the sun, *above right,* can lead to cancer.

to link any of the known cancer-causing agents in our personal environment with major cancers. But that does not mean we should downplay any of those agents. Knowing that they exist helps us to assign a degree of risk to them. We have to look at the evidence objectively.

For example, the Harvard University study linking coffee drinking with pancreatic cancer shows only a possible association. Scientists asked hospital patients about their coffee-drinking habits but did not discern how much or what kind of coffee the patients drank. There was some indication that those people in the study who developed cancer of the pancreas drank decaffeinated coffee primarily. Methylene chloride, the chemical formerly used to remove the caffeine from coffee, is known to cause cancer in animals. Thus, there is a possible association, but one that requires much further investigation. The study did not tell us how coffee or the agent used to remove caffeine might act to cause cancer. The scientist who gave up coffee drinking on the basis of his study may have acted too soon on his own data. Nevertheless, the study is important because it provides leads for further work.

The NCI snuff study was more detailed and yielded more convincing evidence. Scientists had suspected that there was an association between the snuff-dipping habit and cancer of the cheek and gum. The researchers first observed how snuff is used. Finely ground tobacco, suspended in saliva, is held in close contact with the cheek and gums for some time. Cancer appears in those parts of the snuff user's mouth. Since we know that tobacco contains carcinogens, the results come as no surprise.

Saccharin became as much a political as a scientific issue because millions of dollars in diet soft drink profits are at stake. An NCI study published in 1980 showed that artificial sweeteners such as saccharin had some association with bladder cancer but were most likely cancer "promoters" — substances that increase the cancer-causing effects of other agents. The people with the greatest risk, perhaps, are the youngsters who begin to consume large quantities of diet soft drinks early in life. There is also high risk to the babies of women who consume artificial sweeteners while pregnant.

Hair dyes were another focus of controversy when tests performed by the NCI and reported in 1978 showed that 7 of 13 chemicals tested, particularly the derivatives of coal tars, cause cancer in animals. Since hair dyes are applied to the scalp, some of the ingredients can be absorbed by the body.

The atomic bombs dropped on Hiroshima and Nagasaki, Japan, in 1945 gave us a great deal of data on how large doses of radiation cause cancer — particularly leukemias. Trying to relate large doses of radiation and their effects to small doses and their effects has been a difficult task, however, and the results are still far from precise. Scientists have questioned the frequency and amount of radiation used for mammograms, or breast X rays, in women. Their questions are based both on the bomb effects and on studies of periodic X rays. Radiologists today use equipment that is far more precise than was available in the 1950s and 1960s. Thus it is possible to target the doses and keep them to a minimum.

Methapyrilene is a substance that was used in most over-the-counter sleeping pills. In 1979, the NCI reported on animal tests showing that methapyrilene causes cancer in animals. When the results were made public, manufacturers removed methapyrilene and substituted another sleep-inducing chemical. NCI is testing that chemical because it is close in chemical structure to methapyrilene.

Evidence reported by the FDA in 1978 that linked bacon to cancer was based on animal studies of nitrite, a preservative used in bacon and other meats. But in 1980, the FDA announced that this evidence was weak. Yet scientists know nitrite can combine with saliva to form nitrosamines, a class of potent animal carcinogens. Manufacturers have removed some of the nitrites from bacon and other preserved meats and in some cases have added vitamin C, or ascorbic acid, which helps prevent nitrites

Modern technology has brought to the highways, and the coal mines, a faster pace, as well as air that can lead to respiratory cancers.

from becoming nitrosamines.

In the early 1970s, chemist Bruce Ames of the University of California, Berkeley, developed a simple test that would tell if a substance would cause mutagens in bacteria. This test was applied to Tris, a flame retardant used in children's pajamas, and it was announced in 1976 that Tris was mutagenic. NCI tests later indicated that Tris was also carcinogenic in animals. Tris-treated fabrics were quickly removed from the U.S. market, although they are still sold overseas.

Sunlight can cause skin cancer. NCI "cancer maps" showing mortality from different kinds of cancer throughout the United States show that melanoma — the most lethal kind of skin cancer — is most prevalent throughout the Sunbelt. Almost all other kinds of skin cancer are curable. But melanoma, which is linked both to sunlight exposure and to family history and accounts for 2 per cent of all skin cancers, is 98 per cent fatal.

Some cancers are also associated with the workplace. Asbestos and vinyl chloride are two examples of so-called occupational carcinogens. There is a great risk to workers who are exposed to such carcinogens in high concentrations for long periods of time, such as men who work in shipyards where asbestos is used. When inhaled, asbestos fibers cause mesothelioma, a rare form of cancer of the lining of the chest cavity. Unfortunately, it takes 20 to 30 years, and even longer, after exposure for this cancer to show up. Vinyl chloride causes a rare form of liver cancer. Workers in some chemical plants, particularly in the petrochemical industry, are found to have a high risk of bladder cancer. Such workplace exposures, which the Occupational Safety and Health Administration (OSHA) attempts to regulate, can be largely prevented if workers and plant management both work together to minimize exposure.

Obviously, there are many hazards our modern civilization must learn to live with. Fortunately, there are many steps we can take to minimize our exposure to cancer-causing agents. Knowledge is our best tool. Up-to-date information about carcinogens can be obtained from a number of sources — the American Cancer Society, the NCI, and the local Cancer Information Service. In addition, OSHA has local offices throughout the United States.

Most exposures to cancer-causing agents are well within our personal control, and we can follow some simple rules that will keep them to a minimum.

- Don't smoke. Filtered, low-tar and low-nicotine cigarettes are probably safer than others, but there is no "safe" cigarette.
- If you drink alcohol, drink in moderation only. Heavy alcohol consumption increases the risk of cancer of the esophagus. Alcohol may also be a promoter of other carcinogens.
- Eat a varied diet — chicken, fish, lean meats, fresh fruits, and vegetables when possible, and whole-grain breads and cereal. Avoid foods with many additives. Of the hundreds of chemicals added to our food, few have been shown to cause cancer in animals and none has been shown to cause cancer in people. However, only a small number of these non-nutritive additives have been tested. Avoid overuse of diet foods and drinks with artificial sweeteners. All the facts about fiber and fat, and vitamins A and C are not in yet, but extra vitamins are not necessary if you eat a well-balanced diet.
- Avoid sunburn and heavy tanning. Besides aging the skin, overdosing on sunlight causes skin cancer. Tan gradually, wear sunshades and hats, and use a sunscreen that contains the protective agent para-aminobenzoic acid (PABA).
- Avoid overuse of X rays. Those used in diagnosis — for a broken bone, for example, are small doses and necessary. So are dental X rays. But these can be limited. If you move to a new location, take your family's dental X rays with you (X-ray films are your property). The need for a repeat set the first year may be unnecessary.

Follow the NCI recommendation for breast X rays: annual mammography should be considered for women over 50; women over 40 whose mothers or sisters have had breast cancer; and women over 35 who have had breast cancer.

- Discuss the risks and benefits of prescription drugs with your physician. Some forms of estrogen, for example, have been linked with cancer. Reserpine, a drug used to control hypertension, or high blood pressure, has been associated with cancer. There are alternative drugs.
- When using chemicals at home — paint strippers, for example — follow directions and work outdoors or in a garage where there is plenty of ventilation. Avoid breathing the vapors and getting the liquid on your skin.
- Finally, evaluate what you hear and see and do not overreact. If you live a prudent life, you will probably live a longer one.

It is possible today that cancer phobia causes more suffering than cancer itself.

George Washington Crile, Jr., physician and author

127

Dr. Beaumont's Frontier Research

A stomach wound that never closed up provided a 19th-century physician with a window on the workings of digestion

By Darlene R. Stille

It was a beautiful June morning in Michigan in 1822. The beach below the village on the island of Michilimacinac in the straits between Lake Huron and Lake Michigan was crowded with fur traders and Indians who had paddled over to the American Fur Company headquarters in canoes filled with hides and pelts. A few United States soldiers from Fort Mackinac on the hill above wandered among the colorful throng. Many of the fur traders and the voyageurs who transported them to this remote area headed for the company store to buy supplies and catch up on news. One of these was Alexis St. Martin, a 19-year-old French Canadian, who never suspected that his visit to a store on a wilderness island would change the course of medical history.

No one seems sure about what actually happened. St. Martin was apparently standing inside the company store while another trapper was standing nearby with a shotgun. Somehow, the gun went off, and its charge slammed into the left side of St. Martin's body, blowing away flesh and ribs and setting his shirt on fire. The horrified bystanders lifted the wounded young man onto a cot in the store and sent for a doctor from the fort up the hill.

The only doctor at the fort was William Beaumont, the

36-year-old son of a Connecticut farmer. Although his post at Fort Mackinac was a peaceful one, Dr. Beaumont had served as an Army surgeon during the War of 1812, and had a great deal of experience in treating gunshot wounds. When the traders summoned him, Dr. Beaumont rushed down to the company store to attend to St. Martin. "The whole mass of materials forced from the musket, together with fragments of clothing and pieces of fractured ribs, were driven into the muscles and cavity of the chest," Dr. Beaumont later wrote in his journal.

"I saw him in twenty-five or thirty minutes after the accident occurred, and, on examination, found a portion of the lung, as large as a Turkey's egg, protruding through the external wound, lacerated and burnt; and immediately below this, another protrusion, which, on further examination, proved to be a portion of the stomach, lacerated through all its coats, and pouring out the food he had taken for his breakfast, through an orifice large enough to admit the fore finger."

Dr. Beaumont dressed the wound and made the man as comfortable as possible, but he expected him to live no longer than 20 minutes. Nevertheless, St. Martin was still alive the next day. After removing more shot and clothing from the wound, Dr. Beaumont concluded that the wound would heal and that St. Martin would survive.

In fact, St. Martin lived to be almost 80 years old. But the wound never completely healed. And because of this, he became the subject of a series of experiments by Dr. Beaumont that revolutionized the medical profession's understanding of human digestion.

The circumstances that led to this development stemmed from St. Martin's condition 10 months after the accident. He was still a patient in the military hospital, unable even to walk. The town authorities declared him a common pauper and proposed sending him back to Canada. Dr. Beaumont was certain that St. Martin would never survive the journey, so the doctor took his patient into his own home and, over a period of two years, nursed him back to health. But St. Martin was left with an opening under his left breast and a perforation in the lining of his stomach.

Dr. Beaumont saw this as an unprecedented opportunity for medical research. He persuaded St. Martin to allow him to examine the contents of his stomach and observe the process of digestion through the opening. And so, in the sparsely furnished surroundings of a military outpost in the wilds of northern Michigan, Dr. Beaumont set

The author:
Darlene R. Stille is Managing Editor of *Medical Update,* 1982.

130

French-Canadian fur trader Alexis St. Martin, *above,* the patient of Dr. William Beaumont, *above right,* became a living laboratory for Dr. Beaumont's studies of the stomach and digestive processes.

about unlocking some of the mysteries of the body's internal workings.

Dr. Beaumont kept a detailed journal. He performed his first experiment on Aug. 1, 1825 to find out how long it took the stomach to digest various types of food:

"At 12 o'clock, M., I introduced through the perforation, into the stomach, the following articles of diet, suspended by a silk string, and fastened at proper distances, so as to pass in without pain, a piece of high seasoned a la mode beef; a piece of raw, salted, fat pork; a piece of raw, salted, lean beef; a piece of boiled, salted beef; a piece of stale bread; and a bunch of raw, sliced cabbage; each piece weighing about two drachms [drams, or about ¼ ounce]. . . .

"At 1 o'clock, P.M., withdrew and examined them — found the cabbage and bread about half digested: the pieces of meat unchanged. Returned them into the stomach.

"At 2 o'clock, P.M., withdrew them again — found the cabbage, bread, pork; and boiled beef, all cleanly digested, and gone from the string. . . .

"At 2 o'clock, P.M., [sic], examined again — found the a la mode beef partly digested: the raw beef was [generally] firm and entire. The smell and taste of the fluids of the stomach were slightly rancid; and the boy complained of some pain and uneasiness. . . . Returned them again."

In June 1822, St. Martin was accidentally shot in the chest and stomach at the American Fur Company's store on Mackinac Island in the Michigan wilderness.

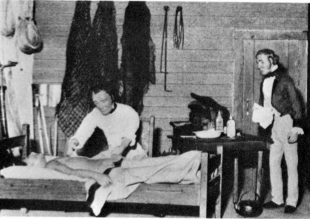

Dr. Beaumont, the Army surgeon stationed at Ft. Mackinac, tended St. Martin's wound in the back of the store but never expected that the young man would survive.

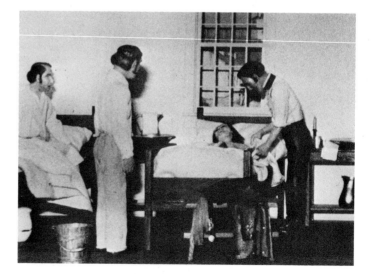

After a ten month stay in the fort's hospital, St. Martin's wound had still not healed. Rather than let the authorities send the sick man back to Canada, Dr. Beaumont decided to move St. Martin into his own home.

In this first experiment, Dr. Beaumont apparently gave St. Martin a very bad case of indigestion.

"The lad complaining of considerable distress and uneasiness at the stomach, general debility and lassitude, with some pain in his head, I withdrew the string, and found the remaining portions of aliment [food] nearly in the same condition as when last examined; the fluid more rancid and sharp. The boy still complaining, I did not return them any more."

The next day, St. Martin was still ill, and Dr. Beaumont could see numerous white spots on the inner surface of the stomach. "I thought it advisable to give medicine; and accordingly, dropped into the stomach, through the aperture, half a dozen calomel pills, four or five grains each; which, in about three hours, had a thorough cathartic effect, and removed all the [indigestion] symptoms, and the diseased appearance of the inner coat of the stomach."

Soon after Dr. Beaumont began his experiments, the Army transferred him to Fort Niagara in New York state. He took St. Martin east with him. But St. Martin did not enjoy being the subject of these experiments, and in the fall of 1825 he ran away to Canada, where he married, began to raise a family, and worked as a voyageur, transporting fur trappers and supplies by canoe to remote forest areas.

After two years of searching, Dr. Beaumont succeeded in tracking him down through American Fur Company agents. After two more years, he convinced St. Martin in 1829 to bring his family to Fort Crawford at Prairie du Chien, Wis., where Dr. Beaumont was then stationed. St. Martin worked as the Beaumont family's personal servant and submitted to more experiments until the spring of 1831, when he and his family returned to Canada.

Dr. Beaumont conducted one more series of experiments on St. Martin in 1832 and 1833 in Washington, D.C., and New York City. But he was never able to persuade St. Martin to take part in any more of these research adventures.

In 1833, Dr. Beaumont published his studies in a book entitled *Experiments and Observations on the Gastric Juice and Physiology of Digestion*. The book contained the details of 238 experiments, plus a table comparing the digestibility of a wide range of foods.

Until this time, very little was known about digestion and the stomach. Some theories held that the stomach was only a storage place for food; others, that it was a grinding mill or a fermentation vat in which food somehow decomposed.

Dr. Beaumont had used the opportunity presented by St. Martin's wound to discover the truth. For example, he was curious about the chemicals that were responsible for digesting food. So he devised a method of removing gastric juice from St. Martin's stomach for analysis.

"The usual method of extracting the gastric juice, for experiment, is by placing the subject on his right side . . . introducing a gum-elastic tube, of the size of a large quill, five or six inches into the stomach, and then turning him on the left side. . . . In health, and when free from food, the stomach is usually entirely empty, and contracted upon itself. On introducing the tube, the fluid soon begins to flow, first by drops, then in an interrupted, and sometimes in a short continuous stream. Moving the tube about, up and down, or backwards and forwards, increases the discharge."

Dr. Beaumont analyzed these gastric juices himself and also sent samples to other doctors for their analyses. They concluded that the main component of the gastric juice is muriatic, or hydrochloric, acid. Doctors later discovered that the gastric juice also contains the enzyme pepsin.

In his primitive surroundings, without the benefit of

In the doctor's office at the fort where Dr. Beaumont began his famous experiments on digestion, artifacts are on display as a monument to Beaumont's role in medical history.

sophisticated laboratory equipment, Dr. Beaumont found a way to determine temperature inside the stomach. He inserted "a Thermometer (Fahrenheit's) through the perforation, into the stomach, nearly the whole length of the stem, to ascertain the natural warmth of the stomach. In fifteen minutes, or less, the mercury rose to 100°, and there remained stationary." After doing this several times, Dr. Beaumont concluded:

"The ordinary temperature of the healthy stomach, may be fairly estimated at 100°, Fahrenheit. Some allowance ought, probably, to be made, in these experiments, for imperfect instruments. It appears . . . that there is probably some difference of temperature in different regions of the stomach, it being higher at the pyloric than at the splenic end."

Dr. Beaumont, the scientific investigator, ever careful and precise in his observations and measurements, was nevertheless sometimes filled with a sense of wonder at what he was witnessing through the window of St. Martin's unclosed wound.

During an examination, he wrote,". . . St. Martin swallowed part of a glass of water, and being situated in a strong light, favourable to an internal view, through the aperture, I distinctly saw the water pass into the cavity of the stomach, through the cardiac orifice – a circumstance, perhaps, never before witnessed, in a living subject. . . . Food, swallowed in this position, could be distinctly seen to enter the stomach."

Medical men of the day debated where the sense of hunger came from and how the act of eating made it go away. Some felt strongly that it was connected with the sense of taste. Others were not so sure. Dr. Beaumont devoted one of his experiments to this question:

"To ascertain whether the sense of hunger would be allayed without the food being passed through the oesophagus, he [St. Martin] fasted from breakfast time, till 4 o'clock, P.M., and became quite hungry. I then put in at the aperture, three and a half drachms of lean, boiled beef. The sense of hunger immediately subsided, and stopped the borborygmus, or croaking noise, caused by the motion of air in the stomach and intestines, peculiar to him since the wound, and almost always observed when the stomach is empty.

"This experiment proves that the sense of hunger resides in the stomach, and is . . . allayed by putting the food directly into the stomach. . . ."

Today, doctors know that the sensations of hunger and

satiety are more complex than that, relying on levels of sugar in the blood and also on signals from the brain. But Dr. Beaumont's observation was a step toward gathering experimental evidence, rather than simply relying on conjecture.

Another area of debate within the medical profession centered on whether gastric juice was always present in the stomach or whether it appeared only when the stomach contained food. In a painstaking series of experiments, Dr. Beaumont inserted his tube into St. Martin's stomach at various times after the young man had eaten and after long periods of fasting:

"Dec. 5, 1829. At 8 o'clock, A.M., after twelve hours abstinence from either food or drinks, I introduced, at the perforation, a gum-elastic tube, and drew off a drachm or two only of the gastric juice. — There was no accumulation in the stomach."

"March 13, 1830. At 10 o'clock, A.M. — stomach empty — introduced tube; but was unable to obtain any gastric juice. On the application of a few crumbs of bread to the inner surface of the stomach, the juice began slowly to accumulate, and flow through the tube. . . ."

"March 18. At 6 o'clock, P.M., after fasting from 8 o'clock A.M., introduced tube — obtained one and a half ounces gastric juice, after having kept up the irritation, by moving the tube from point to point, for twelve or fifteen minutes. No accumulation of free juice in the stomach."

"It would seem, from the preceding experiments," Beaumont concluded, "that the stomach contains no gastric juice, in a free state, when aliment is not present. Any digestible or irritating substance, when applied to the internal coat, excites the action of the gastric vessels. . . ."

In the crude surroundings of the mid-1800's frontier fort, Dr. Beaumont also set about conducting laboratory experiments. He wanted to get a clearer view of the process of digestion by observing it firsthand.

"Dec. 14, 1829. At 1 o'clock, P.M., I took one and a half ounces of gastric juice, fresh from the stomach, after eighteen hours fasting, into an open mouthed vial — put into it twelve drachms recently salted beef, (boiled) and placed it in a basin of water, on a sand bath, and kept it at about 100° (Fahrenheit,) with frequent, gentle agitation. Digestion commenced, in a short time, on the surface of the meat, and progressed in that manner uniformly for about six hours, when its solvent action seemed to cease. The meat was at this time, nearly half dissolved. . . . In twenty-four hours, the digested portion separated into a reddish brown precipitate, and whey coloured fluid.

"I now separated the undigested from the chymous [liquefied] portion, by filtration, through thin muslin. When squeezed dry, it weighed five drachms, two scruples, and eight grains, which, deducted from the twelve drachms of meat put in at first, leaves six drachms and twelve grains, digested in twelve fluid-drachms of gastric juice.

"In this experiment, it appears, that it took twelve drachms of gastric juice to digest six drachms and twelve grains of aliment. No certain rule can, however, be given. Allowance must be made for the purity of the fluid. . . . It is probable, also, that different kinds of diet require different proportions of gastric juice for their solution. . . . There is always disturbance of the stomach when more food has been received than there is gastric juice to act upon it."

The sum of Dr. Beaumont's work changed the medical texts of the time. It revealed the chemical makeup of gastric juice, proved this juice is present only when the stomach contains food, compared rates of digestion in the stomach and in laboratory vials, recorded the motions of the stomach, and compared the digestibility of various kinds of foods.

This great medical research project ended when St. Martin left Dr. Beaumont's employ. In 1840, after retiring from the Army, Beaumont set up private practice in St. Louis. He died there on April 25, 1853. St. Martin lived almost 30 years longer.

Some drugs come in capsule form not to make them easier to swallow but to give them safe passage through the seething stomach. These drugs are meant to act in the intestines, which they will never reach if they are digested by acids en route. Thus, pharmaceutical companies make protective casings from substances that are unaffected by the hydrochloric acid and pepsin in the stomach, but are readily dissolved by trypsin, amylase, or any of the other digestive juices found in the intestines.

Hospices

A new way of caring

By the editors of *MD* Magazine

At Cabrini Hospital in New York City a terminally ill cancer patient is alone in his room. He is fed intravenously, and his only physical contact is with the life-support machines that surround him.

A few blocks north, at the Cabrini Hospice, lies another terminally ill patient. He is surrounded by small children and at the foot of his bed, his dog is curled up asleep. He is sipping a glass of whiskey and eating lasagna, prepared by his wife. The key, says medical director Anthony Bianco, M.D., is "flexibility and sensitivity. Here the patient is king, his individuality and his way of life are respected."

A month earlier at Cabrini Hospice a dying patient was too weak to return home and was distraught at the thought of not having his wife of 40 years share his bed. Arrangements were made for her to live at the hospice. Peter Ungvarski, the director of nursing, says, "Here we don't ask you to check anything at the door, not your property, your genitals, or your mind."

The modern hospice movement developed from several divergent streams of thought. One pioneer was Dr. Elisabeth Kübler-Ross whose book, *On Death and Dying,* became the movement's manifesto. Published in 1969, the book described America as a "death-denying culture." Americans' emphasis on youth and physical beauty has led them to consider death an embarrassment that should not be discussed, she argued, and the denial of death has, in effect, taken away from the terminal patient control over the stages of the dying process. Kübler-Ross

Hospice personnel extend their professional services to encompass natural human emotions.

139

defines them as a natural movement from denial, anger, bargaining, and depression to acceptance.

These death-denying attitudes, says Kübler-Ross, should be countered with special therapies that encourage the dying to share their needs and fears with those around them. She also noted that the heroic medical efforts of modern technology often involved greater heroism on the part of the patient than the doctor. The machines, in effect, isolated the terminally ill in institutions, denying them the warmth of their own homes.

Others contributed to the growing literature of thanatology. Columnist Stewart Alsop, who died in 1974 of leukemia, wrote of his last months in the book *Stay of Execution*. He urged that cancer victims be afforded the illusion of "painless pleasure" that comes from the use of heroin. Academic courses on death and dying became popular in schools and colleges. Others advocated euthanasia, as preferable to an agonizing and impersonal death. The dictum of the British historian Arnold Toynbee that "death is un-American" was no longer true.

By the mid-seventies the hospice movement had taken hold of the nation's imagination. Today there are over 200 scattered throughout the country, and about 100 more are in the planning stage. Their goal is to provide three things to the terminally ill: relief from pain and other symptoms of distress; medical and psychological care; and companionship.

Most hospices have inpatient-care facilities that can be used in emergencies or for symptom relief, but they all urge families to make their first priority home care for the dying. Hospice professionals feel that an active role in the care of the dying prepares the family for the bereavement period and significantly lessens feelings of guilt.

Hospices also provide extensive family counseling both before and after the patient's death. They point to a recent study of mortality rates for widowed women that shows a 700-per cent increase during the first year after the death of a spouse, and to a 70-per cent increase in divorce rates for parents who have lost a child. Hospice professionals describe bereavement counseling as a form of preventive medicine and a matter of simple humanity for those unable to come to terms with a death.

Hospice directors note that practitioners of conventional medicine often seem unequipped, untrained, and psychologically unprepared to treat the dying. Dr. Morris Wessel, clinical professor of pediatrics at Yale University School of Medicine, says health-care professionals have

As reprinted from *MD* Magazine, April 1981

Beyond this grim gate stands one of the first medical establishments to give the dying control over their lives.

become "depersonalized, part of a system that is defined by the rules of third-party payment and the bureaucracy rather than the needs of the patient."

Dr. Balfour Mount, director of Palliative Care Service at McGill University in Montreal, adds that "As physicians we are oriented by our schooling and training toward investigation, diagnosis, prolongation of life and curing. But these patients with advanced disease don't need our hard-won skills, and the patient's other needs are not being recognized. This dilemma, the more you look at it, is a natural product of our information explosion."

The hospice movement says the answer to the dilemma lies in a fundamental change in the attitude of physicians and medical staffs. Dr. Josefina Magno, an oncologist who heads the National Hospice Organization, says institutions that care for the dying must move from "curing to caring." The doctor for the dying, she says, must be "flexible and sensitive, responsive above all to the human as well as medical needs of the patient. He must, for example, be aware of the patient's mood: some want to talk about death, others cannot bear too much reality."

The first hospice in North America was established at the Royal Victoria Hospital in Montreal, in 1973, the second in New Haven in 1974, and the third at St. Lukes Hospital in New York City in 1975. In 1978 the National Hospice Organization (NHO) was formed. They seek out third-party reimbursement for hospice care in the public and private sector, and through their efforts General Electric, Westinghouse, and RCA have agreed to provide hospice benefits to their employees. NHO also establishes

A person with limited time can maintain a sense of self-worth with work that is rewarding.

standards for hospice care and sponsors meetings and symposia relevant to the hospice movement.

The National Cancer Institute, Medicare, and Blue Cross and Blue Shield have all expressed interest in hospice care, both because of its humaneness and its cost. A preliminary study by Georgetown University found that hospice care was less than half the cost of hospital care and that it compared favorably to nursing-home care.

Support for hospices has also come from the Federal Government. There are now 25 million Americans over 65, representing an increase from 4.1 per cent in 1900 to 10.9 per cent in 1977, and it is estimated that in 40 years that number will double. In 1979 the Department of Health and Human Resources awarded two-year pilot grants to 26 existing Hospice Programs for Medicare and Medicaid patients. The cost of the program is being met through the Health Care Financing Administration.

Most hospices in North America take as their model St. Christopher's Hospice in Sydenham, on the outskirts of

Sunshine and fresh air and a nearby friend form a setting of peace that hospice programs assure.

London. The 54-bed hospice, which opened in 1967, is a bright four-story building surrounded by gardens. It has light, colorfully decorated wards, a few private rooms, cheerful family rooms, a play school for staff members' children, and accommodations for some elderly residents who are not terminally ill. Space for a small number of patients who require nursing for chronic illnesses, especially motor neuron disease, is also provided. Because well over two-thirds of St. Christopher's patients are dying of cancer, the hospice accepts patients with long-term illnesses to remove the onus of a "death house" and to provide a sense of permanence for staff members and patients.

More than any other single individual, the founder and medical director of St. Christopher's, Dr. Cicely Saunders, a nurse, social worker, and physician, has set the therapeutic and human standards of the modern hospice. One of her most important contributions is the use of "polypharmacy" to relieve pain, depression, anxiety, and insomnia. Depending upon the severity of the pain, patients at St. Christopher's receive aspirin, propoxyphene, methadone, morphine, or Brompton's "cocktail," a mixture of oral heroin, cocaine, alcohol, syrup, and chloroform water. The use of therapeutic doses of heroin is one of the major differences between hospice practice in the United States and England. The National Institute on Drug Abuse has given $1.9 million to New York's Sloan-Kettering Institute for Cancer Research for a detailed study of heroin and other drugs for the relief of chronic pain.

Our first responsibility, says Saunders, is to erase the fear of recurrent pain. Thus analgesics are not administered "as needed," but on a regular basis, before the effect of the previous dose wears off. Whenever possible, at St. Christopher's oral medications are given. Natural treatments are preferred over artificial ones. "We nourish," says Saunders, "with hot soup, not tubes. . . . We must learn when to stop the prolongation of life and accept a peaceful death. It is far better to have a cup of tea on your last day than drips and tubes in every direction."

In 1968 Florence Wald, former dean of the Yale Nursing School, the Reverend Edward Dobihal, Dr. Ira Goldenberg, professor of clinical surgery, and Dr. Wessel, soon to become president of the New England Pediatric Society, formed a discussion group to look into the experiences of patients in the Yale-New Haven area who were terminally ill.

The discussion group brought Dr. Saunders to New Haven to describe her methods of patient care, and Rev. Dobihal spent a year in England at St. Christopher's. Out of these exchanges came the group's pioneering effort to establish the first hospice in the United States.

The home-care component opened in New Haven in 1974, and in 1980 the group, now called Connecticut Hospice, Inc., opened a 44-bed residence, with a staff of 160, in nearby Branford, Connecticut. Designed by the award-winning architect Lo-Yi Chan, the building is simple and serene. The patient rooms are set into two 22-bed wings that have a central living room and a fireplace. Each room can be entered from a glass-enclosed corridor that offers a view of patios, a large fountain, and gardens.

This is the first building erected in the United States solely for hospice use and it reflects a significant departure from the institutional norms of the hospital and the nursing home. It has large, comfortable rooms for 24-hour family visiting and a day-care center for children of the

When regulations can be relaxed, the hospitalized patient's comfort can be enhanced with the presence of a familiar companion.

144

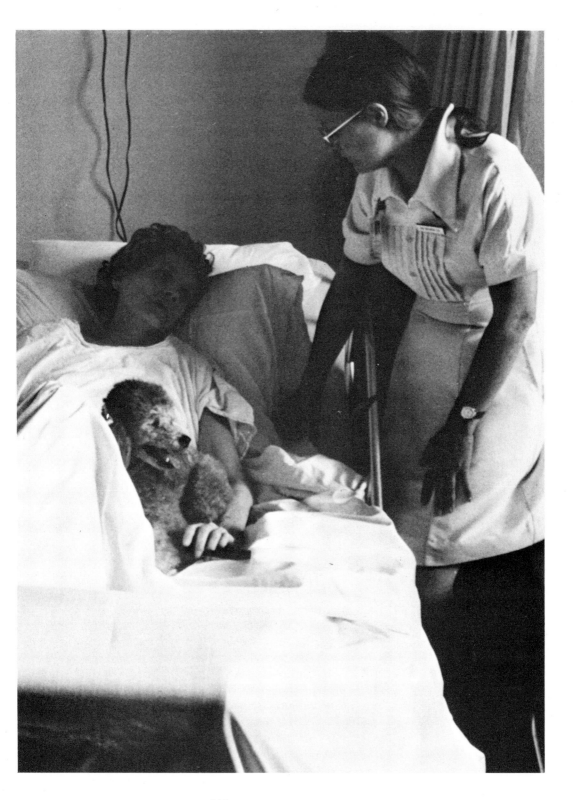

staff and the neighborhood. In good weather the patients can be wheeled out to the patios, and they can rest near the children's play area.

Dr. Wessel sees the preschool child-care center at the hospice as giving great comfort to both the patients and the children who come to visit. The fact that children are nearby, Wessel says, "is a symbol of the unique affection that often exists between the old and the young. Those appointed to take their leave of this life will see it visibly going forward into another generation."

An entirely different setting for hospice care exists at St. Luke's Hospital Center in New York City. Hospice patients requiring symptom control and nursing care are scattered throughout the hospital where they are regularly visited by the hospice team. Out-patients, who visit the clinic, are met by a nurse who expedites treatment and provides emotional support. The major goal of the program is to have the terminally ill taken care of at home, and they have regular visits from counselors and volunteers. The unit of care is always the family. Said one woman: "St. Luke's was my backbone; the hospice held me up so that my hands were free to care for my father."

At the Royal Victoria Hospital in Montreal, hospice patients are admitted to a specific unit within the general hospital. Other centers where hospice care is available are the Riverside Hospital in Boonton, New Jersey, the 39-bed Hilhaven Hospice in Tucson, and the Kaiser-Permanente Health Plan's unit in Los Angeles.

A pioneer in the extension of hospice care to children is St. Mary's Hospital in Bayside, New York. The hospital, founded in 1870, provides long-term rehabilitation for children with severe defects, diseases or injuries. Now with a $1.1 million grant from the New York Community Trust, the 85-bed facility is starting construction of a new floor with a separate six-bed hospice unit.

The medical director of St. Mary's, Dr. Burton Grebin, an assistant professor of clinical pediatrics at Columbia University's College of Physicians and Surgeons, says that "The patient here is not the child, but the child and his family. Our goal is to return the child to his own home."

Dr. Grebin cites the example of a 12-year-old boy with craniopharyngioma. After two surgical procedures and chemotherapy for his slow-growing tumor he was transferred to St. Mary's.

"He came," says Dr. Grebin, "because he was severely depressed and not eating. In fact, he was dying. Six months ago he left St. Mary's with a new lease on life. We were equipped to help him in a way that cannot be done in an acute hospital setting, whose major task is crisis intervention. We arranged for his single father to come to the hospital before work to feed the boy by tube, and by working with them both we were able to teach the boy to feed himself. He regained his appetite and started to go home on weekends. He now lives at home with his eight brothers and sisters. The family benefited from the hospice concept: Expert nursing care, psychological, spiritual, and emotional support."

Dr. Grebin adds that the concept of the hospice has to be redefined when applied to children. Most of the adults in hospice care are cancer patients who die within three to six months, but with children it is difficult to determine lifespan, and it is that "unpredictability" that has such a devastating effect on the family.

One corporation that helps families with seriously ill children is McDonald's. In February 1981, they opened their 21st Ronald McDonald House in Tucson. The houses are hotels for families of very ill children and are located near children's hospitals throughout the country. The fees are nominal, and in hardship cases they are free.

During the 1970s the hospice movement left its mark on American health care, but what of the future? Dr. Richard Geltman, medical director of the St. Luke's Hospice, says, "The concept is not revolutionary but really a return to the tradition of care taught by Florence Nightingale. If those principles became a formalized part of medical education, the hospice might go out of business in a few years."

Dr. Wessel agrees. "If the doctors were all working together," says Wessel, "we wouldn't need hospices at all. But the fact that there are so many means that somewhere the system is failing. Hospice programs give strength to those who work together. Why it isn't possible in all hospitals is difficult to understand . . . but that is the reality."

Terminal cancer patients at Beth Israel Hospital in Boston have benefited from a service designed for the blind – "talking books". These are recordings of classics, novels, mysteries, science fiction, and magazines, distributed through regional libraries and state commissions for the blind. They provide intellectual stimulation as well as a distraction from pain for patients who can no longer hold and turn the pages of conventional books and magazines.

147

On Smell

Notes of a biology-watcher

By Lewis Thomas, M.D.

The vacuum cleaner turned on in the apartment's back bedroom emits a high-pitched lament indistinguishable from the steam alarm on the tea kettle in the kitchen, and the only way of judging whether to run to the stove is to consult one's watch: there is a time of day for the vacuum cleaner, another time for the tea kettle. The telephone in the guest bedroom sounds like the back doorbell, so you wait for the second or third ring before moving. There is a random crunching sound in the vicinity of the front door, resembling an assemblage of people excitedly taking off galoshes, but when listened to carefully it is recognizable as a negligible sound, needing no response, made by the ancient elevator machinery in the wall alongside the door. So it goes. We learn these things from day to day, no trick to it. Sometimes the sounds around our lives become novel confusions, harder to sort out; the family was once given a talking crow named Byron for Christmas, and this animal imitated every nearby sound with such accuracy that the household was kept constantly on the fly, answering doors and telephones, oiling hinges, looking out the window for falling bodies, glancing into empty bathrooms for the sources of flushing.

We are not so easily misled by vision. Most of the things before our eyes are plainly there, not mistakable for other things except for the illusions created for pay by professional magicians and, sometimes, the look of the lights of downtown New York against a sky so black as to make it seem a near view of eternity. Our eyes are not easy to fool.

The smell of burning leaves, now only a memory, once signaled the onset of the fall season.

149

Black-eyed Susans invite the child
in all of us to sample the
pleasure of their fragrance.

The author:
Lewis Thomas is chancellor of the
Memorial Sloan-Kettering Cancer
Center in New York City. He
is the author of two books of
essays: *The Lives of the Cell*
and *The Medusa and the Snail*.

Printed by permission from the New England Journal of Medicine. Vol. 302 No.
13, pages 731–733, March 27, 1980.

Smell is another matter. I should think we might fairly
gauge the future of biological science, centuries ahead, by
estimating the time it will take to reach a complete,
comprehensive understanding of odor. It may not seem a
profound enough problem to dominate all the life sciences, but it contains, piece by piece, all the mysteries.
Smoke: tobacco burning, coal smoke, wood-fire smoke,
leaf smoke. Most of all, leaf smoke. This is the only odor I
can will back to consciousness just by thinking about it. I
can sit in a chair, thinking, and call up clearly to mind the
smell of burning autumn leaves, coded and stored away

New-mown hay evokes a flood of memories for those of us who knew the smell in childhood.

somewhere in a temporal lobe, firing off explosive signals into every part of my right hemisphere. But nothing else: if I try to recall the thick smell of Edinburgh in winter, or the accidental burning of a plastic comb, or a rose, or a glass of wine, I cannot; I can get a clear picture of any face I feel like remembering, and I can hear whatever Beethoven quartet I want to recall, but except for the leaf bonfire I cannot really remember a smell in its absence. To be sure, I know the odor of cinnamon or juniper and can name such things with accuracy when they turn up in front of my nose, but I cannot imagine them into existence.

The act of smelling something, anything, is remarkably like the act of thinking itself. Immediately, at the very moment of perception, you can feel the mind going to work, sending the odor around from place to place, setting off complex repertoires throughout the brain, polling one center after another for signs of recognition, old memories, connections. This is as it should be, I suppose, since the cells that do the smelling are themselves proper brain cells, the only neurons whose axons carry information picked up firsthand in the outside world. Instead of dendrites they have cilia, equipped with receptors for all sorts of chemical stimuli, and they are in some respects as mysterious as lymphocytes. There are reasons to believe

151

Smell's tie to taste is truly experienced in the kitchen after a morning's baking.

that each of these neurons has its own specific class of receptors; like lymphocytes, each cell knows in advance what it is looking for; there are responder and nonresponder cells for different classes of odorant. And they are also the only brain neurons that replicate themselves; the olfactory receptor cells of mice turn over about once every 28 days. There may be room for a modified version of the clonal selection theory to explain olfactory learning and adaptation. The olfactory receptors of mice can smell the difference between self and nonself, a discriminating gift coded by the same H-2 gene locus governing homograft rejection. One wonders whether lymphocytes in the mucosa may be carrying along this kind of information to

152

donate to new generations of olfactory receptor cells as they emerge from basal cells.

The most medically wonderful of all things about these brain cells is that they do not become infected, not very often anyway, despite their exposure to all the microorganisms in the world of the nose. There must exist, in the mucus secretions bathing this surface of the brain, the most extraordinary antibiotics, including electric antiviral substances of some sort.

If you are looking about for things to even out the disparity between the brains of ordinary animals and the great minds of ourselves, the superprimate human beings, this apparatus is a good one to reflect on in humility.

A heady mixture of sweet and healthy smells overwhelms us when we pass by a fruit stand.

The salt smell of sea air combined with the sound of pounding surf is a sensual description of the places where the ocean meets the land.

Compared to the common dog, or any rodent in the field, we are primitive, insensitive creatures, biological failures. Heaven knows how much of the world we are missing.

I suppose that if we tried we could improve ourselves. There are, after all, some among our species with special gifts for smelling—perfume makers, tea-tasters, whiskey blenders—and it is said that these people can train themselves to higher and higher skills by practicing. Perhaps, instead of spending the resources of our huge cosmetic industry on chemicals for the disguising or outright destruction of odors, we should be studying ways to enhance the smell of nature, facing up to the world.

In the meantime, we should be hanging on to some of the few great smells left to us, and I would vote for the preservation of leaf bonfires, by law if necessary. This one is pure pleasure, fetched like music intact out of numberless modular columns of neurons filled chockablock with all the natural details of childhood, firing off memories in every corner of the brain. An autumn curbside bonfire has everything needed for education: danger, surprise (you know in advance that if you poke the right part of the base of leaves with the right kind of stick, a blinding flare of heat and fragrance will follow instantly, but it is still an astonishment when it happens), risk and victory over odds (if you jump across at precisely the right moment the flare and sparks will miss your pants), and above all the aroma of comradeship (if you smell that odor in the distance you know that there are friends somewhere in the next block, jumping and exulting in their leaves, maybe catching fire).

It was a mistake to change this, smoke or no smoke, carbon dioxide and the greenhouse effect or whatever; it was a loss to give up the burning of autumn leaves. Now, in our haste to protect the environment (which is us, when you get down to it), we rake them up and cram them into great black plastic bags, set out at the curb like wrapped corpses, carted away by the garbage truck to be buried somewhere or dumped into the sea or made into fuel or alcohol or whatever it is they do with autumn leaves these days. We should be giving them back to children to burn.

Body scent plays an important role in forming the bond between mother and child. Researchers at Oxford University in England found that, at the age of 6 weeks, sleeping babies will make sucking motions when cotton pads that have been worn inside their mother's bras are passed under their noses. However, they do not suck, and often burst into tears, when confronted with the breast scent of another woman.

Help for
the Headache

Physicians now know better ways
to diagnose and treat the victims
of severe head pain

By David R. Coddon, M.D.

"Daddy, please make the pain go away," my son Johnny
cried one day when he was 12 years old. I had been
called home from my office on an October afternoon to
find him writhing on the floor in agony. He was sweating
profusely and holding his head. His face and lips were
white as a sheet, and his hands were ice cold. He later
became nauseous and vomited uncontrollably.

I was terrified that Johnny had suffered a brain hemorrhage. Unlike most parents, however, as a neurologist I
was able to put my fears to rest. Johnny was severely ill,
to be sure, but he was not having a stroke. He was having
a migraine headache attack. I carried him upstairs to his
bedroom where he eventually fell asleep. When he woke
up the next morning the severe pain was gone. Only a
dull headache and a washed-out feeling remained to
remind him of the terrible ordeal he had gone through.

Johnny is unusual in that his father is a headache
specialist, but he is not a victim of some rare disorder.
More than 20 million Americans suffer the throbbing pain
of migraine headache. Severe as it is, migraine is only one
of several types of chronic and recurrent disabling headaches that afflict more than 10 per cent of the people in
the world. In the United States, as many as 40 million
persons seek medical help each year for relief of severe

head pain; more than half of all visits to doctors are due to headaches. Americans spend billions of dollars annually on over-the-counter remedies and prescription drugs for headache relief. More work time is lost to headache than to cancer, heart disease, stroke, and psychiatric illness combined.

As director of the Headache Clinic at the Mount Sinai Medical Center in New York City and in my private practice, I see thousands of headache sufferers each year. I have learned that headaches respect no age, race, sex, geographic, or other differences. Headache victims are found in all parts of the world, and they live in noisy big cities and on quiet farms.

Headaches have plagued people throughout recorded medical history and probably existed long before. For centuries, the malady was surrounded by myth and misunderstanding. Primitive cultures viewed severe headache much as they did fits or seizures. Victims of severe headaches were believed to be possessed by evil spirits and were sometimes tortured or physically abused. In more modern times, some people have been unwilling to tell others that headache causes their distress, fearing that they will not be taken seriously. Yet many have achieved success in spite of severe, recurrent headaches. Julius Caesar, Thomas Jefferson, Ulysses S. Grant, Frédéric Chopin, Lewis Carroll, Sigmund Freud, Virginia Woolf, Princess Margaret Rose, and Kareem Abdul-Jabbar are just a few among those who have been tormented by headaches.

Those of us who specialize in diagnosing and treating headaches have learned a great deal about them through research in recent years. We have developed elaborate classification schemes for quickly and precisely diagnosing headaches, and treatments ranging from drugs to biofeedback techniques are now widely available. But we are only beginning to understand the underlying cause of headache, in part because headache is a uniquely human condition. Rats, baboons, and other animals that have been valuable as test subjects in other forms of medical research may have headache, but they cannot communicate this condition to researchers.

Many specialists now believe that a change in the rate of blood flow through part of the intricate maze of blood vessels in and leading to the head causes headache. The head contains the body's largest network of blood vessels and pain-sensitive nerves, the neurovascular bed. Headache occurs when the blood flow slows down too much.

The author:
David R. Coddon is an associate professor of neurology at the Mount Sinai School of Medicine in New York City and director of the Headache Clinic at Mount Sinai Medical Center.

From *The World Book Year Book.*
© 1978 World Book-Childcraft
International, Inc.

158

The demons of headache display
their pain-making virtuosity in
this 19th-century cartoon.

This can happen when the blood vessels *dilate* (enlarge),
when the blood thickens, or when the blood is rerouted
unevenly through the intricate channels. In fact, as many
as 90 per cent of the headaches I encounter involve these
vessels and blood flow, even though they are given
different medical names.

Knowing that headaches result from changes in blood
flow helps us to understand why they are triggered in so
many, and often contradictory, ways. For example, many
adults get headaches while they are resting on weekends,
while others get them after strenuous activity. Many children get them after a busy day at school. Physical activity
ensures a steady, even flow of blood to all parts of the
body, thus assuring a rich supply of oxygen to all the
body's cells. But when the activity stops, the blood flow
slows down and becomes uneven in the head and other
parts of the body. Pain may then strike in the head
because there are so many pain receptors in the vessel
walls and in the tissue surrounding the vessels in the
head. These oxygen-sensitive pain receptors send distress
signals to the brain.

Of course, not everyone gets a headache after strenuous activity. In fact, many people rarely get them. The

159

George Bernard Shaw   Kareem Abdul-Jabbar   Princess Margaret   Sigmund Freud

Virginia Woolf   Julius Caesar   Thomas Jefferson

Severe headaches have plagued people from many walks of life.

important point to remember is that people who suffer severe, recurrent headaches differ somehow in the part of the brain that controls blood flow from those who do not get headaches. We have not yet precisely identified this difference, but we hope to find it soon so we can develop more effective ways to prevent and treat severe headaches.

Nevertheless, we do know a great deal about the causes and cures of vascular-flow headaches, chief of which is migraine headache. For example, most migraine sufferers are unable to drink red wine without bringing on a headache. Red wine contains histamine, a substance known for its powerful ability to dilate blood vessels and thus slow blood flow. On the other hand, many drugs that are used to treat headache successfully constrict blood vessels and thus increase blood flow. A well-known cola-based soft drink was originally sold as a headache remedy. It contained cocaine, a pain-killing drug that also constricts blood vessels.

Aspirin is effective for many headaches because it increases blood flow by breaking up clumps of *platelets*—blood cells that cause blood to thicken. It also helps reduce inflammation of the affected vessels and nerves of the neurovascular bed and provides pain-killing action throughout the nervous system.

Migraine headaches, the kind that my son Johnny gets, occur in all races throughout the world. They usually begin in childhood, and can be recognized in children as young as 2 years old. Migraine attacks tend to occur more often and with greater severity in boys until the middle or late teens. Thereafter, males tend to have fewer migraines, but the attacks usually become more frequent and more severe in females with the onset of menstruation. Adult female migraine sufferers outnumber male victims about 4 to 1. The attacks usually last only a few hours in small children and adolescents, but they typically last from one to three days in adult females, and they sometimes last as long as two weeks.

Female hormones play a basic, but still unknown, role in migraine headaches. This is true not only in females, but also in teen-age boys during puberty. A woman's migraine attacks generally disappear during pregnancy, and they become less frequent and severe with advancing age until they disappear at the time of menopause. Migraine attacks are likely to occur more often and be more severe in women who use oral contraceptives than in those who do not take the pill. Taking oral contraceptives can bring on vascular-flow headaches in women who never had them before.

As many as 80 per cent of those who get migraine headaches have a parent, brother, or sister who also suffers attacks. Many migraine victims have allergic reactions to foods and to many medications, particularly penicillin. Most of them suffered from carsickness when they were children.

During the 1920s and 1930s, many physicians believed that migraine headache sufferers shared common psychological traits. For example, migraine victims were thought to be intelligent, hard-working, and overconscientious. Physicians soon spoke of the "migraine personality"—for example, the woman who suffered migraine headaches and arranged all the magazines in the doctor's waiting room into neat stacks. Today we know that no such migraine personality exists. Anyone can develop migraine headaches.

We still do not kow the exact cause and mechanism of migraine headaches, but experiments have demonstrated that a change in blood flow within the vessels carrying blood to the structures in the head is involved. Computerized *axial tomography,* a highly specialized X-ray photo-

Headaches may be brought on by one of the many ways that we experience the world: job tension; certain foods; pollution; drugs, such as birth-control pills; smoking; and even the glare of the sun.

graphic technique that enables us to see inside the head during a migraine attack, has shown some areas of *lucency* (lightness) that represent decreased blood flow. The blood vessels constrict; then they dilate and release certain chemicals that cause inflammation in the affected area. Some headache specialists believe that the pain of the migraine headache is associated with dilation of the blood vessels in the area. Others regard the dilation merely as a result of whatever triggers the migraine attack and not the cause of the migraine attack and its pain.

Because most migraine headaches strike with little warning, a migraine sufferer or parent must act quickly to reduce the attack's severity. If taken soon enough, simple aspirin can prevent or greatly decrease the severity of a child's migraine attack. Adult sufferers can get relief by taking prescription drugs derived from ergot, a substance made by a fungus that grows on rye plants. Ergot preparations must also be taken in the early stages of a migraine attack to be effective.

Ergot medications constrict blood vessels greatly and must be used with care. Too much taken too often can produce unpleasant tingling in hands, feet, legs, and chest, seriously damage blood vessels, and even cause gangrene in the limbs. Ergot preparations produce nausea and vomiting and tend to be addicting. Paradoxically, a patient who takes large amounts of them or one who discontinues taking the medications may get a headache.

Sleep is nature's way of treating migraine. Based on this observation, our clinic developed a special deep-sleep treatment that can be given anytime during an acute migraine attack. More than 95 per cent of the patients receiving this treatment have benefited from it. We administer three medications intravenously— prochlorperazine, diazepam, and amobarbital—in that order, according to a standardized dosage schedule. The patient usually sleeps from three to six hours and, upon awakening, the headache is either gone or much less severe. This sleep treatment appears to be the most effective one now available for acute migraine attacks.

In many cases, the sleep treatment provides long-term relief for headache victims. Several years ago, a 24-year-old woman came to the clinic. She had been suffering recurrent attacks of severe headache, nausea, and vomiting since she was 9 years old. As an attack worsened, she would lose her speech and vision, and her right side would become paralyzed. She was groggy and unable to work for at least a week after an attack. One day when she felt the numbness and speech difficulty coming on, we rushed her to a hospital emergency room and administered the sleep-treatment injections. She slept soundly for five hours and awoke groggy but was able to work the next day. Subsequent attacks were never as severe or disabling as those before she was given the deep-sleep treatment.

Diet is another approach in helping to prevent migraine attacks. The emphasis is on eliminating foods that can trigger migraine, especially chocolate, cheddar cheese, red wine and champagne, nuts, pork, and meats processed with sodium nitrite.

Many drugs have been tried as part of a preventive medication program, and they help about 1 out of 3 patients. During the past two years, our clinic has had very good results with a preventive medication program that combines three prescription drugs, imipramine, propranolol, and chlordiazepoxide. Patients with migraine or other vascular-flow headaches take the medications daily by mouth according to an individual dosage schedule. Three out of four of them now have significantly fewer and less severe acute attacks, and when attacks do occur, they require far less of such strong prescription medica-

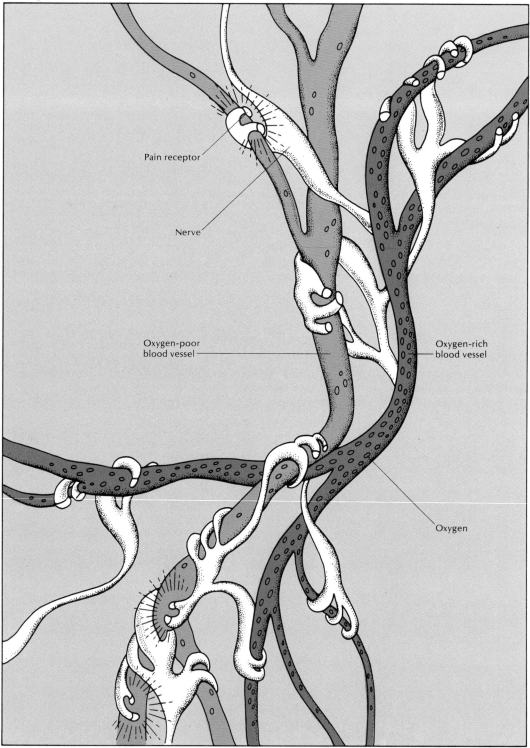

Pain receptor

Nerve

Oxygen-poor
blood vessel

Oxygen-rich
blood vessel

Oxygen

tions as the ergot drugs.

Biofeedback has helped to reduce migraine attacks in children, teen-agers, and young adults. Biofeedback training enables a patient to become aware of muscle tension and to learn to control it. A therapist places electrodes on the patient's forehead and connects them to a gauge that indicates the extent of muscle contraction or relaxation. A temperature-registering device on the fingers is connected to a visual temperature gauge. During treatment sessions, the therapist teaches the patient phrases to repeat and relaxing things to think about in order to reduce tension in the forehead muscles or raise the hand temperature, thereby increasing the flow of blood. Usually, a special tape recording is made so that the patient can practice at home.

However, biofeedback is of little value in treating another kind of severe, disabling headache, the cluster headache. Tom Marbro, a 45-year-old business executive with a strong jaw and weathered skin, is typical of cluster headache victims. An attack usually strikes when Tom is sound asleep. He is awakened by a sharp, knifelike pain in one eye that stays on that side of the head and lasts from 30 to 90 minutes. The pain is so excruciating that Tom gets out of bed and walks around. He may even bang his head against a wall in an effort to gain relief. Cluster headaches are sometimes referred to as killer headaches or suicide headaches because of the extreme measures many victims take during the attacks.

Cluster headaches got that name because they tend to occur in clusters; that is, they may occur daily or every two or three days, almost at the same time each day. Or, several headaches may occur each day over periods varying from a few weeks to a few months. Then the attacks stop completely, only to occur again several months later. Some patients get a cluster headache attack and then do not suffer another one for two or three years. Some suffer the attacks in the spring and fall, others during summer and winter, but in some cases there is no seasonal pattern.

A few headache specialists believe that cluster and migraine headaches are really different forms of the same underlying process. However, other authorities hold just as strongly that they are completely different and represent two different processes. Certainly, the two types of headache differ markedly in who gets them, what triggers them, and the way their victims look and feel during attacks.

Pain receptors in the complex of nerves and blood vessels in the head may be triggered by a lack of oxygen in the blood.

Cluster headaches occur about five times more often in men than in women. The typical victim is a man in his 40s; they rarely occur in males under 13. Cluster headaches are not common throughout the world as are migraines, and they rarely occur in dark-skinned races. Usually, there is no family history of cluster headaches and no history of allergies to foods or medicines. However, most cluster headache patients cannot drink alcoholic beverages during cluster periods, because this will trigger an attack within minutes. Yet they can drink alcohol when the cluster period has ended.

The burning, knifelike pain of a cluster headache differs vastly from the throbbing pain of migraine. Cluster victims are not unusually sensitive to light, sound, odors, and movement and they do not become nauseous and vomit. Rather than being exhausted or washed out when the attack subsides, the cluster victim usually is greatly relieved and can go back to sleep or carry on as if the painful attack had not happened.

Cluster headache patients also look markedly different from migraine sufferers during an attack. They yawn often and sweat on the side of the face where the pain is centered. Characteristically, the eye on that side produces tears, and the pupil is smaller than the other pupil. The affected eyelid usually droops, and the nose drips on that side of the face.

All cluster headaches strongly resemble one another and are easily diagnosed, but patients respond to treatment in a variety of ways. A patient may respond to one type of treatment at one time, but not at another time. The medicines used to treat acute migraine attacks—ergot preparations, for example—may help some cluster headache patients, but not others. Anti-inflammatory drugs used in conjunction with other medications help some patients, while various cortisone preparations are usually effective for others. Cortisone must be used carefully, however, because of the side effects. Long-term use of cortisone medications can cause muscle wasting, bone thinning, excessive weight gain, and even diabetes.

Many other types of headaches can be as painful as severe migraine and cluster headaches. Sinus headaches can occur during or after an infection of one of the sinuses—the cavities in the front or base of the skull. However, correct diagnosis requires X rays or other special techniques. Many headaches are called sinus headaches without any justification, especially in children under 14 years old. The frontal sinuses, just above the

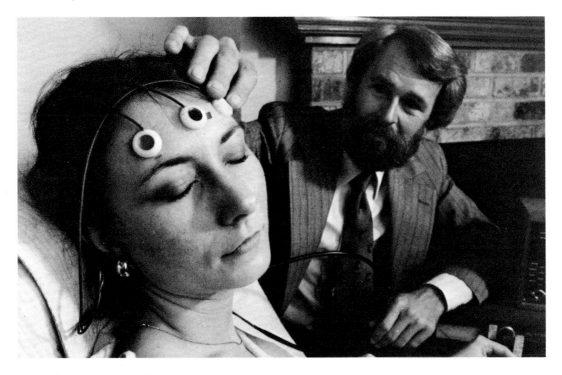

Biofeedback permits some headache sufferers to reduce their pain by helping them to relax tense muscles and increase blood flow.

eyes, rarely are completely formed at that age, so headaches caused by a sinus infection cannot occur in them.

Sinus headaches can be very painful. They are usually most severe in the morning. Pain may be felt anywhere in the head, and sufferers feel throbbing or a dull thud in the forehead when they bend over. Sinus headaches are also referred to as barometric headaches because they are commonly associated with changes in barometric pressure. Flying in an airplane or driving in mountainous areas may also trigger sinus headaches.

A hot shower directed toward the head or medication such as decongestants and antihistamines that promote sinus drainage may relieve sinus headache. Many people who repeatedly get sinus infections go to an ear, nose, and throat specialist for sinus irrigation. However, these treatments often leave the sinus linings more sensitive to smoke and other pollutants that can trigger a sinus headache.

Headaches also result from head injuries, and they can persist long after the injury. But a severe headache does not always result from a severe head injury. In fact, headache pain may last much longer after a head injury that does not fracture the skull than after an injury in which the skull is fractured. The headache may be confined to the injured area, or it may be more widespread. It may be a dull ache or throbbing pain. Simple *analgesics* (painkillers) such as aspirin can be effective in relieving such headaches, but the doctor must be careful to avoid the use of narcotic analgesics. Traumatic and posttraumatic headache may last as long as three to six months. After that, however, the headache may be a psychological and emotional reaction to the head injury.

Some specialists believe that most chronic headaches are also some form of psychological or emotional reaction. This category includes the conversion reaction headache and the headache associated with depression. A conversion reaction headache is related to some psychologically painful situation that the person has experienced. The headache is a substitute that the patient can accept. For example, a teen-age boy trying out for the school basketball team may bump his head slightly during practice. Later, the coach tells him that he did not make the team. Instead of accepting the pain of rejection, the boy complains of a headache. People with long-term depression often have headaches, but there is no clear cause-and-effect relationship.

Other specialists discount the psychological theory of headaches. They point out that such emotionally disturbed persons as psychotic patients rarely complain about headaches. Few patients with chronic headaches thought to have psychological causes find relief through psychiatric treatment.

Tension muscle-contraction headaches are often classified as psychological headaches because they are sometimes triggered by such emotional stress as anger or frustration. Noise, bright flashing lights, pollution, and other environmental stress can also bring on a tension muscle-contraction headache.

Unfortunately, television commercials advertising headache remedies have contributed to misconceptions about tension headaches. Many of these dramatizations depict a situation in which stress causes the victim's neck and head muscles to tighten, bringing on a headache. But the body has a built-in mechanism to prevent prolonged muscle contraction because it is so painful. Headache is more likely the cause of neck pain, rather than the result of tense muscles. Headache victims like to keep their heads still to keep the headache from getting worse. This protective action, in response to a headache, may tense the neck muscles and produce neck ache. The underlying link between stress and headache is unknown, but it may involve hormones as well as a change in blood flow.

Although a change in blood flow underlies most headaches, a few result from serious illness. For example, a patient with a brain tumor usually complains of headache as well as other symptoms such as difficulty in speaking. A patient who complains only of headache, however, rarely turns out to have a brain tumor when given a complete examination.

Blood vessel diseases, inflammation of the brain and its coverings, or eye disorders may also produce headache. Correct diagnosis and treatment require the knowledge and experience of a physician. There are no hard rules for deciding when to seek medical help for the relief of head pain. You are wise to see your family physician if there is a change in your headache condition—a new severe headache that lasts for more than a few hours, for example, or more severe or frequent headaches than usual.

Your family doctor can probably help you, or may refer you to a headache clinic. In the United States there are two such clinics in the New York City area and one each in Albuquerque, N. Mex.; Ann Arbor, Mich.; Boston; Chicago; Encino, Calif.; Kansas City; La Jolla, Calif.; Phoenix; and St. Louis. The National Migraine Foundation in Chicago serves as a primary referral source for headache sufferers in the United States. There are also headache clinics throughout the world, notably in England, Denmark, Sweden, and Norway, as well as in Italy, Austria, and Australia.

And what about Johnny, the migraine sufferer lucky enough to have a headache specialist for a father? He is now 16 and learning biofeedback methods to prevent more severe attacks. He and his Dad look forward to Johnny reaching maturity and leaving his migraines behind with the other discomforts of puberty. And we both hope that by the time Johnny becomes a father, we will know enough about headaches to spare him and millions of others the pain of an attack or the helpless anguish of watching a loved one suffer.

Some people spend the day in complaining of a headache, and the night in drinking the wine that gives it — Johann Wolfgang von Goethe

My agent gets 10 per cent of everything I get, except my blinding headaches — Fred Allen

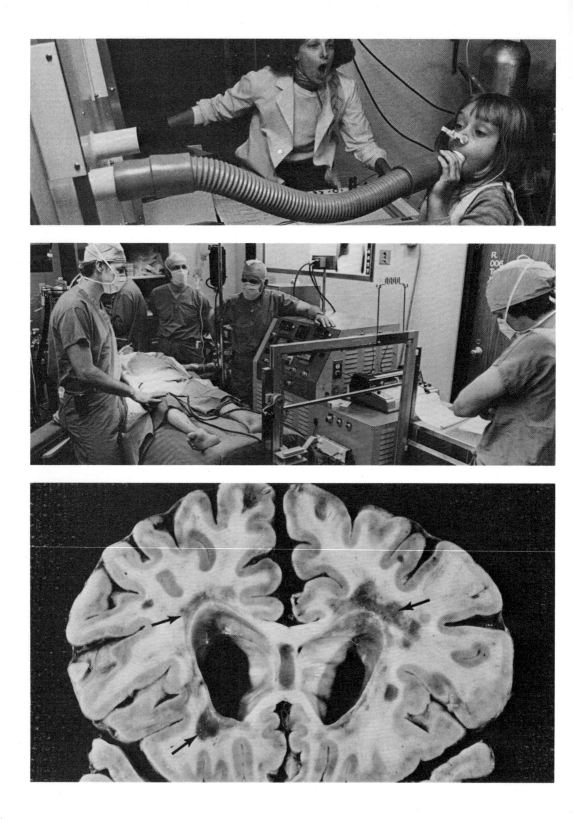

Medical File

Medical Update reports on the year's major developments in medical research. The articles in this section are arranged alphabetically by subject matter.

Alcohol

Alcoholism

Allergy

Bionics

Birth Control

Birth Defects

Blood

Bone Disorders

Cancer

Childbirth

Dentistry

Digestive Disorders

Drugs

Fever

Financing Medical Care

Gynecology

Heart

High Blood Pressure

Hyperactivity

Injury

Kidney

Mental Health

Multiple Sclerosis

Neurology

Nutrition

Occupational Medicine

Skin

Sleep Disorders

Sports Medicine

Surgery

Venereal Disease

Veterinary Medicine

Virus

Vision

Weight Control

Alcohol

Drinking while pregnant increases the risk of birth defects. The National Institute on Alcohol Abuse and Alcoholism advises women to abstain from alcohol during pregnancy.

Studies that report serious birth defects in babies whose mothers drank alcohol while pregnant prompted the United States government in 1980 to advise pregnant women not to drink at all. The warning from the National Institute on Alcohol Abuse and Alcoholism (NIAAA) reversed a 1977 position that had set two drinks per day as the upper limit for expectant mothers. The switch occurred, said government officials, because this limit had given the impression that pregnant women could have at least two drinks per day safely.

The studies show that a pregnant woman who drinks wine, beer, or liquor, particularly during the first two months of pregnancy, may give birth to a baby with a pattern of defects called fetal alcohol syndrome (FAS).

The defects include facial abnormalities: short spaces between the inner eyelids, folds of skin at the inner eye, minimal or no ridge between the nose and upper lip, a flat upper nose bridge, and a thin upper lip. The more serious forms of FAS include mental retardation, heart and skeletal defects, and hyperactivity. FAS babies also have some or all of the signs of underdevelopment – short bodies, small heads, and low birth weights. In the more severe cases, FAS victims never catch up with normal children.

Another reason for the NIAAA switch to a more conservative position was the opinion of many FAS researchers that even fewer than two drinks daily might cause subtle abnormalities that could go unnoticed until the affected child started school.   [Marcia J. Opp]

Alcoholism

The Rand Corporation of Santa Monica, Calif., released results of a four-year study in January 1980 asserting that some alcoholics can safely return to social drinking. This finding confirmed results of a 1976 Rand report on male problem drinking, but it renewed controversy over whether abstinence is the best long-term control for alcoholism.

Alcohol-treatment groups, including Alcoholics Anonymous, and government-sponsored programs have always maintained that total abstinence is the only hope for recovery. Organized citizens' groups and most clinics and hospitals contend that the alcoholic who attempts social drinking is just one step away from becoming a problem drinker again.

The new study "does not recommend that any alcoholic resume

Teen-age drinkers are flirting with danger. The U.S. Department of Health and Human Services estimates that more than 3 million U.S. children 14 through 17 years old are problem drinkers.

However, the report indicated that people over 40 who had strong symptoms of alcohol dependence — tremors, morning drinking, skipped meals, drinking for 12 hours or longer, and loss of control of drinking — should abstain. Some 14.5 per cent of the 922 men studied for the 1976 report died between 1973, when they were admitted to treatment programs, and 1977, when the follow-up study ended. Their death rate was 2½ times the expected rate for normal men of the same ages and racial distribution.

Of the surviving 780 men, 28 per cent had not been drinking for at least four years, and 18 per cent said they were able to drink without problems. However, half of the latter group had more than four drinks a day. Some 54 per cent of the men reported serious drinking problems at the time of the follow-up study.

drinking." However, "for some alcoholics, especially those under 40 and less dependent on alcohol, nonproblem drinking can be regarded as a form of remission," according to the authors, sociologists J. Michael Polich, David J. Armor, and Harriet Braiker. Men in this age group who tried to abstain for long periods were more likely to fall into a drinking pattern again.

The 361-page, $549,000 report, paid for by the National Institute on Alcohol Abuse and Alcoholism, found that 84 per cent of the men had major alcohol-related problems during the four-year period. This probably accounted for the men's lack of social, economic, and psychological improvement, even when they abstained for a while.   [Marcia J. Opp]

Allergy

Robert H. Schwartz, chairman of the Public Education Committee of the American Academy of Allergy (AAA), reported in June 1981 that the medical management of asthma has improved so significantly in recent years that most asthmatics can enjoy a normal life.

"Our understanding of the mechanism of asthma has really expanded in the past year," said Dr. Schwartz.

Drugs used to treat chronic asthma include theophylline, cromolyn, and the sympathomimetic bronchodilators — substances that imitate the action of the sympathetic nervous system to help widen the tubes that carry air to the lungs. These drugs are used alone or in various combinations. Corticosteroids, drugs that imitate certain hormones produced in the adrenal glands, also are often used to control asthma. However, steroid drugs produce many undesirable side effects, so researchers have sought alternatives.

A small group of patients have more severe asthma. These include children who had to take steroids more or less continuously to avoid rounds of hospitalizations and emergency-room visits, and asthmatic patients with a general chronic debilitation. These patients have been treated successfully with theophylline, a nonsteroid that is related to substances found in coffee and tea, reported allergist Edward G. Nassif of the University of Iowa in the *New England Journal of Medicine* in January 1981.

Dr. Nassif and his team tested theophylline on 33 children who were outpatients in the Pediatric Allergy and Pulmonary Division of the University of Iowa Hospitals. They found that theophylline effec-

A technician in a pulmonary function laboratory encourages a child to blow into a spirometer, an instrument that measures how well the lungs are working.

tively relaxed the bronchial smooth muscle, which allowed the children to breathe more easily and also permitted them to exercise. The drug freed the children of asthma symptoms 63 per cent of the time and eliminated both night coughing and interference with normal daytime activities. The Iowa team continued its follow-up study for 2½ years, and concluded that while corticosteroids could still be of value, the young patients' asthma symptoms could be well controlled with theophylline.

Asthma molecule synthesized. Organic chemists Elias J. Corey of Harvard University in Cambridge, Mass., and Bengt Samuelsson of Karolinska Institute in Stockholm, Sweden, reported in March 1980 that they had synthesized a molecule involved in asthma and anaphylaxis, or violent allergic reaction. Anaphylactic reactions can be triggered by such substances as those in bee stings, insect and snake venom, foods, tobacco, and such plants as poison ivy.

The molecule, originally discovered in 1938, is called slow-reacting substance of anaphylaxis (SRS) and minute amounts of it are found in the human body. It is a muscle contractant — similar to histamine in that both substances cause constriction of small airways of the lungs. However, histamine causes muscles to react sharply and then return to normal, while SRS takes effect more slowly but is longer acting.

Dr. Corey said the discovery could lead to new developments in immunology, drug design, and medical research. However, asthma specialist J. L. Beets of Brompton Hospital in London said SRS is only one of several molecules involved in allergy responses and might not be the most important one. Nevertheless, Dr. Corey stated that it may now become possible to develop anti-SRS drugs that act much like antihistamines, and thus prevent the possibly fatal effect of anaphylaxis.

Penicillin allergy may not last for a lifetime, reported Kevin Hepler of the University of Missouri-Columbia Medical Center in Columbia. He said so-called allergic reactions may be just sensitivity, and if penicillin therapy is needed, an individual should be retested carefully to see if he is truly allergic.

Heart attack or allergy? Robert Levi of Cornell University Medical School in New York City suggested at the American Heart Association Science Writers' Forum held at Hilton Head Island, S. C., in January 1980 that some apparent heart attacks may be allergic reactions.

He said that anaphylaxis can produce symptoms that could be mistaken for those of a heart attack, including difficulty in breathing and collapse of the cardiovascular, or heart and blood vessel, system.

Dr. Levi thinks the allergic reaction causes the heart to release histamines and other substances that affect that part of the heart that controls rhythm, producing arrhythmia, or abnormal rhythm. Other substances in the body then magnify the arrhythmia. Levi concluded, "It is quite conceivable that a number of incidences of sudden cardiac death may have an underlying and overlooked allergic origin."

Allergy tests flunked. The AAA published a statement in May 1981 about the validity of five controversial diagnostic and therapeutic procedures. According to the AAA, the procedures are either ineffective or illogical, and are of unproven value. The techniques included:

■ Cytotoxicity testing, or Bryan's test, used to diagnose food and inhalant allergies, is based on the belief that a specific allergen will kill leucocytes, or white blood cells, in a blood sample from an allergic patient. The AAA said controlled trials showed the test to be ineffective.

■ Autoinjection of urine, which involves injecting a patient's freshly collected and sterilized urine into a muscle in his body, is used to treat various allergic diseases. The AAA reported that the treatment is "potentially dangerous" and that there is no underlying reason or immunological basis for administering it.

■ Skin titration, or the Rinkel method, used to determine the starting dose of an antigen, is simply not a good test, said the AAA. In the Rinkel method, an antigen, such as ragweed pollen, is injected into a patient to stimulate the production of an antibody and so eventually make the person less sensitive to it.

■ Subcutaneous provocation and neutralization test, a technique for allergy diagnosis and treatment that involves using just enough antigen to produce symptoms and then applying a weaker or stronger dilution to correct the symptoms, has no scientific basis, according to the AAA.

■ Sublingual provocative test, used to diagnose food-induced respiratory or gastrointestinal symptoms, involves placing an antigen under the patient's tongue. If the test is positive, typical symptoms of the patient's allergy should appear within 10 minutes. The AAA said controlled studies showed that this method was ineffective and incapable of discriminating between an inactive substance and certain food extracts.   [Virginia S. Cowart]

Bionics

A host of "replacement parts" for the human body premiered in 1980 and 1981. Among the most notable were devices designed to provide insulin automatically to victims of diabetes. See *Dealing with Diabetes*.

The Salt Lake City arm. One of the most sophisticated artificial arms ever designed was fitted to an amputee in December 1980. The arm, made of lightweight plastic, was developed by Stephen C. Jacobsen at the University of Utah in Salt Lake City.

Complete with operating parts, and batteries in the elbow, it weighs only 2½ pounds, about half the weight of a real human arm. The messages that tell the arm to bend or extend come from two electronic sensors in the socket, or sleeve, that slips over the user's stump. These sensors pick up minute electrical signals from the biceps and triceps muscles — the muscles that control major arm movements — in the stump.

Nickel-cadmium batteries power the arm for a full day — an average of about 3,000 bends and extensions. The batteries are then easily removed and recharged. Because the arm is assembled in sections, its parts can be easily removed for replacement or repair. The sophisticated electronic sensors, for example, are contained in two removable packs in the elbow.

The arm has a smooth and natural motion and operates quietly enough to be unnoticed during a normal conversation. Dr. Jacobsen and the manufacturers — Motion Control, Incorporated, of Salt Lake City, Utah — insist that prospective clients come to Salt Lake City for fitting and training so that the researchers can continuously evaluate the arm's performance. The $12,000 price tag includes fitting

and two training sessions. They plan to have fitted 20 arms by January 1982.

The Hershey heart. Scientists at Milton S. Hershey Medical Center in Hershey, Pa., are working on an artificial heart that shows great promise. In doing so, they have solved a problem associated with all previous attempts to design an artificial heart — how to get the heart, which is basically a mechanical pump, to vary its pumping speed with the constantly changing needs of the wearer.

The Hershey scientists turned to a tiny solid-state switch called the Hall effect switch to solve the problem. The Hall effect is a phenomenon in which a magnetic force is applied to an electrical conductor in such a way that its electrical voltage is increased. A Hall effect switch turns on the voltage when the magnet comes close to the conductor and turns off the voltage when the magnet moves away.

In the Hershey heart, the left chamber, which receives oxygenated blood to be pumped out to the body, contains a pusher disk with a tiny magnet in its center. As the cylindrical chamber fills, it pushes the disk to the opposite end of the chamber where it comes close enough to a conductor to trigger the voltage that drives the heart. This thrusts the disk in the opposite direction, which pumps the blood out of the chamber and into the body. With the disk and magnet at the far end of the chamber again, the voltage cuts off and the process begins again.

Since the filling time of the chamber depends upon blood pressure in the body and blood pressure is related to the blood requirements of the body, the Hall effect switch operates the heart at the correct pace.

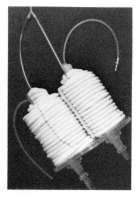

Coiled teflon tubing is the basis of an artificial lung developed at Brown University. The tubing is placed inside an oxygen-filled plastic bag and hooked up to the patient's blood supply. The blood picks up oxygen as it passes through the tubing, much as it would inside a human lung.

The Hershey scientists are working on making the heart lighter. It currently weighs 2 pounds without its external battery pack, almost twice as much as a human heart. They are also testing its reliability. The Hall effect switch has been tested and proved reliable for 12 billion cycles, which means that it could keep an artificial heart beating for about 300 years.

The left, or pumping, half of the heart is being tested in calves as a left-ventricular assist — a device to aid a heart so weakened that it cannot support life alone. The device, in effect, adds crucial pumping power until the heart heals enough to resume its full burden. There were perhaps 100 such devices in use in human patients in 1981.   [Michael Reed]

Birth Control

The booming interest in a century-old contraceptive device that has not been approved by the United States Food and Drug Administration (FDA) prompted that agency to clamp down on its distribution in January 1981. Thousands of women have begun to use cervical caps over the last several years. These thimble-shaped, molded-rubber devices work somewhat like the diaphragm, which has FDA approval as a safe and effective means of preventing pregnancy. The cervical cap fits over and blocks the cervix, the opening to the uterus, thus preventing sperm from uniting with an egg.

The FDA ruled that every health center and physician who prescribes this contraceptive device must become part of a government-sanctioned research project. In 1953, the U.S. government had funded a thorough investigation of the cervical cap, finding it 92.4 per cent effective in preventing conception. But the FDA cited several recent studies of cervical caps that had high failure and low acceptance rates and said that it would thoroughly investigate all data before approving any cap.

By the summer of 1981, some 240 researchers in 50 clinics had begun to study caps manufactured in England and custom-made caps. Caps are not mass-produced in the United States. The researchers noted how easy or difficult the caps were to insert and remove, whether they caused side effects, how women accepted them, and how well they prevented pregnancy.

Researchers say that a cap is harder to insert and remove than a diaphragm, but a woman can leave it in place longer. Some models can be worn for three days. A cap developed by obstetrician-gynecologist Uwe Freese of Chicago Medical School and University of Chicago dentist Robert A. Goepp can be worn indefinitely. A one-way valve in this custom-made device allows menstrual fluids to flow from the uterus, but keeps sperm out.

Gynecologist James P. Koch of Brigham and Women's Hospital in Boston revealed in 1981 that 372 women who used an English cap for 3 to 22 months became pregnant at a rate of 8.4 per cent per year, about the same rate as that of the diaphragm. Dr. Koch and his colleagues are working on a cap that they hope will reduce the failure rate to 1 per cent.

Oral contraceptives. Two reports published in 1980 reversed a trend of negative publicity on oral contraceptives. News accounts in 1975 that the pill increased the risk of heart attacks had caused purchases to decrease by 25 per cent.

The 1980 reports, however, indicated that the pill may not be as dangerous as many women and their physicians fear.

A study coordinated by Boston University Medical Center showed that women who used an estrogen and progestin pill developed cancer of the endometrium, or lining of the uterus, at only half the rate of other women, while the Walnut Creek Contraceptive Drug Study of 16,638 Kaiser-Permanente Foundation Health Plan members near San Francisco concluded that pill users face only a "negligible" overall health risk and no increased risk of death from all causes.

The San Francisco area women ranged from 18 to 54 years old. Most of them were white, young, and middle class. Some 61 per cent had used or were using oral contraceptives when the study began.

Researchers compared the incidence of disease and death in women who had used the pill with those of women who had not. Epidemiologist Savitri Ramcharan confirmed that the pill may prevent fibrocystic breast disease and provide strong protection against endometrial cancer and some protection against cancer of the ovary.

The Walnut Creek study did not confirm other researchers' reports that linked heart attacks and stroke to pill use, and it strongly suggested that the pill is not implicated in breast cancer.

However, the study turned up links between pill use and an increase in malignant melanoma, a serious skin cancer; high blood pressure; depression; certain eye diseases; thyroid cancer; rheumatic disease; gastrointestinal disease; benign tumors of the cervix and uterus; benign endocrine tumors; and glaucoma.

In contrast to other research, the Walnut Creek study showed "no significant risk" of heart attack, certain kinds of heart disease, or symptoms leading to strokes. Pill users who smoked heavily also faced higher risks of other diseases and death.

Of the 170 deaths that occurred during the study period, 45 per cent were due to malignant neoplasms, or abnormal growths of tissue; 19 per cent to accidents or violence; and 15 per cent to cardiovascular disease.

Natural birth control. The Human Life and Natural Family Planning Foundation in Alexandria, Va., reported in late 1980 that nearly 100,000 women in the United States are opting each year for two new natural birth control measures. These methods – the ovulation method and the symptothermal method – rely on natural changes in a woman's body that

Boston gynecologist James P. Koch indicates on a model of the female reproductive system where to place a contraceptive device called a cervical cap. Dr. Koch is trying to develop a cap that will reduce the pregnancy risk to 1 per cent per year.

indicate peak fertility times, when a woman is most likely to become pregnant.

In the ovulation method, women learn to discern changes in their cervix and in vaginal mucus – both of which can help determine when an egg is released. Women who use the sympto-thermal method take their temperatures daily, and also monitor the mucus changes.

Obstetrician-gynecologist Hanna Klaus, a foundation director, reported a 1 per cent pregnancy rate with the ovulation method, but other investigators have reported much higher rates. For example, in 1979, Maclyn E. Wade, head of obstetrics and gynecology at Cedars-Sinai Medical Center in Los Angeles, reported a 27 per cent rate.   [Marcia J. Opp]

Birth Defects

Physicians found new uses in 1980 and 1981 for amniocentesis – a medical procedure performed during pregnancy to determine the health of an unborn baby. In amniocentesis, the doctor inserts a thin needle into the sac containing the fetus and withdraws a small amount of fluid. Tests of the fetal chromosomes – the rodlike structures containing genes – in this fluid sample can determine if the infant has certain serious defects.

Pediatrician Henry L. Nadler of Northwestern University School of Medicine in Chicago reported in November 1980 that it may be possible to diagnose cystic fibrosis by amniocentesis. Cystic fibrosis (CF) – a disease in which thick mucous secretions block the bronchial tubes – is the most common fatal genetic disease among people of northern European descent. Although doctors can drain the lungs of CF victims to clear them temporarily, mucous secretions blocking other body organs usually result in death before the patient is 20 years old. Dr. Nadler's diagnostic procedure consists of a triple set of tests done on a sample of amniotic fluid.

Amniocentesis has been bitterly attacked by abortion foes who feel that the diagnosis of a birth defect may encourage women to end the pregnancy. This controversy was fanned by a case reported in June 1981 telling how a 40-year-old pregnant woman underwent amniocentesis and discovered that one of the twins she was carrying had Down's syndrome – a condition characterized by mental retardation. Doctors were able to stop the heart of the twin with the defect, leaving the normal twin to develop to full term. However, the mother said that if that procedure had not been available, she would have chosen to have an abortion, ending the lives of both twins.

Amniocentesis may also lead to treatment rather than abortion of the fetus. For example, Debra Whitmore had given birth in 1978 to a son with an inability to make the vitamin biotin, which the body needs to convert fats and carbohydrates into energy. When she became pregnant again in 1980, doctors at Moffitt Hospital at the University of California in San Francisco advised her that there was 1 chance in 4 that the second child would also inherit the disorder. Amniocentesis confirmed that the second child was also affected and Whitmore was given large doses of biotin. Her daughter's entry into the world was uncomplicated. By receiving large doses of biotin, both Whitmore children can be expected to lead normal lives.   /

Sickle cell disease, seen in black people almost exclusively, can cause strokes and death in its severest form, even in children. Unlike normal round red blood cells, sickle cells cannot pass easily through blood vessels and may form blood clots. They are also more fragile than normal red cells and are easily broken as they circulate. Thus, sickle cell victims have fewer red blood cells to carry oxygen and are severely anemic.

Hematologist Robert P. Hebbel of the University of Minnesota in Minneapolis reported that he had established a link between the severity of sickle cell anemia and the form of the sickle cells themselves. Red blood cells from patients with the worst form of sickle cell disease tend to adhere to the inner walls of blood vessels more than do those of patients with milder disease. Dr. Hebbel predicted that researchers may find ways to reduce the stickiness of the cells and, thereby, to treat the disease.

Immune system disorders. The March of Dimes reported advances in treating a genetic deficiency that is connected with the failure of the immune system to respond to infection. Children lacking adenosine deaminase (ADA), an enzyme found in all body cells, die of illnesses that would not be severe in a normal baby. They may also have some nervous system abnormalities.

Rochelle Hirschorn, a researcher at New York University in New York City, reported that she had treated an infant with this defect by periodically exchanging a small amount of the baby's blood for blood with normal red blood cells containing ADA. The child, 2 years old in June 1981, had not suffered a serious infection since she was 14 months old. In addition, her nervous system was functioning almost normally.

A report issued by dermatologist Eugene A. Bauer of Washington University in St. Louis in 1981 offered hope to children with recessive dystrophic epidermolysis bullosa (RDEB) — a genetic disorder in which the skin is so sensitive to friction that even wearing shoes may be impossible.

RDEB victims characteristically develop massive blisters in the deepest layers of skin. The blisters eventually break, leaving open wounds that are easily infected. Such continuous skin destruction often results in disfiguring scars, particularly on the hands and feet. However, Dr. Bauer has successfully used the anticonvulsant drug phenytoin to reduce skin destruction.   [Virginia S. Cowart]

Blood

Blood "washing," or plasmapheresis, is a medical technique that was rapidly growing in popularity in 1981. It is used to treat a number of diseases and physical conditions, including myasthenia gravis, multiple sclerosis, rheumatoid arthritis, some forms of cancer, and kidney-transplant rejection.

During plasmapheresis, doctors connect the patient's veins to equipment that takes blood from the body, and separates the red cells, white cells, and platelets, or colorless blood cells, from the protein-rich solution called plasma. It then returns the cells — together with a plasma substitute — to the patient. The procedure takes three to four hours and may have to be repeated many times during the course of treatment.

The blood plasma is removed because it contains autoantibodies

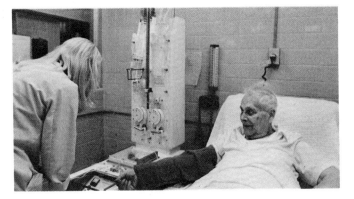

A hospital technician turns on a plasmapheresis machine that will remove the patient's blood, and separate the plasma from blood cells. It will then return the cells, along with new plasma or a plasma substitute, to the patient.

and other factors that are thought to contribute to or cause the disease being treated. Autoantibodies are molecules made by the body that attack other natural body molecules, producing so-called autoimmune diseases. Doctors have reported dramatic improvements in some patients with autoimmune diseases, such as myasthenia gravis, following plasmapheresis.

In other variations of the technique, only white blood cells or both white cells and plasma are removed. The latter procedure is particularly useful in averting kidney-transplant rejection because white blood cells are involved in rejection.

In addition, new equipment that removes only specific proteins or antibodies from the blood is being tested. At the Mayo Clinic in Rochester, Minn., for example, doctors are experimenting with the removal of bile acids and cholesterol.

Despite the promise shown by plasmapheresis, doctors are cautious in recommending it. The procedure is somewhat unpleasant and costly — the typical charge for one session is $1,000, and may need to be repeated. In addition, it may reduce calcium levels in the body or cause allergic reactions. And, finally, except in kidney-transplant rejections; Crohn's disease, an intestinal inflammation;

and some rheumatoid arthritis, the value of plasmapheresis is far from established.

Transfusions. There continued to be a shortage of blood donations for transfusions in 1981. Such donated blood is usually separated into its components. This allows doctors to give only cells when oxygen needs to be transported in the blood; granulocytes, a kind of white blood cell, when a recipient is fighting off an infection; or platelets, which aid in blood-clotting, when a patient is bleeding.

Researchers are even attempting to separate red cells into old and young cells. Dr. Richard Propper of Boston's Children's Hospital, and Dr. Laurence M. Corash of the National Institutes of Health in Bethesda, Md., note that young red cells have a longer life span than do older cells. If they are given to a patient with thalassemia, one of the hereditary anemias, for example, fewer transfusions will be needed. This means that there will be less accumulation of iron in the body. Iron that enters transfused blood can build up to cause serious consequences, including death.

Blood cells. The clumping of platelets is believed to cause some heart attacks and strokes and blood vessel disease elsewhere in the body. Thus, researchers are testing many drugs that reduce platelet clumping. Aspirin is one such drug. The possibility that taking a small dose of aspirin each day may reduce the chance of stroke, eventual death after a heart attack, or other disorders is under study in many research centers. See *Aspirin and Your Heart.*

Anturane, a drug used in the treatment of gout, also inhibits platelet clumping. Doctors are studying Anturane to see if it might reduce cases of sudden death after heart attacks.

Blood (cont.)

Other drugs that inhibit clumping are Persantine and the prostaglandins PGE$_1$ and prostacyclin. Prostacyclin, which causes blood vessels to dilate, may be useful for treating angina pectoris or chest pain due to heart disease, and serious vein and artery disease in the legs, according to Dr. Andrew Szczeklik of Krakow, Poland.

Platelets tend to cling to the tubes and other parts of heart-lung machines that recycle blood during heart surgery. Thus some physicians, such as Dr. Kjell Radegran of the University of Göteborg, Sweden, Dr. Michael Kaye of the Mayo Clinic, and Dr. Eugene Blackstone of the University of Alabama in Birmingham are using prostacyclin to keep platelets from clogging the machines.   [Gail McBride]

Bone Disorders

In the spring of 1981, researchers at Harvard University in Cambridge, Mass., announced that they had repaired particularly challenging bone deformities in a large number of patients. They used a technique based on many years of research in several laboratories. The technique causes bone to grow and even creates bone where none existed before.

The key element is demineralized pieces of bone or bone powder used to trigger new growth. The bone pieces or powder come from the bones of cadavers (dead bodies) or of the patients receiving treatment.

The Harvard researchers reported on 34 patients treated by this method and claimed to have found evidence of bone healing in at least 31 of them. Most of the patients were children born with malformed heads or faces.

A dramatic example of the work is a 5-year-old boy suffering from a birth defect called cloverleaf syndrome — a grotesque, three-lobed skull. Three operations had failed to correct the condition and surgeons at Boston's Children's Hospital Medical Center decided to try the new technique.

First, the surgeons removed the entire top of the boy's skull and crushed it into pieces about the size of a penny. The pieces were soaked in hydrochloric acid for three hours to remove all minerals. They were then washed in distilled water and other liquids and sterilized with radiation. The surgeons re-covered the outer membrane of the child's brain with the now-demineralized bone pieces and then "iced" the entire area, like a cake, with a paste made from demineralized bone powder. There was evidence that bone had formed in the area within four months and, after a year, the boy had a relatively solid, normally shaped head.

Other successes with the new technique include fashioning a nose for a 7-year-old born without one, and healing jaw cysts in a 16-year-old and a 59-year-old.

The technique has great potential in other areas also. For example, it may be useful in the repair of fractures, deteriorating bones in the aged, and damage caused by bone cancer and dental diseases. Despite the doctors' success, they do not know just why the new process works. Research is continuing at Harvard and at the University of California, Los Angeles, in an effort to discover the biological mechanism behind the technique.

Damage to runners' bones. Reports at the January 1981 meeting of the Radiological Society of North America in Dallas indicated

182

that people who jog or run regularly can damage their leg bones in an unusual way. The peculiar injuries were described by radiologists Richard H. Daffner of Duke University in Durham, N.C., and Helene Pavlov of Cornell Medical College in New York City.

The injuries, which appear on the tibia or shinbone about 5 inches below the knee, are fractures described by Dr. Pavlov as ". . . very subtle and easy to overlook in a routine inspection or review of X rays." Dr. Daffner warned that the telltale cracks of the injury, when first spotted, often lead to an erroneous diagnosis of bone cancer because of their "mottled" look and because they occur where tumors are often found.

Dr. Daffner said that these characteristic fractures are caused by the prolonged and repeated pounding of runners' feet and legs on hard or uneven surfaces with

the arms swinging and the body in the typical forward-leaning position of a runner. The fractures are painful and become more so if running continues. If the victim stops running, the pain disappears in about two weeks and the fractures heal without treatment in six weeks.

Dr. Daffner said that when a person who runs regularly complains of leg pain and damage at the spot on the shinbone where stress fractures typically occur, doctors should not suspect cancer and immediately do a biopsy. (In a biopsy, a tissue sample is taken and examined closely for signs of cancer.) "As long as the patient isn't acutely ill," he said, "it's better to wait 10 days or 2 weeks and X-ray again. By then, there should be sufficient evidence of bone healing to indicate stress fracture."

Bone length tells fetal age. Researchers at Georgetown University Medical Center in Washington,

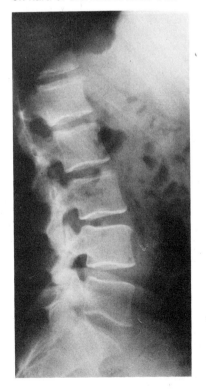
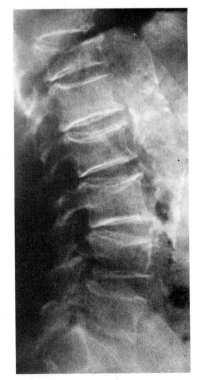

The lower region of the spine in a normal person, *left,* appears much denser in an X-ray photo than the same region in a person with osteoporosis, *right.* In this condition affecting older people, bones become porous due to loss of body calcium and are easily broken.

D.C., and King's College Hospital in London reported in March 1981 that they had successfully used ultrasound measurement of a bone to determine the age of a fetus, or unborn child, in the second trimester of pregnancy. The bone measured is the femur, the leg bone from the pelvis to the knee.

Estimating the age of a fetus is an important part of prenatal care. A physician needs to know the exact age of the fetus as accurately as possible both to administer tests that detect developmental problems and to make decisions concerning the delivery.

Of all the means of determining fetal age, the history of the expectant mother's menstrual periods can be the most accurate. But in more than 40 per cent of pregnancies, women are unable to recall the exact date of their last period.

Brain
See Neurology

Burns
See Better News About Burns

Other methods of determining fetal age are either more difficult and expensive or less accurate than the new ultrasound technique.

The researchers, including John T. Queenan of Georgetown and Stuart Campbell of King's College, established the method by measuring the femurs of 180 fetuses of known prebirth ages between 12 and 23 weeks. From these measurements, they developed a growth curve, a correlation between femur length and fetus age, that proved to be 95 per cent accurate within six days of the true fetal age.

Ultrasound is a technique that is similar to sonar. High-frequency sound waves directed at living tissues send back echoes that are analyzed by computers. Different tissues send back different echoes that the computer uses to form an image.   [Michael Reed]

Cancer

Although zealots may remain unimpressed, there is now firm evidence that the substance called Laetrile has no value in the treatment of cancer. The National Cancer Institute (NCI) sponsored an 11-month, four-center study of 178 cancer patients that was reported in April 1981. It showed that Laetrile did not extend the life span of the patients and did not decrease their symptoms. In only 1 of 156 patients who could be evaluated at that time was there even a regression of a tumor, and that lasted only 10 weeks.

Oncologist Charles G. Moertel of the Mayo Clinic in Rochester, Minn., which coordinated the study, said that the amygdalin, a substance derived from apricot pits, was "structurally identical" to that of the major Mexican product used by "Laetrile practitioners" and was given in the same doses.

The patients in the study also were put on the same diet used by Laetrile practitioners. The diet was high in fresh fruits, vegetables, and whole grains, and low in meats, dairy products, and refined sugars and flours. Patients were also given special enzymes and vitamins.

At the start of the study, most of the patients had colorectal, lung, or breast cancers. They had failed conventional treatment — surgery, radiation, or chemotherapy — or such treatment was not offered because their cancer was not advanced. More than two-thirds of the patients were able to work part time or full time; none were totally disabled. "These emphatically were not patients in their terminal episode," said Dr. Moertel, although all the patients had proven cancer "beyond any hope of cure or therapy known to extend life expectancy."

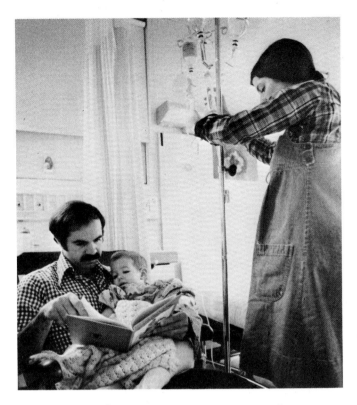

A young cancer patient responds better when her parents are closely involved in the therapy.

As of April 1981, 104 patients had died. The median survival for these patients was just 4.5 per cent, with only 20 per cent still alive after eight months. "Median survival among specific tumor types seemed consistent with anticipated survival if these patients had received no treatment whatsoever," Dr. Moertel said. He concluded that "amygdalin in combination with so-called metabolic therapy does not produce any substantive benefit in terms of cure or improvement of cancer."

Oncologist Vincent T. DeVita, Jr., director of NCI, said the findings "present public evidence of Laetrile's failure as a cancer treatment. The hollow promise of this drug has led thousands of Americans away from potentially helpful therapy of scientific validity. Now the facts speak for themselves."

Breast surgery that removes only a quarter of the breast may be as effective as a radical mastectomy for women with early breast cancer, according to a 7½-year controlled study of 701 women performed at Italy's National Cancer Institute in Milan. The study was reported in the July 1, 1981, *New England Journal of Medicine* by Dr. Umberto Veronesi.

All the women had tumors about 0.8 inch or less in diameter. It appeared that their lymph nodes were not involved. The women were randomly assigned to receive either radical mastectomy or "quadrectomy" of the section of the breast where the tumor was found, plus removal of the lymph nodes in the armpit. Those in the quadrectomy group also received radiation for six weeks after the surgery. The survival rate after 7½ years was greater than 85 per cent for both groups.

Tumors 0.8 inch in diameter can be diagnosed by women using self breast examination, as well as by doctors' examinations or mammography. About 14 per cent of breast cancer patients are discovered with tumors this small.

Snuffing out your life. "Snuff-dipping," the practice of keeping finely ground tobacco tucked between the gum and the cheek, is dangerous to your health, according to a report in March 1981 by epidemiologists from the NCI. The researchers studied groups of women in North Carolina where snuff-dipping is a common habit and compared those who had oral and pharyngeal cancers with healthy women. They found that using snuff increased the risk of oral and pharyngeal cancer four-fold, and the risk of cancers of the gum and cheek fiftyfold. They found no cancer association with the textile industries where many of these women work. The association between snuff and cancer was not connected to cigarette smoking or alcohol consumption, although smoking alone, or smoking and drinking together, both increased the risk of mouth cancer.

NCI researcher Deborah Winn, who reported the study, said that scientists do not know the exact constituents of snuff, but a prime suspect is N'-nitrosonornicotine (NNN), which can induce tumors in laboratory animals. NNN is present in cigarette smoke but there is more of it in snuff and chewing tobacco. The NNN in tobacco begins to develop during the curing process. More of it is generated when the user "incubates" the tobacco with saliva, through the action of nitrites in saliva.

Heavy advertising campaigns by the tobacco industry have encouraged the use of smokeless tobacco as a substitute for cigarettes, as have medical reports. As a result, total U.S. production of smokeless tobacco rose from 98 million pounds in 1971 to about 134 million pounds in 1980. See *Reducing the Risks of Cancer.*

More interferon trials begin. The NCI launched seven clinical trials with "natural" human interferons at U.S. research institutions in February 1981. The agency began similar trials with interferon produced by recombinant DNA technology in March. The American Cancer Society sponsored a number of earlier trials.

Phase 1 of the NCI trials is designed to determine the maximum safe level of dosage, the dose that will give the maximum biological effect, and the best schedule for administering the drug. The trials are not intended to test anticancer effects, although the researchers will note if patients respond to the drug. Phase 2 trials, scheduled to

begin sometime in 1982, will test how well interferons work against various cancers.

Interferon is produced in all vertebrate cells, for a very short time and in minute amounts, in response to an invasion of viruses. It acts as an early alarm system among the cells by provoking natural killer cells and other lymphocytes to attack foreign invaders. Scientists have shown that some tumors respond to it as well as viruses.

The natural interferons being used on about 200 cancer patients are harvested from human disease-fighting cells such as leucocytes and lymphoblasts, and repair tissue called fibroblasts. About 80 patients were expected to be enrolled in the trials of the genetically engineered interferon.

Some of the first results have been disappointing. Interferon action against various cancers was not significantly better than that of cancer-fighting chemicals. However, all of the natural interferon harvested from human cells was notably impure. Researchers hope that the interferon produced by genetic engineering techniques will have fewer impurities, and also be considerably cheaper to produce in quantity.

Coffee and pancreatic cancer were associated in a statistical study reported in March 1981 by Brian MacMahon and his associates at the Harvard School of Public Health. The research did not indicate a cause-and-effect relationship, however.

Pancreatic cancer is the fourth most common cause of cancer deaths, accounting for about 20,000 fatalities in the United States each year. What causes it is unknown.

The Harvard group interviewed almost 400 pancreatic cancer patients and more than 600 hospital patients with some other, unrelated, disease. The patients were asked how many cups of coffee and tea they drank on a typical day before they were hospitalized. They were also asked about their smoking and alcohol consumption. The data showed a weak association between smoking and pancreatic cancer, none between alcohol or tea and pancreatic cancer, but a strong association with coffee drinking. Since tea seemed not to be involved, caffeine as a possible cause was ruled out.

The risk of getting pancreatic cancer was twice as great for people who drank two cups of coffee a day as it was for those who drank none, and three times as great for those who drank five cups of coffee a day.

Dr. MacMahon said he gave up coffee on the basis of this study.

A cancer patient is treated with whole-body hyperthermia in which his blood is shunted through a heat exchanger that heats or cools it as the treatment requires.

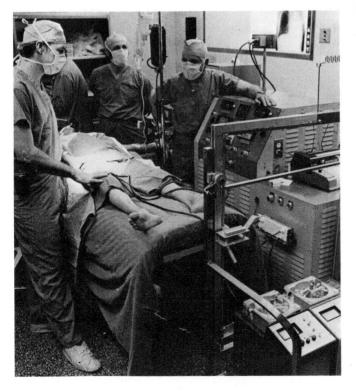

But there were a number of researchers who pointed out that the study was far from conclusive. The interviews did not dwell on past coffee habits, especially what kinds of coffee were drunk. There have been other studies implicating decaffeinated coffee with cancer, but these were not strong associations, either.

Putting the heat on cancer. The use of hyperthermia, or heat therapy, for cancer tumors is still experimental, but continuing research in 1981 has been exciting enough to kindle interest in the procedure in many leading U.S. medical centers. For example, F. Kristian Storm, Donald L. Morton, and Larry R. Kaiser of the University of California School of Medicine at Los Angeles reported in June 1981 that they had achieved deep internal hyperthermia with a magnetrode – a magnetic loop induction coil that transmits high energy radio waves.

Scientists have known for some time that tumor cells are more sensitive to heat than are surrounding body tissues, and that delivering heat to a cancer tumor causes some form of cell death. The researchers are trying to find the best way to deliver the heat, at what temperatures, and for how long.

Tumors are thought to be heat-sensitive because they lack some of the network of blood vessels that can act as heat exchangers and cool them down. At a body temperature of 108°F. a number of things appear to take place within the tumors that kill them: vital enzyme systems become altered; the synthesis of DNA and RNA slows down; membranes become more permeable; and lysosomes, or cell enzymes, are released. At 113°F. and above, normal body tissue dies.

In studies conducted in the mid

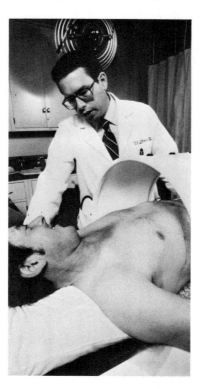

A magnetic device generates electric currents that heat and destroy tumors in the interior of the body.

Cardiology
See Drugs; Heart

1970s, researchers immersed cancer patients in molten wax or in hot-water blankets and found significant tumor regression. Such whole-body hyperthermia was hard on some patients, however, particularly those with very large tumors or with major organs affected by tumors. Recent efforts have therefore concentrated on local hyperthermia, or selective heating.

Ultrasound, microwaves, and radio-frequency waves are among the techniques being considered. The energy they produce would be turned into heat at the tumor site.

With the University of California's magnetrode, temperatures up to 122°F. could be achieved in some tumors, with no damage to normal surrounding tissue which could dissipate the heat. The researchers found the degree of heat that could be attained was directly related to the size of the tumor. They also found that temperatures above 113°F. had the greatest effect on the tumor.

Dr. Storm and his co-workers suggested that the greatest potential of hyperthermia might be in its combined use with other therapies. Because high heat causes blood clots and blood vessels within the tumor to constrict, it might be helpful to use hyperthermia before surgery to remove a tumor. And because it increases the permeability of cell membranes, it might increase the action of chemotherapy. In preliminary studies, Dr. Storm and his co-workers have seen both improved responses and improved rates of survival when they combined hyperthermia with chemotherapy for melanoma and for colon cancer that had metastasized to the liver.   [Harriet S. Page]

Childbirth

Despite strong objections from organized medicine, large numbers of couples in the United States are spurning hospital maternity wards in favor of the psychological comfort of their homes or clinics for the birth of their babies.

In 1977, the latest year for which national statistics are available, more than 36,000 women had babies outside hospitals. This represents 1.1 per cent of the total, up

slightly from 1976. Data from some states, however, show a dramatic shift. In Oregon, for example, there was a 56 per cent increase from 1976 to 1977. Some 3.9 per cent of all babies in Oregon in 1977 were born outside hospitals.

The reason for this increase may be found in an article in the May 1980 issue of the *Journal of the American Medical Association* (JAMA). Expectant parents enumer-

A woman of the 1600s gives birth in the traditional sitting position, *above,* a practice that lasted until the 1700s. Now, vertical delivery is returning, aided by a motorized birthing chair, *below,* that raises, lowers, and tilts.

ated complaints about hospitals that included previous unpleasant birth experiences, impersonal attitudes, mandatory tests and procedures, intervention in an otherwise natural event, and high cost.

The issue of home birth is frustrating for doctors, according to Dr. Warren H. Pearse, executive director of the American College of Obstetricians and Gynecologists (ACOG). "Physician concerns for the well-being of both mother and newborn seem not to be shared by some pregnant couples [sic], who speak of experiences instead of outcomes," Dr. Pearse commented.

People who favor home births and those who are opposed cite studies that compare the risks involved in difficult deliveries. But obstetricians G. David Adamson of Stanford University Medical Center in California and Douglas J. Gare

of Toronto General Hospital in Canada noted in the JAMA article that current data on merits and deficiencies in both home and hospital settings "are limited and do not conclusively support either opinion."

An ACOG study based on statistics from health departments in 47 U.S. states showed that babies born outside hospitals ran a 2 to 5 times greater risk than babies born in hospitals. California, Iowa, Kansas, and Oklahoma reported that between 18 and 23 fetuses and newborns died for every 1,000 deliveries in hospitals, compared with a perinatal mortality rate of between 42 and 104 deaths for every 1,000 out-of-hospital deliveries. The perinatal mortality rate is the death rate during the period shortly before and after birth.

"Stillbirths are a major risk of home delivery, particularly where the birth attendants are untrained," said Dr. Pearse. Equipment that diagnoses fetal distress before birth and apparatus for rescuing fetuses in distress are not available in homes. Pearse cited California statistics presented in 1976 – 25 stillbirths per 1,000 births for out-of-hospital deliveries, compared with 9.9 stillbirths per 1,000 births in hospitals.

Many advocates of home births point to a 1977 report of 1,146 healthy pregnant women in California by family practitioner Lewis E. Mehl. That study showed a perinatal death rate of 9.5 per 1,000 for home births.

Midwives. The American College of Certified Nurse-Midwives reported that 2,200 certified nurse-midwives were practicing in the United States in 1981, twice as many as in 1971. These are registered nurses who have completed additional training in the care of babies and pregnant women, deliv-

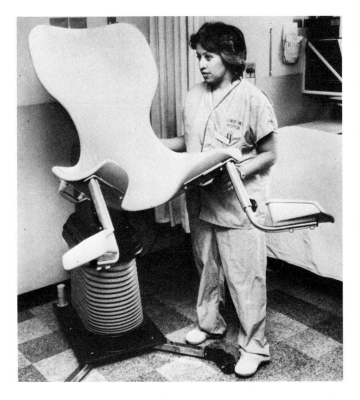

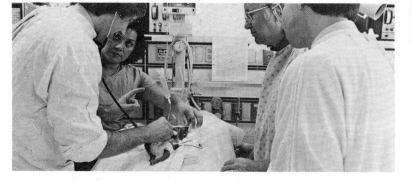

A doctor listens to a tiny baby's heartbeat in Stanford University Hospital's neonatal intensive care unit. Each year the unit treats more than 800 critically ill infants.

Children's Diseases
See Bone Disorders; Hyperactivity

Circulation
See Blood; High Blood Pressure

Contraception
See Birth Control

ery of babies, and family planning.

Diane Boyer, president of the Chicago Chapter of the American College of Certified Nurse-Midwives, cited studies showing that infant mortality rates drop after nurse-midwives arrive in cities and rural areas. Even so, the legal position of midwives is unclear in many states because some health departments interpret midwifery as

the practice of medicine without a license.

At Chicago's Cook County Hospital, where physicians supervise midwives, 18 midwives delivered 1,500 babies in 1980, nearly one-third of the hospital's normal deliveries. The midwives concentrate on low-risk patients while obstetricians deal with complicated deliveries.   [Marcia J. Opp]

Dentistry

A pneumatic device sends a series of split-second pulses of force against a tooth in a new orthodontic technique. The pulsed pressure moves the tooth along the jaw more quickly than the constant pressure of orthodontic braces.

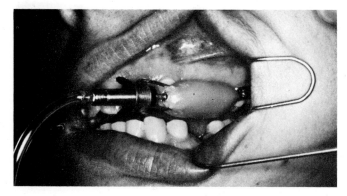

A vaccine to stop tooth decay moved a step closer to reality in 1981. Dental researcher Thomas Lehner and his associates at Guy's Hospital in London disclosed that they have successfully inoculated monkeys with a vaccine that fights *Streptococcus mutans,* the bacteria that causes tooth decay.

S. mutans lives on tooth surfaces and converts sugar in the diet to

acids that eat into tooth enamel and infect dentin, the material beneath the enamel surface. Ultimately, the tooth nerve is attacked, causing toothache. If uncared for, the tooth is lost.

Proper diet and dental care can control decay, and water fluoridation has been shown to help prevent it. But dental researchers have long sought a method to attack the decay-causing bacteria.

Dr. Lehner's vaccine contains highly purified proteins from the bacteria. When injected into the body, these proteins stimulate the body's immune system to make antibodies, proteins that attack and destroy the bacteria, eliminating the conditions in the mouth that cause decay.

Vaccinated rhesus monkeys, fed a sugar-rich diet similar to the average diet in developed countries such as the United States, had 70 per cent fewer cavities than monkeys who were not given the vaccine. The test monkeys suffered no side effects from the vaccine. Eventually, the vaccine will be tested on humans.

Cleft lip and cleft palate are fairly common birth defects, occurring about once in every 1,000 births. In cleft palate, the two halves of the fetal palate fail to grow together to form the roof of the mouth. Such a defect produces an opening between the mouth and the nasal cavity, interfering with eating, drinking, and speech. Researchers at the University of North Carolina's Dental Research Center in Chapel Hill announced in May 1981 that these birth defects may sometimes be caused by a drug that is commonly prescribed to prevent convulsions, such as epileptic seizures, in adults.

Dental researchers Guillermo Millicovsky and Malcolm C. Johnston tested the drug — called phenytoin, or Dilantin — on pregnant mice. They found an unusual number of cases of cleft palate and cleft lip in the offspring of these mice. Their research indicates that phenytoin, which is used to treat epilepsy and other convulsive disorders, slows down heart and breathing activity. This reduces the amount of oxygen taken into the body, and, in pregnancy, cuts down the amount of oxygen available to the developing fetus. It is this lack of oxygen, the researchers believe, that causes the malformations of palate and lip.

Giving oxygen to pregnant women who must take phenytoin may help prevent the development of cleft palate and lip in their offspring.   [Paul Goldhaber]

Digestive Disorders

In recent years, a great deal has been learned about a common gastrointestinal problem — traveler's diarrhea, also known as Montezuma's revenge, or turista — which has spoiled vacations for many people. Norman Noah, a consultant epidemiologist at the British Public Health Laboratory Service's Communicable Disease Surveillance Centre in Colindale, England, discussed this problem in an August 1980 issue of *New Scientist* magazine.

Noah wrote that the disease has been blamed on a variety of causes, including rapid changes in climate, and the consumption of cheap wine, spicy foods, or foods cooked in cheap oil.

However, evidence points to an infectious origin of diarrhea. The most common cause of traveler's diarrhea for United States citizens is the intestinal bacterium *Esche-*

richia coli, or *E. coli*. Travelers to foreign countries may contract other infectious agents that cause diarrhea, such as salmonella bacteria, which cause food poisoning; shigella bacteria, which cause dysentery; and other organisms whose role in causing diarrhea is not well understood.

E. coli bacteria normally inhabit the intestines of healthy people, but three strains of *E. coli* apparently cause diarrhea. An enteropathogenic group (EPEC) causes infant or neonatal diarrhea, which is more common in bottle-fed babies than in breast-fed babies, although the method of infection is not fully understood. Enteroinvasive *E. coli* (EIEC) penetrates the intestinal lining and leads to a dysenterylike illness in adults and children. But EPEC and EIEC strains are not frequently found in traveler's diarrhea. Rather, they are more likely

"Yes, I mind *very much* if you
talk about constipation!"

Drug Abuse
See The Perils of PCP;
Alcoholism

to be associated with outbreaks of diarrhea due to food poisoning.

The major strain of *E. coli* in traveler's diarrhea is the entero-toxic (ETEC) type, which may be present in food and water. ETEC produces two poisons that cause the release of enzymes in the intestinal wall. These enzymes cause fluids to move into the intestine.

One poison produces diarrhea in less than 1 hour, while the other takes more than 2 hours. This difference may explain why traveler's diarrhea strikes its victims twice.

Whether or not ETEC produces poison depends on factors such as the stomach's production of hydrochloric acid, which aids digestion; the presence of digestive enzymes; the state of the mucous lining of the intestine; and the number of antibodies that are produced in the intestine.

Young children and the elderly are especially prone to fluid loss, but all diarrhea victims should replace fluids. Other treatments include settling bowel activity and attacking the infection.

Antidiarrheal medications such as Lomotil, kaolin, and codeine phosphate settle the intestine but they may do more harm than good if used repeatedly. Such medications and antibiotics tend to upset the interaction of intestinal factors further and prolong or shift the infection.

Research on the problem includes attempts to alter normal intestinal organisms so that they cannot produce poisons, developing substances to absorb the poisons before they exert their effect on the intestinal wall, and using prostaglandins to reduce the outpouring of fluid.   [Donald F. Phillips]

Drugs

In April 1981, the Food and Drug Administration (FDA) approved the use of a new drug to treat hypertension (high blood pressure). Captopril, developed from the research of physician John H. Laragh and his associates at New York Hospital-Cornell Medical Center in New York City, should help many hypertensive persons.

Medical authorities estimate that 15 to 20 per cent of all adults in the United States suffer to some extent from high blood pressure. It is the most important risk factor associated with heart and kidney disease and stroke.

High blood pressure is caused, in part, by the constriction of blood vessels and the retention of salt and fluid. Captopril acts by keeping the body from manufacturing a blood protein called angiotensin II. This protein, produced by the action of a kidney hormone called renin, constricts arteries and veins. Angiotensin II also increases salt and water retention.

Second heart attacks may be prevented by a drug that passed a major testing goal in 1981. A Norwegian study group, coordinated by cardiologist Terje Pedersen of the University of Bergen, studied the effects of timolol – a beta-blocker – on patients who had already suffered heart attacks. Such persons run a high risk of having a second attack.

Beta-blockers work by reducing or preventing the effects of the hormone adrenalin on the heart. This produces a slower heart rate and fewer heartbeat irregularities.

The researchers found that timolol users had 28.4 per cent fewer second heart attacks than did the members of a control group who took a *placebo* (inert substance). In addition, the sudden death rate went down 44.6 per cent.

Angina pectoris is the chest pain caused by spasms of the blood vessels that lead to the heart. In March and April 1981, scientists reported on two drugs that may help victims of angina.

Both substances belong to a group of drugs called calcium-blockers that inhibit the action of calcium, a chemical essential in the pumping operation of the heart. Calcium-blockers also relax and dilate the body's blood vessels. The drugs have been used in other parts of the world for years, but only recently have clinical tests been carried out by scientists in the United States.

In a nine-month test conducted by internist Stacy M. Johnson and associates at the University of Texas Health Science Center in Dallas, the calcium-blocker verapamil was tried on victims of Prinzmetal's variant angina, a form of angina that strikes during periods of rest. Those who used the drug had only 2 to 5 attacks of angina per week. Control patients, who did not take the drug, suffered 12 to 26 angina attacks per week. Verapamil had no serious side effects, according to test results.

Another calcium-blocker, nifedipine, was tested against severe angina by physician Dennis M. Krikler of the Royal Post Graduate Medical School in London. The drug, administered during periods of exercise, proved effective in reducing the number and severity of angina attacks.

Researchers are working to assess the value of calcium-blockers in other heart problems, such as irregular beats and high blood pressure.   [Marcus M. Reidenberg]

Emphysema
See Calling it Quits; Reducing the Risks of Cancer; Cancer

Epilepsy
See Neurology

Eyes
See Vision

Fever

Several medical investigators reported in 1981 that fever is not necessarily a harmful symptom; it can be an important body defense against infection. Rather than trying to lower the patient's body temperature to the normal 98.6°F. with cold baths, aspirin, or other antifever treatments, doctors have begun to consider using fever to fight disease.

Although scientists do not yet know exactly what triggers a fever, they do know many of the ways in which fever affects the body. The heart beats faster and the metabolism rate increases when a person is running a fever. A fever also activates the body's natural defense system, causing white blood cells to multiply and speed to the site of the infection to engulf and destroy bacteria. When the body temperature climbs above 98.6°F., iron,

A moderate fever is not necessarily an ominous sign; it may be one of the body's best weapons against infection.

which many bacteria need to survive, is withdrawn from the blood and stored in the liver.

Internist Philip Mackowiak of the University of Texas Health Science Center in Dallas reported at a March 1981 meeting of the American Society for Microbiology that antibiotics kill some bacteria more easily during a fever than when body temperature is normal. Dr. Mackowiak speculated that if patients were allowed to run a fever while taking antibiotics for an infection, they might recover in three days. But if their fevers were suppressed, they might need five days to get well. He asserted that fever may be valuable in treating infections in patients whose immune systems are weakened, perhaps from anticancer drugs.

Physiologist Matthew J. Kluger of the University of Michigan demon-

strated that humans and warm-blooded animals are not alone in benefiting from fevers. He injected lizards with a potentially fatal dose of bacteria. The reptiles, which cannot raise their body temperatures internally, sunned themselves on rocks or crawled under a heat lamp to warm their blood. Dr. Kluger found that 75 per cent of the lizards who raised their temperatures from 101°F. to 104°F. survived the infection. In a control group in which no heat source was available, 75 per cent of the infected lizards died.

Although other researchers have been able to reduce tumors in terminal cancer patients by raising their body temperatures to 106°F. or 107°F., Dr. Kluger cautioned that fevers of 105°F. or more may produce convulsions or brain damage.   [Eleanor Dunn]

Financing Medical Care

The cost of health services and supplies and health-related research and construction activities in the United States reached $227.7 billion in June 1980. This represents an increase of 13.7 per cent over 1979 and accounts for 9.2 per cent of the gross national product. Personal health care expenditures amounted to $898 for each person in the United States.

Four factors account for the rapidly rising costs of health care. They are inflation; development of health programs for the aged and the poor; fee-for-service payments to physicians that encourage them to offer increased services; and a reimbursement system for hospitals that encourages them to add services that increase the costs of health care.

Until recently, consumer-patients had little reason to be concerned over costs since their health

services were largely covered by insurance companies or by the government. By 1981, about 90 per cent of the population was insured for hospital expenses. About 90 per cent was also insured for other medical expenses through third-party plans or programs, such as Blue Cross-Blue Shield, private commercial insurance companies, and government-funded Medicare and Medicaid programs.

During the 1970s, however, insurance companies were unable to keep pace with the rising costs of health care. As a result, the cost of insurance premiums has risen dramatically and coverage for services or benefits has been cut back.

These high insurance premiums are forcing consumers to dig deeper to pay for health care. Although consumers are paying a smaller percentage of their health care costs directly than they paid in previous years, direct payments are costing consumers increasingly larger sums of money. Out-of-pocket expenses have climbed from $34 billion in 1973 to $71 billion in 1980. Health insurance premiums also continue to cost consumers a mounting portion of their income. In 1973, health insurance premiums constituted 2.7 per cent of disposable income. By 1980, they had risen to 3.4 per cent.

How can you help stem the rising costs of your health care? There are a number of ways. In seeking health insurance, for example, you should know that there is a considerable difference in premiums and benefits between group insurance policies and individual and family policies. In a group insurance program, you will generally pay a lower premium and receive greater benefits.

If you must take out an individual policy, you should consider health insurance policies that have deductibles, where you pay some of the "first dollars" before the insurance company starts to reimburse you. Another plan is co-insurance, in which the consumer pays a fixed percentage of the total medical bill. Co-insurance gives consumers an incentive to examine the costs of their care and to be more prudent about what services they accept. Some private insurance companies encourage this. For example, by paying only 80 per cent of hospital costs, but 100 per cent of outpatient costs, the insurer gives the consumer reason to use less-expensive outpatient services rather than expensive hospital treatment.

Another approach to cost-cutting is prepaid group insurance. In these health plans, you pay a flat monthly premium regardless of how much or how little care you or

your family receives. Physicians who work for a prepaid plan receive the same pay regardless of the number of services they provide or the number of patients they see.

By pooling premiums paid by thousands of plan members, a group of physicians can provide all the care necessary for the group. Furthermore, since the physicians are paid a fixed amount of money, they are encouraged to provide only necessary services. More important, they place greater emphasis on prevention and early detection of illnesses, before those illnesses become costly to treat or require hospitalization.

Prepaid group practices are also called health-maintenance organizations (HMOs). The first HMO in the United States, the Ross-Luce Plan, began serving municipal employees in Los Angeles in 1929. Later, the Kaiser-Permanente Plan was established, which in 1981 was serving about 6 million people in six Western states.

A 1973 federal law established a grant and loan program to aid in the development of these prepaid medical plans. A new HMO can receive more than $2.25 million in grants and $4 million in federal loans. HMOs cannot rely on the government to subsidize their losses, however. They must become financially secure after five years, or go out of business.

There are three types of HMOs. One is the staff model. It is essentially a loose confederation of physicians sharing administrative and secretarial chores. Another type is the group practice or closed panel. These have medical centers where staff physicians provide services in a clinic setting. In the third type of HMO, the independent practice association, doctors maintain their own offices, but have a contract

Soaring Medical Bills
Americans and their
medical insurance
companies have been
paying for medical care
at a steadily increasing
rate. The chart's
scale is logarithmic to
keep the bars of
projected costs from
running off the page.

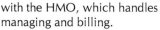

Fractures
See Bone Disorders

Genetic Research
See Birth Defects

Geriatrics
See Arthritis Is
Everyone's Disease

with the HMO, which handles
managing and billing.

By the end of 1980, there were
235 HMOs in the United States
with nearly 8.2 million members.

HMOs are not open to the
public — only employees of firms
that offer the plans can become
members. However, an amendment to the 1973 HMO law states

that an HMO must open its enroll-
ment to everyone who applies for
limited periods after it has 50,000
members, has been reviewed and
qualified by the federal government, and is financially solvent.
Therefore, HMOs in the future can
be expected to play an increasingly
large role in community health.
[Donald F. Phillips]

Gynecology

Toxic shock syndrome (TSS), an illness first reported in 1978 and not
known to exist before 1970, became one of the most discussed
and feared diseases of 1981. TSS
occurs primarily in otherwise
healthy young women and there is
a striking association with menstruation and, more specifically, with
the use of tampons.

The onset is usually sudden, with
high fever, vomiting, and diarrhea.
Many patients also have a sore
throat, headache, and muscle pain.
A sunburnlike rash develops and
the skin eventually peels. Shock
and coma may follow and there
may be respiratory distress and irregularities of the heart rhythm.

A patient who survives TSS will
improve within 7 to 10 days, but
the skin will peel for some time.
Peeling is most prominent on the
palms of the hands and soles of the
feet but can occur on the face,

torso, and even on the tongue. Skin
may come off in sheets.

Pathologist John Blair of St. Louis
University School of Medicine told
his colleagues at the International
Academy of Pathology meeting in
March 1981 in Chicago that doctors did not recognize the effects of
TSS until the late 1970s. He re-
called performing an autopsy on a
15-year-old girl who had died suddenly in 1975. The autopsy disclosed small blood clots in the
lungs, liver damage, ulceration of
the vagina, and swelling of the
brain. Pathologists had not yet associated these tissue changes with
TSS, so the cause of the girl's death
had eluded Dr. Blair.

Pediatrician James Todd and his
colleagues at the University of Colorado's Children's Hospital in Den-
ver first described TSS in a 1978
article in *The Lancet*. They discussed seven TSS patients who

were from 8 to 17 years old. In January 1980, epidemiologists in Minnesota and Wisconsin reported 12 cases to the Centers for Disease Control (CDC) in Atlanta, Ga. A flood of cases followed.

The CDC reported that the incidence of TSS reached a peak of 797 cases in the United States in 1980. By June 15, 1981, the CDC had received reports of 1,128 cases, all but 15 of them in women. There have been 84 deaths – a fatality rate of 7.4 per cent. TSS has been reported in 48 states and in Canada, Great Britain, The Netherlands, Sweden, and West Germany.

Even after a year of effort to compile data on this disease, there still are many unanswered questions. Investigators know that a poison produced by *Staphylococcus aureus* bacteria causes the disease, but they had not identified the poison by July 1981. The role of tampons is unknown.

Rely tampons, the brand most associated with TSS, were withdrawn from the market in September 1980, though no one could show why that particular superabsorbent tampon seemed more closely linked with TSS than other brands. In October, the American College of Obstetricians and Gynecologists (ACOG) said "it would be prudent, at present, to discontinue use of the newly developed superabsorbent tampons until more conclusive scientific research has been conducted. When tampons are used, they should be changed frequently, at least every six to eight hours, to reduce the risk of potential infection."

That statement was promptly challenged by doctors who said that frequent changes could increase the risk of vaginal abrasions through which the bacteria could enter the bloodstream. Some women reportedly changed tampons as often as every hour.

The CDC reported that the incidence of TSS apparently was on the decline by the summer of 1981. However, states such as Minnesota, Texas, Utah, and Wisconsin that have TSS surveillance programs report a leveling off in TSS incidence, but no decline.

The CDC received reports of only 94 new cases between January 1 and May 15, 1981. The agency thinks the most likely cause of the apparent decline is that women have changed their tampon-use habits. A survey of tampon manufacturers showed the proportion of menstruating women who use tampons declined from 70 per cent to 55 per cent after TSS received national attention.

Epidemiologist George P. Schmid of the CDC outlined this theory and others at an ACOG meeting in Las Vegas in the spring of 1981. He also suggested that women are now more aware of the disease, so when they have early TSS symptoms, they stop using tampons and go to the doctor. Consequently, they do not develop reportable cases of TSS, so the disease seems to be on the decline.

However, some doctors remain concerned with such mild cases of TSS, especially since women who have suffered one episode of the disease are more likely to have another. Pediatrician P. Joan Chesney of the University of Wisconsin in Madison stated in a June 1981 letter to the *New England Journal of Medicine* that "accurate diagnosis of mild cases of TSS is important in preventing more severe episodes. We suspect that an increasing number of mild manifestations of this disease will be reported, as women learn to discontinue the use of tampons with the appearance of symptoms and physicians recognize that the spectrum of TSS includes milder illnesses."

Women who have had a mild episode of TSS should not use tampons for several months, said Dr. Chesney, and they should be treated with antibiotics that have proved effective in preventing recurrence of TSS.

CDC conducted a study in 1980 showing that tampon absorbency alone or the number of tampons used during a menstrual period apparently did not determine the risk of TSS infection. The CDC report concluded that "women who have not had TSS have a low risk of its development (6.2 cases per 100,000 menstruating women) and probably do not need to change their patterns of tampon use." [Virginia S. Cowart]

Headache
See Help for the Headache

Heart

New drugs introduced in 1980 and 1981 expanded the possibilities for treating heart disease, the number-one killer in the United States. Although the overall death rate from heart disease is dropping, heart attacks account for some 550,000 deaths in America each year.

Two types of drugs — calcium antagonists and beta-blockers — are especially important. Calcium antagonists prevent calcium, which speeds up the heart rate, from entering the heart. Beta-blockers prevent nerve impulses from reaching special sites called beta receptors in the heart and blood vessels, and so reduce both the heart rate and the force of heart muscle contractions. Both types of drugs can reduce high blood pressure, which often leads to heart disease.

Verapamil. The U.S. Food and Drug Administration (FDA) in 1981 approved the calcium antagonist verapamil for intravenous injections. Verapamil is used to treat arrhythmia, or abnormal heart rhythms, and angina, a squeezing or pressurelike pain in the chest. It has been used in Europe since 1970, but it was not until 1981 that the FDA approved it.

Verapamil is especially effective in controlling arrhythmia. The heart rate is regulated by a natural pacemaker, a group of cells that generate the electrical impulses that make the heart beat. If too much calcium reaches the pacemaker, the heart rate may jump to 160 to 200 beats per minute — a rate that could be fatal if left uncontrolled. Verapamil reduces the amount of calcium that gets through so that the pacemaker gives off fewer electrical impulses. As a result, the heart rate drops to 80 to 100 beats per minute.

Verapamil also relieves the chronic irregular heartbeat, a less dangerous but very uncomfortable condition that occurs in people with rheumatic heart disease. The drug also appears to relieve the major forms of angina. It enables patients with exertional angina — chest pain during exercise — to exercise for longer periods without pain and reduces the incidence of angina attacks in resting patients. Resting angina often precedes a heart attack.

Beta-blockers. These drugs show enormous promise in reducing the risk of a second, and fatal, heart attack. But until recently, no studies had proven conclusively that they work. Only 3 of some 12 different beta-blockers used throughout the world are approved for use in the United States.

Cardiologist Terje R. Pedersen of the University of Bergen in Norway reported in 1981 on a 1,884-patient study in which timolol, a

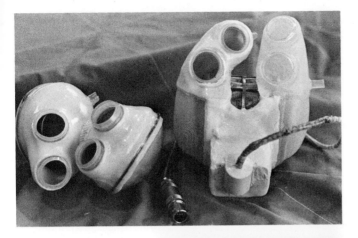

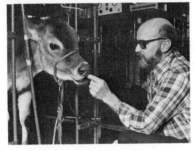

Artificial hearts, *above*, developed at the University of Utah include a device driven by compressed air (left) and an electrically powered model (right). Tennyson the calf, *right*, whose natural heart was removed, survived a record 268 days with an artificial heart.

to block circulation. However, sometimes a person with a potentially fatal blocked artery may have little or no cholesterol build-up inside the vessels. If the clot can be dissolved quickly — before the heart muscle begins to die — the patient can recover.

Cardiologist William Ganz, professor of medicine at the University of California at Los Angeles and senior research scientist at Cedar-Sinai Medical Center in Los Angeles, reported on his method of thrombolysis at the American Heart Association meeting in the fall of 1980. Dr. Ganz threads a narrow tube through the artery to a position very close to the clot and runs the drug through the tube. This method enables him and his colleagues to open coronary arteries in 20 of 21 heart-attack victims. The average length of the procedure is 20 minutes.

Previously, the outlook for heart attack victims with blocked arteries was bleak. The patient was simply monitored in an intensive care room and given oxygen and drugs to prevent heart failure or arrhythmia while the heart attack ran its course.

Heart surgery. A panel of scientists assembled by the National Institutes of Health in Bethesda, Md., reported in February 1981 that bypass surgery represents a major advance in heart disease treatment and that it not only increases life expectancy but also improves the quality of the patient's life.

The panel, composed of two statisticians, six cardiologists, four surgeons, and one family practitioner noted that the types of patients who benefit most from bypass surgery are those with a major block of the left coronary artery, and those with disease in three of the major vessels. Approximately 100,000 by-pass operations are

beta-blocker not approved for use in the United States, reduced by 40 per cent the number of fatal heart attacks in Norwegian patients surviving a previous heart attack. Timolol treatments were started within 28 days of the first heart attack and continued for up to 33 months. The FDA was expected to approve the drug late in 1981. See *Aspirin and Your Heart.*

Dissolving blood clots. Thrombolysis, a technique for dissolving blood clots in coronary vessels, has enabled physicians to open blocked arteries within an hour after a heart attack occurs, according to a report issued in 1981. The drug streptokinase is used to dissolve the clot.

In some forms of arterial disease, cholesterol deposits form on the walls of the arteries, narrowing them significantly. In these cases, a blood clot may plug up the artery

Widening the Wall

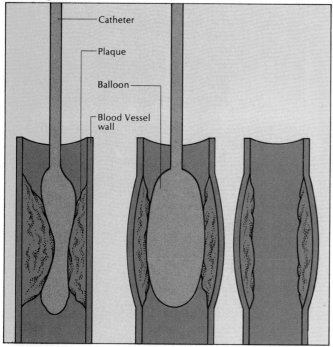

Catheter

Plaque

Balloon

Blood Vessel wall

A balloon catheter expands against built-up plaque in an artery, flattening the plaque against the wall and opening the blood vessel.

nique that enables physicians to detect signs that the transplanted heart is being rejected much earlier than was previously possible.

The surgeons insert a thin flexible wire with a clipper at the end into the patient's jugular vein and thread it into the transplanted heart to snip a small sample of tissue. This tissue is then analyzed for signs of rejection. If the heart appears to be under attack by the body's immune system, the doctors can increase dosages of drugs to ward off the reaction. One such drug – cyclosporin A – which can suppress the immune system without hampering its ability to fight infections, has also contributed to Stanford's increased success rate.

The new rejection-sampling technique and cyclosporin A enabled Dr. Shumway and cardiovascular surgeon Bruce A. Reitz to perform in March 1981 the first heart and lung transplant operation in almost 10 years. The transplant recipient, Mary D. Grohlke, was suffering from pulmonary hypertension – a form of high blood pressure that weakens both the heart and lungs. Although the three previous human heart-lung transplant patients had died within a few weeks, Mrs. Grohlke had resumed many normal activities by July.   [Virginia S. Cowart]

performed in the United States each year.

Heart transplant surgery has become increasingly successful, with surgeons at Stanford University in Palo Alto, Calif., reporting a survival rate among transplant patients of 70 per cent one year after surgery. The Stanford team, led by cardiovascular surgeon Norman E. Shumway, is using a new tech-

---

High Blood Pressure

The risk of serious heart and blood vessel disorder is twice as high in people with mild hypertension, or high blood pressure, as in individuals with normal blood pressure, according to the 1980 report of the Joint National Committee on Detection, Evaluation, and Treatment of High Blood Pressure. The report was drafted by various medical groups and federal agencies. It drew heavily on findings published

in 1979 by the Hypertension, Detection, and Follow-up Program Cooperating Group.

A normal blood-pressure reading ranges between 100/60 and 140/90 for persons between the ages of 18 and 45. The top number in the ratio refers to systolic pressure, which measures how hard the heart works to pump blood to the vessels. The bottom number in the ratio refers to the diastolic pressure,

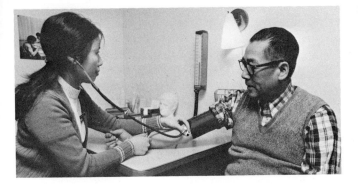

A health-care professional measures a patient's blood pressure. Regular blood-pressure checks are essential in the battle to control high blood pressure, the "silent killer."

Hospital
See Dr. Beaumont's Frontier Research; Hospice

which measures the blood pressure when the heart relaxes between beats. Mild hypertensives have a diastolic pressure of 90 to 104.

In the National Committee study, the researchers reviewed records of 10,940 hypertensive patients from 14 communities for 5 years. The men and women, who ranged in age from 30 to 69, were assigned either to an intensive antihypertensive treatment program or to the regular care of their family physician or local health center.

The five-year mortality rate was 17 per cent lower for people assigned to the intensive-treatment group than for those in the regular care group. Significantly, two-thirds of the people in the intensive-treatment group stuck with their treatment programs, which would explain their superior blood-pressure control and lower death rate. More than one-half achieved their desired pressure.

The Joint Committee report stressed that it is especially important for mild hypertensives, who represent a significant proportion of the population, to reduce their blood pressure. With daily medication, these patients can reduce risk of death from strokes and heart disease by 20 per cent.

The report also recommended that mild hypertensives adopt a salt-free diet, low in animal fats. If people with high blood pressure

smoke, they should stop. If they are not exercising, they should gradually begin.

The report emphasized that medical treatment lowers the complications that can result from even mild elevations in blood pressure. These include stroke; congestive heart failure, in which blood backs up in the veins leading to the heart; enlargement of the heart's left ventricle; and a continued rise of blood pressure.

Elevations in blood pressure rarely cause obvious problems. In fact, because the first symptom may be either a heart attack or stroke, hypertension has been called the "silent killer." Often, persons with diagnosed high blood pressure stop taking their antihypertensive medicine on the grounds that they feel no apparent physical change. This failure to continue medication is the major obstacle in controlling hypertension, according to the report, and physicians should strongly emphasize that hypertension can be controlled, but not cured. Invariably, the blood pressure shoots up again as soon as the patient goes off the drug regimen.

No drugs? For years, physicians and other medical personnel have debated whether hypertensives should try to lower their blood pressure without drugs before using medication. The 1980 report recommended that young patients who have uncomplicated mild hypertension and no heart or blood vessel disorders should try to bring their pressure down by a change in diet—particularly by cutting their intake of salt and fattening foods.

Some people have lowered their blood pressure with such methods as biofeedback, psychiatric counseling, and relaxation. But the committee considers these experimental.   [Marcia J. Opp]

Hyperactivity

By working with parents, two researchers have found that they can lower the level of hyperactivity in children suffering from that problem while at the same time reducing the dosage of drugs the children require. Kathy Kirmil-Gray and Laurie Duckham-Shoor of Stanford University in California found in their doctoral studies that a key to calming hyperactive children lies in helping parents to be more consistent in how they treat the children.

Specialists estimate that up to 20 per cent of the school-age children in the United States are afflicted to some degree with hyperactivity, also known variously as attention-deficit disorder, hyperkinesis, or minimal brain dysfunction. Its symptoms include: short attention span, fighting, truancy, and academic failure.

In the past, doctors and behavior specialists have treated the problem with tranquilizing drugs, and assured parents that the children would "grow out of it." But research reported during 1980 contradicts this notion. The condition continues to affect many young people, causing various forms of maladjustment as they mature.

Dr. Kirmil-Gray and Dr. Duckham-Shoor studied eight hyperactive boys ranging from 7 to 10 years of age at Stanford's School of Education. The researchers point out that boys tend to be more hyperactive than girls by a factor of 7 to 1 and attribute this to early experience, physiology, or social role modeling. They compared the hyperactive boys with eight boys from similar backgrounds who were not hyperactive. In their study, the hyperactive boys were divided into two groups — a group made up of six "actives" and a group made up of two controls. The two controls were kept on full medication during the three-month study, while medications for the other six were gradually reduced. Paradoxically, hyperactive children are given stimulants, such as methylphenidate (Ritalin), permoline, or dextroamphetamines, rather than tranquilizers, to control their boisterous behavior.

Kirmil-Gray and Duckham-Shoor worked with the parents of all the children at night for about 20 hours during the study and worked with the boys at school and at the university, giving them a course of 48 lessons in self-control. In working with parents, the researchers found that, like most other American families, discipline with children was inconsistent. Mothers and fathers enforce discipline differently and they differ on when to discipline their children, so that the children never know quite what to expect.

The researchers taught the parents to set up "minicontracts" with their children, spelling out definite limits. They urged the parents to follow through on the contracts — to praise when praise was appropriate, and to ignore some types of behavior. The parents learned to punish by banishing the boys to a room where nothing was going on and it was boring. The researchers

A child's hyperactivity level can be lowered substantially when all members of the family become involved in the treatment.

reported that the isolation technique was "very effective" with all the children.

After therapy started, two of the hyperactive boys improved so much that they could be taken off medication completely. Two others were able to function on 25 per cent of their original dosage, and the other two on 50 per cent.

While the researchers acknowledged that their study represents a small sample, they emphasized that it demonstrated that "the parents, rather than the boys themselves, were the key."

James R. Morrison, a psychiatrist at the University of California, San Diego, reported in the *Journal of Clinical Psychiatry* in 1980 on a study in which he found that adults who were hyperactive as children are likely to be more violent, less successful professionally, and in

more trouble with the law than adults who were not hyperactive as children.

Dr. Morrison studied 48 adults who had hyperactivity symptoms as children and compared these subjects with 48 similar adults who were not hyperactive as children. His conclusions agreed with the Stanford study on the parental role in hyperactivity. Morrison said that lack of parental control might encourage "an already abnormally rambunctious child to range further and further outside of social norms, eventually resulting in adult antisocial behavior." He noted that most of the adults who had been hyperactive children were from homes in which the father was often absent, and more of them had been separated from one of their parents during the formative years.   [Charles-Gene McDaniel]

Hypertension
See High Blood Pressure

Immunization
See Dentistry

Injury

People who drink in a hot tub do so at their peril. If alcohol clouds a bather's thinking, he or she may overheat drastically without realizing it, and suffer heatstroke.

About 4,000 people die each year in the United States of heatstroke, usually caused by strenuous exercise in hot weather. The increasing popularity of hot tubs in the United States has been linked with death due to heatstroke, according to physicist Albert A. Bartlett of the University of Colorado in Boulder and oncologist Thomas J. Braun of

the Memorial Sloan-Kettering Cancer Center in New York City. They reported this finding at the annual meeting of the American Association of Physics Teachers in New York City in January 1981.

When the body needs to get rid of a large amount of heat, it opens up blood vessels near the skin surface. These vessels lose heat if the skin is in contact with a cooler environment.

However, if the environment is warmer — as in a hot tub — the blood cannot cool down. The hot environment may even heat the blood further. In this case, the blood vessels near the skin surface remain open, increasing the body's demand for blood flow and causing the heart to beat faster. The resulting strain can cause a weak or diseased heart to tire, putting the victim in great danger. Furthermore, as more blood goes to the

skin, the blood supply to the brain may drop, leading to unconsciousness and death.

Hot tubs pose an additional risk to pregnant women. A July 1981 study by Mary Ann Sedgwick Harvey, a research associate in the University of Washington School of Medicine's Department of Pediatrics in Seattle, showed that prolonged hot-tub use can raise a woman's body temperature to 102° F, which can be a hazard to the fetus' central nervous system.

Hopping into and out of the tub according to how hot she feels may not prevent adverse effects, Harvey warned, because her feeling is based on skin temperature, which returns to normal much more rapidly than does internal body temperature.   [Donald F. Phillips]

Intestinal Disorders
See Digestive Disorders

Kidney

The kidney problem that attracted the most attention in 1980 and 1981 was money. Many people with damaged kidneys are kept alive by the technique of kidney dialysis, in a process that filters out the body wastes normally removed by the kidneys. Since 1972, dialysis has been primarily supported by Medicare; this includes both hemodialysis carried out at home or in special centers, and peritoneal dialysis carried out at home. The cost to the taxpayer has risen tremendously in that time, partly because of inflation but largely because the number of U.S. patients needing dialysis has risen for some reason from about 5,000 in 1972 to more than 55,000 in 1980. Thus, the cost for dialysis, according to the Federal Government's Health Care Financing Administration, has risen from $150 million to over $1 billion per year.

Dialysis at home costs only about half as much as other forms, and a trend has begun toward the cheaper method, although about 94 per cent of hemodialyses are still done in dialysis centers.

In hemodialysis, the patient's blood is pumped through equipment that filters out various toxins and other materials. A newer method of dialysis, which patients can manage on their own, is gaining favor, however. In this technique, called continuous ambulatory peritoneal dialysis (CAPD), dialysis fluid flows from a bag held by the patient into his abdominal cavity through a permanently installed abdominal tube, or catheter. There the fluid picks up urea and other wastes. Three or four times a day, the patient allows the old fluid to drain out of his body and replaces it with sterile fluid.

Many dialysis patients experience a greater sense of freedom with CAPD. However, they must keep the catheter, the bag, and the fluid sterile. Otherwise, peritonitis (infection of the lining of the abdominal cavity) can occur.

Currently, more than 300 dialysis centers have made CAPD available to more than 3,000 patients. The technique was developed in 1975 by nephrologist Jack Moncrief of Austin, Tex., and bioengineer Robert P. Popovich of the University of Texas.

An even newer approach is continuous-cycling peritoneal dialysis (CCPD). In this technique, patients do not exchange the fluid during the day but do three exchanges during the night with the aid of an automatic cycling machine that drains the old fluid, delivers the new, and monitors the entire operation. In the morning, just before disconnecting themselves from the machine, patients perform a fourth exchange that leaves four pints of dialysis fluid in the abdomen for the entire day. The incidence of peritonitis seems to be reduced with CCPD and the patient does not have to be bothered with fluid exchanges during the day.

Yet another modification of dialysis comes from Israel, where researchers at Tel Aviv University have developed a portable artificial kidney. The briefcase-sized, lightweight machine produces its own sterile dialysis fluid from ordinary tap water.

Kidney transplants are the alternative to dialysis. Although the success rate of kidney transplants has risen in recent years, the number of transplants of kidneys taken from cadavers, or dead bodies, compared with kidneys taken from living relatives, has declined. One reason for this, according to John J-S. Cheigh and his co-workers at New York Hospital-Cornell Medical Center in New York City is that an increasing number of potential kidney-transplant recipients have had blood transfusions and prior kidney transplants. This gives them so much "experience" with foreign tissues that their immune systems have become sensitized and more likely to reject foreign kidneys.

Of 140 patients waiting for kidneys, Dr. Cheigh reported that 92 per cent showed varying degrees of such sensitivity — the more transfusions, the greater the sensitivity. Only 6.4 per cent of these sensitized patients had received neither transfusions nor prior transplants.

On the other hand, Doctor Gerhard Opelz and his colleagues at the University of California, Los Angeles, School of Medicine have collected evidence from 33 medical centers showing that recipients of cadaver kidneys who have had frequent preoperative blood transfusions have a better rate of one-year transplant survival than those who have not had transfusions. In 22 patients who received no preoperative transfusions, the graft survival was 23 per cent after one year. For 31 patients who had received more than 10 transfusions, the graft survival rate was 85 per cent. Only 28 per cent of the 152 patients who had received transfusions became sensitized against foreign tissues; 72 per cent did not. The investigators believe that the multiple transfusions made the patients' immune systems unresponsive to foreign tissues. Yet their immune response to bacteria and other infectious agents was not impaired.

Nevertheless, there is always a possibility of rejection in kidney transplants. Various drugs are used to suppress the body's immune system and therefore its attempts to reject a foreign kidney. An experimental agent called cyclosporin A is showing great promise in studies at the University of Minnesota and four other centers.

High blood pressure. Reaming out obstructed kidney arteries with a balloon-tipped catheter continues to be useful in the treatment of hypertension caused by such blocked kidney arteries. According to radiologist Eric Martin of Columbia University in New York City, the technique — also used to clean obstructions in coronary arteries — is as effective as surgery. In this method, a balloon-tipped catheter and guide wire are inserted into a major blood vessel and guided to the site of kidney obstruction. Then the balloon is inflated to push the blocking material back against the vessel walls. This treatment for this form of hypertension may eliminate the need for antihypertensive drugs or surgery, such as a vascular by-pass.   [Gail McBride]

Shock treatment, or electroconvulsive therapy (ECT), may have some value in treating schizophrenia, the most common of the serious mental illnesses, according to research reported in 1980. However, British psychiatrists Pamela Taylor and J. J. Fleminger reported that most of the improvement they noted in schizophrenic patients receiving ECT disappeared quickly, and they pointed out that chronic schizophrenics "are notoriously unresponsive to most forms of treatment, including ECT."

Drs. Taylor and Fleminger studied 20 schizophrenic patients from 18 to 50 years of age at Guy Hospital in London. They reported in June 1980 in *The Lancet,* a British medical journal, that the patients receiving ECT "showed significantly greater improvement" than a comparable group who did not receive ECT. However, most of the benefits disappeared within about 12 weeks. The researchers suggested that longer-lasting improvements might be achieved with a lengthier series of treatments, or that a more extensive study might indicate whether ECT is effective in treating schizophrenia.

Schizophrenia is a mental disease characterized by severe disturbances in perception – delusions, disturbances in mood and behavior, withdrawal from reality, and thinking in illogical, confused patterns.

Introduced in the 1930s as a treatment for schizophrenia, ECT was the most common therapy for this disease and was considered by many to have had a dramatic and favorable impact on the illness. The therapy consists of administering an electric shock to the patient through a set of electrodes placed on the head. The current causes a convulsion that may last for about a minute. The patient may be in a stupor for about an hour after ECT and may experience amnesia for several weeks.

Taylor and Fleminger reported that by the late 1970s, ECT "seems to have lost favor." They cite an American Psychiatric Association survey in which 25 per cent of the psychiatrists polled said they think ECT is an appropriate treatment for schizophrenia and 8 per cent said it is their first choice in treatment. But 59 per cent said ECT is inappropriate in schizophrenia. ECT has also been used, but again is controversial, in the treatment of depression.

Psychiatrist Carl Salzman of Harvard Medical School and the Massachusetts Mental Health Center,

"We in the psychoanalytic field don't refer to your problem as 'depression' any more, Mr. Chetham. We simply say 'temporary recession.'"

in a comprehensive survey of studies on the use of ECT in treating schizophrenia, said in the *American Journal of Psychiatry* in September 1980 that, "ECT does not alter the fundamental psychopathology [the basic disease] of schizophrenia. Given the variable quality of reports, often contradictory findings, and abundance of different and passionate opinions regarding ECT in schizophrenia, further research is indicated. ECT offers little hope for lasting improvement in chronic schizophrenic patients. It controls behavior and temporarily reduces symptoms, but relapse rates are very high.

"The studies show that ECT is better for some types of schizophrenia than for others," Dr. Salzman reported. "The best results are with patients who have been ill for one year or less."

Drugs such as the phenothiazines, introduced about 15 years after ECT was first used, supplanted ECT as the favored treatment. But these drugs have now been shown to produce serious and irreversible brain damage in many cases.

Taylor and Fleminger divided their patients into two groups of 10, and each patient received drug therapy for at least two weeks. Both groups were prepared for ECT in the usual way, with brief anesthesia and muscle relaxants, and each patient received oxygen through a face mask just before and after treatment. But only one group actually received ECT.

After six treatments, both groups showed significant improvement, but the change was greater in the group that received the ECT. When the course of treatment was completed after four weeks, the control group showed little further change, but there was "significant further improvement" in the patients who received ECT. Taylor and Fleminger found that the difference between the group receiving ECT and the control group was minimal three months after the treatment ended.

The British researchers offered four possible explanations for the initial improvement shown by the control group: delay in response to the medication; removal from the stressful environment of their regular lives when they entered the hospital; specific effect of the anesthesia; or placebo response — the response to a nontreatment that often occurs when patients are given inert substances, such as sugar pills.

Out of the depths of depression. Other recent studies have marked advances in understanding the biochemistry of mental illness, and this may lead to improved treatment and perhaps prevention in some instances. A research team headed by pharmacologist Donald S. Robinson, chairman of the Department of Pharmacology at Marshall University in Huntington, W. Va., reported to the American Society of Clinical Pharmacology and Therapeutics in March 1981 that they had identified a possible link between depression and a little-known chemical found in the body. This discovery may lead to a means of identifying a person's susceptibility to depression, differentiating it from normal grief, and determining what would be effective therapy.

The substance — 3,4-dihydroxyphenylglycol (DOPEG) — can now be measured in a single drop of blood through the use of a sophisticated new test that was developed by another member of the research team, Garland A. Johnson of the Upjohn Company in Kalamazoo, Mich.

Dr. Robinson said DOPEG may

be a possible marker for depressive disorders — that is, a chemical indicator that the disease is present or could be developed.

DOPEG is a metabolic product of norepinephrine, a hormone produced in the adrenal glands, peripheral nervous stem, and brain.

Dr. Robinson and his team studied the effect of two widely used drugs — amitriptyline, a tricyclic antidepressant, and phenelzine, a monoamine-oxidase inhibitor — on 48 patients, divided in two equal groups. Each drug produced about the same amount of improvement in depression, and DOPEG levels dropped when the patient improved, regardless of the drug used.

Coping with stress. Psychiatrist Joel Dimsdale of Harvard University has studied Jewish survivors of the Nazi Holocaust living in Jerusalem, Israel, and in the San Francisco Bay area to learn how they coped with extreme stress. From this study, begun in 1970, Dr. Dimsdale has developed a "classification of coping strategies" that might serve as a guide to health-care professionals for treating patients who have experienced other stressful situations of catastrophic proportions, such as serious illnesses; natural or civil disasters; or major personal crises.

These coping strategies, reported in the *Harvard Medical Area Focus* in February 1981, are: hopefulness or optimism; group affiliation; psychological numbing; religious belief; and information-gathering.

Dr. Dimsdale said that information-gathering and group affiliation are the two main strategies that health-care professionals, including doctors, nurses, psychologists, psychiatrists, and therapists, can show people how to use. "With information, people are not solely victims of fate; they can maintain some sense of mastery over what is going to happen to them," he said. These specialists, he pointed out, can ensure that patients know about the treatment they will undergo and what they might expect afterward.

By fostering group affiliations of seriously ill heart patients, the specialists "can help them realize that other people can be just as devastated as they are, and that they are not unique or losing their minds because they are so anxious after a heart attack," the psychiatrist said.

While attending doctors and therapists cannot engender optimism in someone who is not a "congenital optimist," he added, they can help by maintaining an "optimistic stance" themselves. [Charles-Gene McDaniel]

Multiple Sclerosis

A faulty immune response in the central nervous system has been implicated in multiple sclerosis (MS), a crippling disorder of the nervous system. A research team headed by neurologist Barry G. W. Arnason, professor and chairman of the Department of Neurology at the University of Chicago, disclosed major discoveries involving abnormalities in the lymphocytes (white blood cells) that comprise

the immune system.

One finding was reported by neurologist Joel Oger in April 1981. Dr. Oger found new evidence that MS may result from a simultaneous attack on two cells known to play a vital part in the disease process. These "target cells" are a type of lymphocyte called the T-suppressor cell, and the oligodendrocyte — a brain cell that makes and maintains myelin,

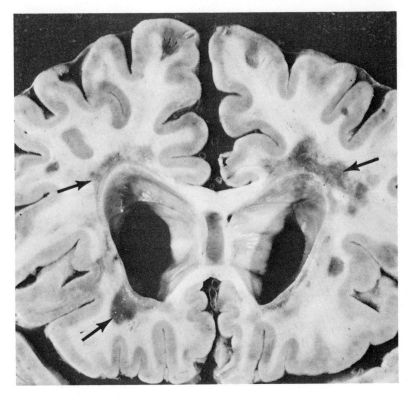

Gray patches (arrows) in a cross section of the brain of a patient who died of multiple sclerosis are areas where the myelin sheath that insulates the nerves was destroyed.

the sheath that insulates the nerves. The surface of the T-suppressor cells in the blood and the oligo-dendrocytes in the brain are similar. Because the similarities may play a part in the MS attack, the finding may help scientists find a way to halt the disease process.

In 1980, neurologist Azertano B. C. Noronha reported that lymphocytes, stimulated by foreign bodies, travel from the brain to the cerebral spinal fluid in MS patients. According to Dr. Noronha, this supports the view that there is an active immune response in the central nervous system. Activity in the spinal fluid is a mirror of activity in the brain.

This relates to another important discovery at the University of Chicago. In 1978, neurologist Jack Antel had published evidence that the T-suppressor cell disappears from the blood before an attack of

MS. When the patient is in remission, these cells reappear.

MS usually affects people between the ages of 15 and 50. Approximately 250,000 persons in the United States have MS, and another 250,000 persons have related disorders.

Current methods of treatment can only relieve symptoms and do not keep the disease from progressing. But scientists are optimistic that someday MS can be prevented. They believe that "MS can go the way of polio."

In MS, sections of myelin become inflamed and are eventually destroyed. This interrupts the conduction of nerve impulses and brings on the disabling symptoms of MS.

These symptoms include faulty vision, loss of coordination and staggering, slurred speech, loss of bladder and bowel control, sexual difficulties, numbness, weakness, spasticity, and general fatigue.

The course of the disease is unpredictable. An MS victim will have remissions — relief from symptoms — and relapses with exacerbations — when the symptoms recur and can become more severe. The symptoms and severity of the disease vary considerably. Some patients have relatively mild attacks followed by long remissions; others have a more severe case. MS victims are seldom totally incapacitated, however. During the active phases, patients are usually treated with the drug ACTH and corticosteroids such as cortisone and prednisone. These drugs reduce inflammation and act as agents that suppress the nervous system.

Many researchers believe that MS is an autoimmune response. Autoimmunity represents a sort of confusion of identity on the part of the immune system. Other scientists believe that MS may be triggered by the presence of a latent virus. The virus may have persisted since childhood and may have changed, or mutated. The measles virus has been suspected, but it could be any common virus.

The immune system normally produces antibodies to fight infectious agents. However, when an infectious agent, such as a virus, resembles one of the body's own parts or components, the immune system attacks the "self" component — healthy tissue — as if it were a foreign agent. In MS, the myelin is the attacked self.

Other researchers, including some at Albert Einstein College of Medicine in New York City believe that the combined action of two white blood cells — monocytes and lymphocytes — brings on the inflammation and destructive disease process. An immune reaction causes them to leave the bloodstream. Once outside the bloodstream, the monocyte changes into a larger cell called a macrophage. The macrophage releases enzymes that eat and digest protein and other components of the myelin sheath.

Evidence of malfunction of the immune system in MS is based on changes in the lymphocytes, particularly T cells. There are three major types of T cells. In addition to the suppressor cells that blunt or "turn off" the immune response when it is no longer needed, there are the effector cells that call up other immune cells, such as macrophages; and helper cells that enhance the immune response.

In MS, the turn-off mechanism may fail, setting off an autoimmune reaction.

Scientists believe that effective clinical treatment of MS — and its eventual prevention — can only take place when the exact mechanism of the disease is understood. In the meantime, however, they are conducting clinical trials based on promising research findings.

One such trial is underway in 1981 at the Scripps Clinic and Research Foundation in La Jolla, Calif., and the University of California, San Francisco. It involves the use of interferon, a natural protein produced in very minute amounts by the body, usually during a virus infection.

Interferon is not only an antiviral agent but also acts as a biological-response modifier that selectively suppresses certain of the body's immune responses.

Work on transfer factor was reported by doctors at the University of Sydney in Australia in September 1980. MS patients were given extracts of pooled white blood cells from people who lived with them and probably had been exposed to the same viruses. Those patients with mild to moderate MS showed some slowing of disease progression 18 months after treatment started.

New immunosuppressive drugs such as azathioprine (Imuran) and cyclophosphamide (Cytoxan) are also being tested. Another type of immunosuppressant treatment is plasmapheresis. In this dialysislike procedure, medical personnel re- move the plasma from the patient's blood; the plasma supposedly contains antibodies and other substances that are harmful to the nervous system. The red and white blood cells are then returned to the patient's bloodstream. Plasmapheresis is often accompanied by treatment with various types of conventional immunosuppressive drugs.

[Shirlee Kempner]

Nephrology
See Kidney

Neurology

Neurologists and other health-care professionals involved in treating epileptics in the United States intensified their efforts in 1981 to educate the public about the nature of epilepsy. "Social alienation is usually the major problem these people [epileptics] must face," said neurologist Albert Ehle, associate professor of neurology at the University of Texas Southwestern Medical School.

Although there is no cure for epilepsy, Dr. Ehle states that about 80 per cent of all epileptics can control their symptoms with medication. So the social discrimination they suffer — shunned by acquaintances, refused certain jobs, turned down by insurance companies, and in some states even denied the right to marry — is often more damaging than the disease itself.

About 2 million Americans suffer epileptic seizures. A seizure occurs when nerve cells in the brain release a sudden burst of electrical energy. Seizures may be caused by brain damage due to head injury, infection, a major illness, or a tumor. Some victims inherit a genetic tendency to develop the disease. In others, doctors cannot find any cause.

There are three main types of epilepsy. A grand mal, or "major attack," lasts several minutes and the victim becomes rigid, falls down, and loses consciousness. The victim then experiences irregular breathing, jerking movements of the muscles, clenching of teeth, and general convulsions.

Petit mal, or "little sickness" attacks are most common in children from 6 to 14 years old. These attacks involve "blank spells" and a slight twitching or blinking, which may last only a few seconds, but may occur dozens or even hundreds of times a day. These seizures are hard to recognize and are often mistaken by parents and teachers for daydreaming.

Psychomotor epilepsy, unlike grand and petit mal, involves nerve cells in only one part of the brain. Psychomotor epilepsy can occur at any age, and the nature of the seizure depends on what part of the brain is affected. Usually, the person experiences mental confusion, along with violent twitching or pointless movements, such as chewing motions, hand rubbing, or walking about aimlessly. These seizures are often mistaken for the physical effects of alcohol or drug abuse.

Although the events of a seizure are well recorded, little is known about why a given seizure occurs when it does. Some attacks occur with no warning, and thus a person can suffer the embarrassment of having an epileptic seizure in a

Nursing Homes
See Hospice

public place.

But some victims experience the first signs of abnormal electrical discharges in the brain in the form of "auras." This can give them time to get to a safe place before a seizure and thereby avoid its social embarrassment. These auras may take a variety of forms — smelling odors, seeing hallucinations, or hearing voices.

For help in dealing with problems surrounding epilepsy, persons with this disorder can call their local chapter of the Epilepsy Foundation of America. The foundation offers information about low-cost medication, special group life insurance, and guidance in finding support groups to help deal with the social problems epileptics face.

[Donald F. Phillips]

Nutrition

Food scientist Ken Lee of the University of Wisconsin in Madison reported at the 1981 American Chemical Society meeting that only 1 per cent of the iron in spinach, whether it is fresh, canned, or frozen, can be assimilated. The rest is in a tightly bound insoluble form. One out of 5 Americans has an iron deficiency because the body cannot absorb many forms of iron in food. The effects of food processing on iron, said Lee, are unpredictable. Sometimes they make iron suitable for body needs; sometimes they make it useless.

One reason iron is so important is that it works with other nutrients to make hemoglobin, which helps to transport oxygen through the bloodstream. Lee and other researchers are investigating ways to make iron more accessible to the

body. Combining citrus fruit with spinach or liver may be one way to do this, because vitamin C, found in oranges and other citrus fruits, increases the absorption of iron.

Coffee break. Coffee is not relaxing; it actually increases muscle tension and stress, reported researcher Mary F. Asterita at the April 1981 meeting of the Federation of American Societies for Experimental Biology in Atlanta, Ga. Asterita said caffeine stimulates the nervous system and the heart, and increases gastric acid secretion. It speeds up respiration and increases the levels of free fatty acids and glucose in the blood and raises blood pressure.

Asterita and her colleagues at Indiana University School of Medicine in Bloomington held five biofeedback sessions during which they trained 18- to 58-year-old volunteers to control involuntary muscle tension. Then another five biofeedback sessions were held. At the start of each session, half the volunteers were given coffee containing 120 to 140 milligrams of caffeine while the other half drank decaffeinated coffee, but neither group knew which they were given. The investigators found that coffee with caffeine interfered immediately with the subjects' ability to control muscle tension but decaffeinated coffee did not.

According to a 1981 report by Charles F. Ehret, a geneticist at Argonne National Laboratory near Chicago, drinking coffee or tea in the morning can make a person feel sleepy during the day and restless all night. Ehret, who was studying ways to help workers adjust and remain alert when they change shifts or work at night, said the traditional British late-afternoon tea time is preferable.

Ehret noted that coffee gives a person an immediate "lift" by increasing blood sugar, but within 90 minutes the body's insulin overrides the boost. Even black coffee does this by setting up a chemical reaction that breaks down glycogen, an energy-storing carbohydrate in the body, and releases its sugar into the blood.

Caffeine in coffee and theophylline in tea delay the build-up of epinephrine, or adrenalin, the chemical messenger needed to start a person's "body clock." Epinephrine levels usually are highest in late afternoon, then subside as the body produces a chemical called serotonin to aid relaxation and sleep. Drinking coffee or tea in the morning delays the cycle and drinking them at night speeds up the cycle. So in both cases, they work against the natural tendency to be alert during the day and relaxed at night. Ehret said it is best to have caffeine-containing drinks around 3:30 P.M. or 4 P.M., because then their effect on the body's cycle is neutral.

Cardiologist Charles A. Bertrand contradicted claims made after a 1978 study showing that coffee causes high blood pressure. Dr. Bertrand based his argument on the size of the study, which included only nine subjects, all of whom were in their 20s. In articles published in 1979 and 1980, Dr. Bertrand, who is the cardiologist consultant for International Business Machines (IBM) Corporation, presented data from multiphasic health tests that IBM has conducted continuously since 1968 on volunteer employees over age 35. Studies of 72,100 coffee drinkers showed no relationship between high blood pressure and caffeine.

Vitamin E for breasts. Robert S. London and his colleagues at Johns Hopkins University School of Medicine and Sinai Hospital in Baltimore reported in September 1980 that women with fibrocystic disease may be helped by large doses of vitamin E.

One in 5 women in the United States have fibrocystic disease. It causes painful swelling of the breasts and lumps that must sometimes be subjected to biopsy. Women with benign fibroid cysts have a higher risk of developing breast cancer. London found that 600 international units of vitamin E taken orally each day for eight weeks brought significant relief to about 85 per cent of the patients studied.

In a separate study of fibrocystic breast disease, researcher John P. Minton of Ohio State University College of Medicine in Columbus found that many patients obtained relief by avoiding cigarettes and caffeine. Neither vitamin E nor avoidance has been tested for the ability to prevent cancer.

Food additives. The Select Committee of the Federation of American Societies for Experimental Biology reviewed the 415 food additives on the Food and Drug Administration's (FDA) list of substances generally recognized as safe (GRAS), and reported in May 1981 that more study was needed on 110 items. All the items had been in use and considered safe when the food additives amendment to the Food, Drug, and Cos-

Nutrition (cont.)

metic Act was passed in 1958. Re-evaluation was deemed necessary after cyclamates, chemicals used as artificial sweeteners, were found unsafe in 1970.

To compile its 1981 report, the committee grouped the additives into five categories. Remaining on the GRAS list are 305 items in Class 1, which includes substances that are safe for use at current levels and at future anticipated levels. These include aluminum compounds, benzoates, casein, protein hydrolyzates, tartrates, and vegetable oils. The 68 ingredients in Class 2 are considered safe for use at current levels but need more research on whether significant increases would create dietary hazards. Among them are alginates, some zinc salts, iron and some iron salts, tannic acid, sucrose, and vitamins A and D.

Additional studies were recommended for 19 substances in Class 3, including caffeine and two preservatives, butylated hydroxyanisole and butylated hydroxytoluene. Class 4 covers salt and four modified starches. The committee urged the FDA to establish safer conditions of use for Class 4 substances or to prohibit them. Although there is no evidence that salt harms most people, salt reduction in processed food would benefit those suffering from high blood pressure. The committee reported there was insufficient data for evaluating the 18 substances in Class 5, which includes glycerides, certain iron salts, and carnauba wax. The FDA published new regulations for some GRAS food additives and is preparing to act on the remaining recommendations within the next three years.   [Eleanor Dunn]

Obstetrics
See Childbirth

Occupational Medicine

Ethylene oxide (ETO) is a chemical widely used to sterilize hospital instruments and as a fungicide in agriculture. It may also have the potential to make men who work with it sterile and cause other medical problems. American Hospital Supply Corporation of Chicago, a major manufacturer of medical devices, reported in 1980 that it had screened workers regularly exposed to ETO and found indications that the chemical might damage blood cell chromosomes, cause leukemia, and reduce sperm counts.

Use of ETO gas has caused some concern in federal agencies. The National Institute for Occupational Health and Safety (NIOSH), the Occupational Safety and Health Administration (OSHA), and the Environmental Protection Agency (EPA) have had the chemical under study for several years, along with

other substances on a lengthening list of workplace hazards.

OSHA recommends that workers should never breathe more than 50 parts per million (ppm) of ETO – a level 100 times higher than is allowed in Russia. The safe level is also 50 ppm in West Germany, while in Sweden it is 20 ppm. Following its discovery of potential medical problems, American Hospital Supply reduced the maximum exposure level at its plants to 10 ppm and notified federal authorities of its findings.

Ronald Abrahams, the corporation's director of regulatory compliance, reported that 12 of 46 men working with ETO were found to have sperm counts lower than 20 million per cubic centimeter(cc), (compared to the normal 60 to 80 million per cc) but said that not enough specimens have been examined to draw a causal link be-

The chemicals in many artists' materials are toxic or are suspected carcinogens. They can be hazardous if they get on the skin, or if their fumes are inhaled.

used in U.S. health-care facilities and that about 75,000 workers could be exposed to ETO.

The chemical is registered with EPA as a fungicide for fumigating books, dental, pharmaceutical, medical, and scientific equipment and supplies made of glass, metals, plastic, rubber or textiles, drugs, leather, motor oil, paper, soil, bedding for experimental animals, clothing, furs, and furniture, and transportation vehicles such as jet aircraft, buses, and railroad passenger cars. ETO has also been used to kill bacteria and fungi in foodstuffs such as spices, cocoa, flour, dehydrated eggs, shredded coconut, dried fruits, and dehydrated vegetables, as well as to accelerate the maturing tobacco leaves.

These widespread uses mean that thousands of other workers are exposed throughout the world. U.S. production of ETO totaled 4.7 billion pounds in 1976 and has steadily increased. ETO is one of the top 25 chemicals produced in the United States; Japan and several European countries are also major producers.

The potential of ETO to cause changes in genes in humans is in line with recent experimental work with animals. This research has shown that ETO has a mutagenic effect on at least 13 biological species. According to a 1977 NIOSH study, "Continuous occupational exposure to significant concentrations of ETO may induce an increase in the frequency of mutations in human populations."

The study also indicated that ETO might cause cancer. "Whenever alternative sterilization processes are available which do not present similar or more serious hazards, they should be substituted for ETO sterilization" it recommended. [Charles-Gene McDaniel]

tween the gas and the low counts. More disturbing is the finding that the gas might have a mutagenic effect — that is, alter the structure of the genes.

Affected workers in plants in California and Puerto Rico were found to have mutagenic changes — abnormalities in chromosomes — many of which are thought to be precursors, or forerunners, of leukemia. American Hospital Supply has moved the affected workers to other jobs.

ETO is especially useful in sterilizing equipment and supplies that may be damaged if exposed to high levels of heat. Only 0.02 per cent of the total amount of ETO produced in the United States in 1976 was used to sterilize equipment, but this accounted for about 1.1 million pounds. Federal reports estimate that more than 10,000 ETO sterilizers are being

Orthopedics
See Bone Disorders

Pancreas
See Dealing With Diabetes

Prenatal Care
See Alcohol, Birth Defects

The American Academy of Dermatology and the Food and Drug Administration (FDA) undertook a joint effort in December 1980 to obtain data on the skin's reaction to drugs. Previously, such data were available only from clinical tests and hospital reports. Under the new program, dermatologists are encouraged to report to the academy reactions to specific drugs such as hives, welts, swelling, itching, rashes, eruptions, target-shaped sores, patchy color changes, and peeling skin. Academy reports are relayed monthly to the FDA's computer. When potentially dangerous medications are identified, the FDA sends warnings to doctors and requires manufacturers to put warnings on all drug labels.

Skin tests. A new method of skin patch testing, announced in April 1981, has enabled researchers at the dermatology clinic at the University of California, San Francisco, to determine the exact substance to which a person is allergic. The patch test involved applying a small amount of each substance to a strip of aluminum tape and sticking it on the patient's back. If the skin under the tape appeared irritated when the tape was removed two days later, the patient would be allergic to the substance.

Toby Mathias, director of the Dermatology Division of the Northern California Occupational Health Center, cited an example of the test's value. According to Mathias, when the standard epoxy resin patch test was used on a boatbuilder who got a skin rash while using an epoxy resin, the results were negative, indicating no allergy. However, the rash persisted, so the man came to the health center.

After phoning the manufacturer to obtain the product's chemical composition, technicians at the center applied patch tests of each ingredient in the resin. The tests revealed that the boatbuilder was allergic to only one ingredient. He found a different epoxy resin without that particular ingredient and continued his work, free from further problems.

Only 20 per cent of all occupational skin diseases are caused by allergies. Most are caused by irritation from soaps, detergents, solvents, acids, and alkalis.

Sun and psoralens. Doctors in the United States and Great Britain in 1981 warned about the increased danger of contracting skin cancer after exposure to natural sunlight or ultraviolet lamps combined with any of a group of drugs called psoralens. Although the medical benefits of treatments with sun or ultraviolet radiation and the psoralen, 8-methoxypsoralen, outweigh the cancer risks for psoriasis sufferers, the use of a similar drug, 5-methoxypsoralen, in some tanning lotions is too risky simply to promote a tan.

Dermatologist Thomas Fitzpatrick of Harvard University Medical School reported that bergamot oils from the rinds of a citrus fruit used in some perfumes also contain psoralens and that the risk to the wearer is too great to justify their use.

Faster healing. Researchers reported in 1981 that a nutrient solution containing carbohydrates, amino acids — the building blocks of proteins — and vitamin C was used to speed healing and control a variety of skin conditions including infected bedsores, thermal and chemical burns, varicose ulcers, and diabetic skin lesions.

Anthony N. Silvetti and his associates at Bethany Methodist Hospital in Chicago reported at the 1981

A sunbather soaks up the warm rays, unaware that her tanning lotion or perfume might contain psoralen, a chemical that, in the presence of sunlight, may cause skin cancer.

meeting of the Federation of American Societies for Experimental Biology that they successfully used the nutrient solution on patients who did not respond to other types of treatment. The solution, when applied directly to the affected area, appears to inhibit bacterial growth and provide glucose for energy needed to promote the formation of healthy cells and tissues.

Artificial skin. Scientists reported in 1981 that an artificial skin made from cowhide, shark cartilage, and plastic has been used to replace tissue damaged by third-degree burns over 50 to 90 per cent of patients' bodies. Three of the first 10 recipients probably would have died without the new skin, according to surgeon John F. Burke of Massachusetts General Hospital who developed the skin replacement with physical chemist Ioannis V. Yannas of Massachusetts Institute of Technology.

Unlike skin from pigs or other sources, which eventually must be replaced with skin grafts from elsewhere on the patient's body, the new artificial skin can remain in place. The inner layer is made of a connective material found in cowhide and a chemical derived from shark cartilage. The outer layer is plastic. Because these materials are similar to substances in human skin, they support new skin tissues as they grow. See *Better News About Burns*.

Heat on acne. Dermatologist Walter F. Schwartz of Pasadena, Calif., reported in May 1981 on the effects of heat on acne. Dr. Schwartz studied 150 acne patients — males and females, aged 14 to 28 — each having more blemishes on one side of the body than on the other. He found that most of his subjects had slept on the more heavily blemished side or had exposed that side of the body to the sun more than the other side while sunbathing, playing, or working. Dr. Schwartz noted that these practices increased skin temperature on the affected side, and that oil secretion increased 10 per cent for each degree that skin temperature rose. Excessive oil is a major cause of acne.   [Eleanor Dunn]

Sleep Disorders

Scientists and doctors in 1980 and 1981 experimented with a variety of treatments for sleep disorders, which affect an estimated 50 million Americans.

Although individual requirements for sleep vary widely, surveys show that about 13 per cent of the United States population has trouble sleeping "often" or "all the time." An additional 22 per cent say they have trouble sleeping

"sometimes."

Since our sleeping patterns vary, what constitutes sufficient or insufficient sleep is highly subjective. Physicians usually diagnose insomnia if a patient reports long delays in falling asleep, waking up frequently for periods that total more than 30 minutes per night, inability to return to sleep after only a few hours of rest, less than six hours of sleep nightly, or a drop in daily performance as a result of inadequate sleep.

New drugs. Kingman P. Strohl, an internist at Harvard University Medical School reported in 1980 that a new drug can help some sufferers of a sleep disorder called apnea. Apnea victims stop breathing temporarily while asleep. They wake repeatedly to catch a breath and are therefore deprived of a chance to fall into deep sleep. Doctors believe apnea can trigger heart and neurological complications or even sudden death. The new drug, medroxyprogesterone acetate, acts as a breathing stimulant by increasing muscle activity in the upper air passages and chest.

Scientists were also experimenting with safer drug treatments for sleep disorders caused by emotional or mental conditions, such as anxiety, depression, schizophrenia, and manic-depressive psychosis. Psychotherapy is primarily used to treat sleep disorders due to depression caused by a specific event, such as grief over the loss of a loved one. In cases of chronic emotional or mental disorders, doctors often prescribe sedatives to promote sleep. But these drugs have unpleasant side effects and could be deadly if the patient takes too many or combines them with alcohol.

Some sleep-inducing drugs are habit-forming, and some lose their effectiveness after several weeks of constant use. So scientists are studying tryptophan as a "natural" remedy for insomnia. Tryptophan is an amino acid, or building block for protein, found in meat, fish, and dairy products. It causes brain cells to release a biochemical that promotes sleep.

Neurologist Ernest Hartmann, director of the Sleep Research Laboratory at West-Ros-Park Mental Health Center in Boston, predicted in June 1981 that tryptophan will replace the mild sleeping pills that are taken by some insomniac patients.

There are also behavioral causes of insomnia, such as a change in working hours and drinking coffee, tea, cola or other stimulants before bedtime. Jet lag, caused by crossing several time zones in an airplane, can seriously disrupt sleep patterns. Sometimes, after repeated bouts of sleeplessness, the patient begins to associate preparations for going to sleep with failure to sleep, and this perpetuates insomnia.

Other treatments. Sometimes behavior-modification therapy, such as scheduling regular hours for sleep and reading or taking a bath before bedtime, is beneficial when sleep patterns are irregular. At the Dartmouth Sleep Disorders Center in Hanover, N.H., psychologist Peter Hauri is experimenting with biofeedback techniques to help patients with behavioral sleep disorders fight insomnia. He teaches patients to recognize and sustain certain brain waves, called sleep spindles, that are associated with the ability to sleep. An electronic device receives information about brain waves from sensors attached to the patient's scalp. The device then signals when the patient's brain is producing sleep spindles. In ways that scientists do not understand, this biofeedback causes the brain to unconsciously produce more sleep spindles. Dr. Hauri said in June 1981 that biofeedback has helped about 50 per cent of his patients.

Neurologist Elliot Weitzman, director of Montefiore Hospital's Sleep-Wake Disorders Center in New York City, is conducting ongoing experiments with a method called chronotherapy to treat victims of delayed sleep-phase syndrome, which accounts for 5 to 8 per cent of all insomnia cases. Persons with this disorder cannot fall asleep until it is time to get up. Scientists believe this condition arises in persons who are unable to control their natural biological clocks, which operate on a 25-hour cycle, and have difficulty in adjusting to the conventional 24-hour day. Using his chronotherapy technique, Dr. Weitzman asks patients to postpone going to bed by three hours each day and to continue this postponement on each succeeding day, until they finally reach their desired bedtime. Dr. Weitzman reports that most patients using this method find that once their biological clock is reset, they fall asleep at night soon after going to bed.   [Donald F. Phillips]

Smoking
See Calling It Quits; Reducing the Risks of Cancer; Cancer

Sports Medicine

Almost everyone knows an athlete or a former athlete who has had a "torn cartilage" or had "cartilage removed." Such people – often football, hockey, or soccer players – have usually had a knee injury involving a crescent-shaped piece of cartilage called the meniscus.

The surgical procedure to treat such an injury is called a meniscectomy. Until recently, most meniscectomies have been total, but today many surgeons are performing partial meniscectomies, or "miniscectomies," reported orthopedic surgeon Daniel N. Kulund of the University of Virginia, Charlottesville, in 1981.

The menisci of the knee joint are found between the femur, or thigh bone, and the tibia, the larger of the two leg bones. They act as buffers between the bones and help to bear weight and absorb shock. The menisci also enlarge the contact area between the femur and tibia, thus guiding and synchronizing knee motion, and improving knee stability.

There are two menisci in the knee and both can be torn in sports accidents. The medial meniscus, toward the inner side of the leg, is C-shaped; the lateral meniscus, toward the outer side of the leg, is O-shaped. The most common tear in athletes is the longitudinal, or up-and-down, tear in which the separated part of the meniscus produces a bowstring or "bucket handle" that can lock the knee. In older athletes, however, a horizontal tear is more common. This produces a flap that may rotate painfully, causing the knee to "give out."

If a piece of torn meniscus is caught between the femur and tibia, it will stress and eventually break down the cartilage connecting the two bones. When a tear interferes mechanically with the knee's function, producing pain or concentrating stress to break down the cartilage, doctors perform a meniscectomy to remove the involved portion of the meniscus.

However, a total meniscectomy, whether it is lateral or medial, removes an important shock absorber, and the forces generated by

Hyphema, or blood in the front portion of the eye, is a common injury in such sports as squash and racquetball. It is caused by hemorrhaging after the eye is struck by a racket or ball.

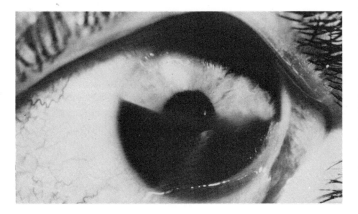

219

body weight and motion on the knee's cartilage are increased. The medial meniscus normally carries 60 per cent of the load on the inner side of the knee, and the lateral meniscus carries 75 per cent on the outer side. After a total meniscectomy, the motion of the knee is disrupted, sometimes leading to a breakdown of the joint. If possible, therefore, the menisci of the knee should be preserved.

In a miniscectomy, the surgeon usually uses an instrument invented in Japan in 1918, but little used in other countries until after World War II, called an arthroscope, about the size of a ballpoint pen, to view and evaluate the type, location, and extent of a meniscal injury. With the arthroscope, a surgeon can look through a small hole into the knee area rather than surgically opening the knee joint. The surgeon looks at the structures in the knee through the eyepiece of the arthroscope or attaches the scope to a television camera and views the joint on a screen.

In arthroscopic surgery, the surgeon uses a probe, grasper, scissors, and surgical knives to cut out the torn piece of the meniscus.

An arthroscopic meniscectomy is most effective for older individuals with horizontal tears, athletes with displaced bowstring tears, and for minor tears in the otherwise normal menisci of young athletes. The removal of a minor tear gives an athlete many additional years of normal meniscus function.

After a total meniscectomy, there is often pain, swelling, muscle and knee weakness. It usually takes an athlete more than 2 1/2 months to return to athletic activity after a total meniscectomy. With miniscectomies, however, pain is reduced, postoperative bleeding is rare, convalescence is rapid, and the athlete can quickly return to sports. Often the athlete can return to limited activities the day after the miniscectomy and return to sports in two weeks. Furthermore, the remaining tissue still serves a useful function, preserving the joint and guiding its movement.

A competitive ebb. In the past few years, more and more female athletes have reported menstrual irregularity. Although the problem is most common among long-distance runners and ballet dancers, it has also been reported among body builders and skaters.

Investigators such as endocrinologists Michelle Warren, of Roosevelt Hospital in New York City, and Edwin Dale, of Emory University, Atlanta, Ga., have suggested since 1979 that the physical and mental stress of training could be responsible. These stresses could, for instance, trigger hormone changes that result in menstrual irregularity. In a recent study, a researcher found that the degree and incidence of menstrual irregularity was in direct proportion to the degree of physical exertion. Other researchers have suggested that a critical level of body fat is necessary for menstruation.

New York City gynecologist Mona Shangold has studied the problem for several years. She notes that many past studies have produced conflicting results and suggests that this confusion may result from differences in terminology. Along with other gynecologists, Dr. Shangold believes that *primary amenorrhea* should be defined as the failure to menstruate at all by the age of 16. *Secondary amenorrhea* includes missing three regular cycles, or the failure to menstruate at all for six months. *Oligomenorrhea*, is infrequent or scanty menstruation, or a gap of two months or more between menstrual periods.

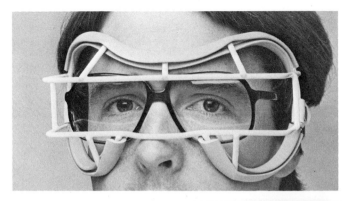

Among the best forms of protective eyewear available today for athletes are wire guards designed for those who must wear glasses, *above,* and guards equipped with plastic lenses for those who do not wear glasses, *right.*

Shangold warns that it is a mistake for an athlete to assume that changes in her menstrual cycle are due to her training regimen. She says: "If a woman has been menstruating regularly and suddenly stops menstruating, she needs to be evaluated, regardless of how strenuously she's exercising, or even if she's not exercising at all."

Dr. Shangold and many other investigators believe that the key to poor menstrual function in athletes is psychological. In a recent discussion she said, "It has been shown in a number of studies that amenorrheic women tend to be lighter and have lower ratios of weight to height than women who have regular menstrual periods. However, there are psychological factors that may confuse the picture. This brings us to a point that is often forgotten: The brain acts as an endocrine gland; it secretes hor-

mones in response to signals from the outside world. Psychological factors can certainly alter hormones that lead to or are associated with menstrual irregularity or amenorrhea. It's difficult to separate all the variables . . . ."

Dr. Shangold pointed out that in the course of a vigorous training program a woman is subjected to more than the effects of the exercise itself. In addition to the physical stress, she is likely to experience the emotional stresses of training and coordinating her other activities.

Most research so far has looked at what has happened after a woman starts training. In a survey of women who entered the 1979 New York City marathon, Dr. Shangold asked the runners about their menstrual history. She found that women who had regular periods during training also had regular periods before training, and that those who had irregular periods during training had irregular periods before they began training.

This suggests, she says, that the exercise may not be responsible for the irregularity. "It also suggests that perhaps there is something different about the type of woman who is attracted to a long-distance training program. Perhaps she is more likely to develop menstrual irregularity because of whatever that factor may be."

Even though a definitive answer to this problem has not been found, most researchers add one heartening note: Poor menstrual function in athletes seems to be reversible. Ken Foreman, a Seattle track coach who was among the first to recognize the phenomenon of poor menstrual function in athletes, says that he trained two women who didn't menstruate for seven years. Each has since borne two children.

221

Foreman says that regular periods often resume when the athlete stops training, but that resumption of normal menstruation can also take place when an athlete changes her attitude and looks at running as a recreational, rather than a competitive, pursuit. Other researchers have noted that ballet dancers have regular menstrual periods when they are on vacation or when an injury prevents them from training.

Circuit weight training. The American College of Sports Medicine, a national professional group, advised in 1981 that to develop and maintain cardiorespiratory fitness, or a healthy heart and lungs, and good body composition with a desirable percentage of body fat, a healthy person should exercise for 15 to 60 minutes three times a week with the heart beating at about 85 per cent of the person's age-predicted heart rate. You can calculate this rate by subtracting your age from 220.

The types of exercise the college recommends are those that use large muscle groups and can be done continuously, such as running, jogging, walking, swimming, bicycling, cross-country skiing, skipping rope, and rowing.

A number of studies in 1980 and 1981 have shown that circuit weight training (CWT) builds heart and lung endurance. CWT is a series of exercises in which the participant lifts weights at about 50 per cent of his or her capacity — the maximum amount of weight that can be lifted one time. In this exercise course, there are usually 10 exercises. The exerciser repeats each exercise several times, and rests about 15 to 30 seconds before going on to the next.

In one of the first CWT studies, investigators compared three groups: runners; a group that did CWT; and a control group that did not exercise. The subjects in the CWT group showed significant improvements in percentage of body fat and in strength, but only modest improvements in cardiorespiratory endurance. Exercise physiologist Larry R. Gettman, then director of the Institute for Aerobics Research in Dallas, concluded in 1979 that a person who for some reason, such as an injury, could not run or jog, could maintain fitness in a CWT program. CWT could be a useful alternative to running or jogging because it takes less time, puts less stress on the weight-bearing joints, and can be done indoors. But, Dr. Gettman added, an individual who wants to develop high cardiorespiratory endurance will find that a running program is more effective. [Frances Caldwell]

Stomach
See Dr. Beaumont's
Frontier Research

Surgery

Eye surgery that could correct myopia in near-sighted people and eliminate their need for eyeglasses produced considerable controversy in medical circles in 1981. The operation, called radial keratotomy, calls for a series of spokelike incisions in the cornea, the transparent window of the eye. Svyataslav Fyodorov, a Russian ophthalmologist, pioneered the technique in the late 1970s.

The surgeon makes about 16 "bicycle-spoke" cuts that penetrate the cornea to a depth of about three-fourths of a millimeter. Internal eye pressure stretches the cuts and distorts the cornea to a flatter shape, thus changing the focal length of the eyeball and improving vision. Modern microsurgical techniques should make the operation a safe procedure. About 55 per cent of radial keratotomy patients

Mary D. Gohlke, left, and Charles Walker appear at a press conference at Stanford University Medical Center, after successful operations in which doctors replaced their hearts and lungs with transplants.

can function without glasses after surgery and the vision of the remaining 45 per cent almost always shows some improvement.

However, many eye specialists question the long-term value of the surgery and express concern over possible later degeneration of the cornea. Even the operation's supporters warn that there is inadequate data to assure patients that the improvement will last and will have no permanent side effects.

Ophthalmologist Carl Kupfer, head of the National Eye Institute in Bethesda, Md., has pointed out the lack of any systematic research or evaluation program in animals or patients. In an effort to prevent the widespread use of the operation before its safety and value can be established, eye researchers are drawing up guidelines concerning its use. See *Vision*.

Spinal charges. New treatments for scoliosis, a curvature of the spine that can result in the so-called hunchback, have been successfully tested in 1980 and 1981. Traditional treatment of this orthopedic affliction, which strikes its victims — usually girls — at the onset of puberty, included awkward and heavy body braces, and, occasionally, the surgical implantation of metal rods along the spine.

The causes of scoliosis are not well understood, but most doctors suspect that an imbalance of muscle tension in the deep, spine-supporting, muscles of the back is involved.

In the new methods, an electrical current is applied to these deep muscles. The current is applied at night while the patient is asleep, leaving the patient free to live a normal life during the day. The researchers feel that the stimulation helps to correct the muscular imbalance.

Orthopedic surgeon Wallace Bobechko, of the Hospital for Sick Children in Toronto, Canada, surgically implants electrodes under the skin. Dr. John C. Brown, an orthopedic surgeon at Rancho Los Amigos Hospital in Los Angeles, positions electrodes on the surface of the skin. Both methods stimulate muscular contraction.

Data on the long-term success of these methods are not yet available. But orthopedists are hopeful that the treatment will stabilize the maturing spine long enough to prevent permanent curvature.

Growing skin . . . Burn victims may someday receive skin transplants grown in the laboratory from their own skin cells, if experimental work at Massachusetts Institute of Technology in Cambridge proves successful. In two separate projects, biochemists Eugene Bell and Howard Green have been able to culture and grow "test-tube" skin.

Bell, who has worked only with animal skin so far, takes small squares of skin from test animals and grows them in a nutrient medium. In as little as three weeks, the area of cultured skin can grow 100 times. The multilayered skin lacks only the oil and sweat glands and hair follicles present in normal skin.

Green grows a single-layer of human skin from human skin cells. By growing the skin on forms, he is able to mold it into shapes to cover specific body areas. He has also been able to maintain a high rate of growth.

Such test-tube skins would avoid the common rejection by a burn victim's immune system of skin grafts from other donors. Natural skin would also provide a more effective barrier to infection than some of the artificial skins that have been developed.

The new techniques may ultimately be applied to other organs or tissues. Vein or artery grafts for blood-vessel surgery might be grown around a tube rather than on a flat surface, for example. See *Better News About Burns.*

...And bone. At Children's Hospital Medical Center in Boston, Harvard University researchers are perfecting a technique that uses ground-up and demineralized bone to persuade human fibroblast cells to make new bone tissue. The bone powder has been successfully used in a number of operations to correct bone-related birth defects. See *Bone Disorders.*

Brain surgery before birth. Surgeons at Brigham and Women's Hospital in Boston used hollow needles to draw off excess fluid from the brain of a fetus in what may be the first brain surgery on an unborn child. The operation, reported in April 1981, was performed to relieve a condition called neonatal hydrocephalus, a birth defect that occurs in about 2 of every 1,000 babies. In neonatal hydrocephalus, the excess fluid produced during fetal development compresses brain tissue, causing permanent impairment.

The Boston doctors used ultrasound waves to pinpoint the position of the fetus in the womb, then inserted the needle through the mother's abdomen and womb into the fetal skull just above the ear. In six operations over a period of nine weeks, the surgeons drew off more than a quart of fluid.

The child, who was born prematurely, suffered some retardation despite the surgery. Yet doctors believe the new technique has great promise.   [Frank E. Gump]

Teeth
See Dentistry

Venereal Disease

The latest results of research on a drug that may alleviate the symptoms of genital herpes was announced in July 1981 by doctors at Johns Hopkins University School of Medicine. Dr. Rein Sarel and his colleagues conducted the experiment with the drug acyclovir on bone-marrow transplant patients who had been given immunosuppressive drugs and who consequently were highly susceptible to herpes infections, including cold sores.

All of the patients who were injected with acyclovir remained free of any herpes symptoms. Ordinarily, about 70 per cent of such patients break out with some form of the disease.

The medical researchers pointed out, however, that the drug probably does not eradicate the virus, but simply keeps it inactive.

Herpes simplex virus has emerged as "the most prominent" sexually transmitted disease of the 1970s in the United States, a panel of experts concluded in a federal report issued in 1980. The disease causes "chronic recurrent infection with frequent complications in perhaps 20 per cent of sexually active adults of all socioeconomic strata," the panel said, and leads to "a devastating, often fatal infection of infants."

Because of the potential for causing death among the newborn and a possible connection with cervical cancer, genital herpes has become a cause for alarm.

Mary E. Guinan, an expert on the disease at the Centers for Disease Control in Atlanta, Ga., believes the threat may be somewhat exaggerated. "The prevalence is greater than the incidence," she pointed out. That is — people who get it, keep it. Dr. Guinan said there is no documentation of an epidemic. But, as she observed, those who have it are a vocal minority and increasing attention is being paid to the disease.

Nevertheless, the American Social Health Association (ASHA) in Palo Alto, Calif., publishes a newsletter, *The Helper,* that is devoted solely to news about herpes infection. The newsletter, started in

1979, reports results of research aimed at curing or preventing the disease and correcting the symptoms, calls attention to myths and unproved treatments, and encourages victims of the disease to lobby the Congress of the United States for more money for research to develop effective treatments and a cure. ASHA has also created HELP, an organization of mutual support groups, to aid herpes victims. In mid-1981, the organization had 25 chapters in the United States and 5 more were being formed.

There are two types of herpes simplex virus (HSV). Type 1 causes fever blisters, or cold sores on the lips. Type 2 is associated with genital infection. Blisters appear on the genitalia and sometimes on the buttocks and thighs, break open, and form crusted sores. The sores clear up quickly in some victims, but they persist in others. ASHA says that infections caused by both viruses are now being seen both on the mouth and the genitalia because of "increasingly liberal sexual attitudes and practices."

The federal study, sponsored by the National Institute of Allergy and Infectious Diseases (NIAID), estimated that 300,000 to 500,000 new cases of genital herpes occur in the United States each year. Dr. Guinan says the disease affects het-

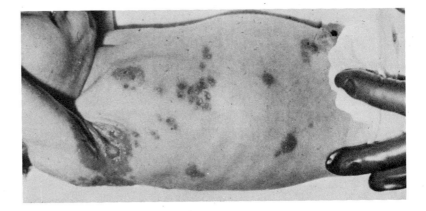

A newborn infant's body is covered with sores caused by the genital herpes virus, which was transmitted from the mother to the baby as it passed through the birth canal.

erosexuals and whites primarily. It differs from other sexually transmitted diseases, such as syphilis and gonorrhea, in that it is chronic, occurs frequently, and lacks effective treatment or prevention. The recurrence of the disease is unpredictable and is sometimes associated with stress or anxiety. Sores appear, urination becomes uncomfortable and at times agonizingly painful, and victims sometimes require hospitalization. During its active phase when sores appear, genital herpes can be transmitted to newborn babies. Obstetricians who are aware that the mother has the disease prefer to deliver the baby by Caesarean section so that the infant does not have to pass through the birth canal and thus be exposed to the herpes virus.

Two University of Pennsylvania researchers reported in *The Helper* in 1980 that "ocular herpes is the most common cause of infectious blindness in the United States." Irving Raber of the Scheie Eye Institute's Division of Corneal and External Diseases and Herbert A. Blough of the Division of Virology and Membrane Research said the cause can usually be traced to HSV-1, although HSV-2 has been implicated occasionally. In most cases, the virus affects the cornea — the window of the eye — causing keratitis, or inflammation of the corneal tissue.

Surgical treatment and chemotherapy are used, but the two researchers said, "One of the most difficult problems for both the doctor and the patient is the tendency for ocular herpes to recur." However, the disease does not affect both eyes unless the virus is transmitted to the previously uninvolved eye. They point out that HSV may also cause conjunctivitis ("pink eye"), uveitis (inflammation

of the middle coats of the eye), glaucoma, and cataracts.

The Helper reported that "inadvertent transmission by individuals with recurrent herpes lesions of the genitalia appears to be rare. To keep that risk at a minimum, regular use of soap and water before touching or rubbing the eyes should be strictly adhered to during the course of an attack."

Other forms. There are more than 50 herpes viruses known to affect humans. (Herpes is a Greek word meaning *creep.*) Another herpes virus that can be sexually transmitted is the cytomegalovirus (CMV), which NIAID describes as the most common known cause of fetal infections and the leading cause of deafness in newborns." In addition, CMV adds "at least 6,000 children a year to the ranks of disabled and retarded citizens."

NIAID said that this virus generally does not cause symptoms in the carrier and, even though large amounts of it are found in the genital tracts of women and in semen, it may be transmitted in nonsexual ways.

The Helper concluded, as a result of a survey of antiviral drug research, that the possibility of seeing treatment and preventive vaccine for herpes simplex disease in our lifetime "appears overwhelmingly optimistic."

King K. Holmes of the University of Washington and the U.S. Public Health Service Hospital in Seattle, who is chairman of the NIAID panel, reported that the growing number of diseases other than syphilis, gonorrhea, and other recognized sexually transmitted infections might be considered the "new generation" of these diseases. He cited "the dramatic increase in incidence of venereal disease caused by *Chlamydia trachomatis* and herpes simplex

Social Diseases are Soaring

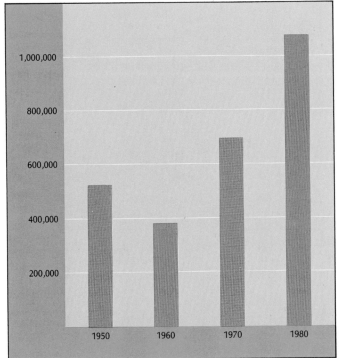

The annual number of venereal disease cases, after an encouraging drop between 1950 and 1960, soared over the following 20 years. More than 1 million cases were reported in 1980.

ganism causes more than half of the 500,000 annual cases of *epididymitis* (Inflammation of a tiny tube lying on the testes). Epididymitis may cause sterility.

And because of chlamydial infection, the panel reported, more than 11,000 women of childbearing age will become involuntarily sterilized each year and 3,600 will suffer ectopic pregnancies (development of the embryo outside the uterus), which account for 10 per cent of maternal deaths. Of the more than 155,000 infants born to chlamydia-infected mothers each year, the panel said, 75,000 develop conjunctivitis and 30,000 develop pneumonia. Chlamydia can be treated effectively, but diagnosis is complicated and expensive.

Gonorrhea vaccine. Further progress was reported in 1981 toward developing a gonorrhea vaccine. Researchers discovered that the bacteria that cause gonorrhea have pili, or hairlike proteins, on their surfaces that play a role in causing the disease. The researchers reported that gonorrhea vaccine made from killed gonorrhea bacteria failed to protect against the disease in the 1960s because it did not include the pili. Edward Tramont and Jerald C. Sadoff of the Walter Reed Army Institute of Research in Washington, D.C., and Charles Briton of the University of Pittsburgh tested a vaccine made of gonorrhea pili in 1980 and reported it was safe for humans and developed antibodies against the pili.

Robert Seid of Walter Reed and Dr. Sadoff reported at the annual meeting of the American Society for Microbiology in Dallas in 1981 that they tested a revised vaccine incorporating the pili in mice and found that it developed antibodies against the pili and against other important components of the gonorrhea bacterium called lipopoly-

virus," not only in North America but also in Europe.

"Owing to the lack of practical diagnostic tools, control techniques, and of specific treatment in some cases, the incidence of these diseases is increasing faster than that of gonorrhea or syphilis," he said. Holmes added that these diseases are contributing to miscarriages, infertility, infant illness and death, and maternal death.

Some researchers say that chlamydia is now the number-one sexually transmitted disease in the United States. It primarily affects heterosexual whites.

NIAID reported that more than 3 million Americans suffer the serious consequences of epidemic chlamydia infections each year and named it as "the major cause of nongonococcal urethritis in men, which is twice as common as gonorrhea." NIAID said the microor-

saccharides. This vaccine is yet to be tested in human beings.

NIAID reported that gonorrhea rates have been stabilized through efforts to control its spread, educational programs, and effective therapy. It added, however, that "It is likely that complete control of the disease will require development and deployment of an effective vaccine."

A vaccine against hepatitis B, another widespread sexually transmitted disease, has reached the stage of human testing and has been administered to homosexual volunteers at a number of centers in the United States. NIAID estimates that at least 500,000 persons are afflicted with the disease each year. It is particularly prevalent among homosexuals.

There are three types of hepatitis: A, B, and non-A, non-B hepatitis. The A-type virus can be transmitted through food and water; the B-type through blood transfusions and contaminated needles, as well as through sexual contact. The non-A, non-B type is transmitted mainly through transfusions. All forms of the disease affect the liver.

Immunization against hepatitis A with serum globulin "has been very effective," NIAID said. However, the agency questioned how well it worked to prevent hepatitis B.

Non-A, non-B hepatitis resembles type B more closely than type A. Among other things, it occurs following injection of blood or illicit drugs, occurs more commonly among the less affluent, and appears most often in homosexual men. Doctors know less about this virus than they do about the other two.   [Charles-Gene McDaniel]

Veterinary Medicine

Veterinarians in 1981 continued their campaign against canine parvovirus (CPV) disease, a viral infection that was unknown prior to 1978. CPV disease struck the United States dog population with devastating impact in the spring of that year.

Diagnosing and treating what quickly became an epidemic was complicated by the fact that the disease has two forms: a highly contagious enteritis, or inflammation of the intestine; and a heart condition that causes seemingly healthy puppies to die suddenly.

Combating CPV is one of the greatest concerns among veterinarians. For the past 2 1/2 years, scientists at Cornell University's James A. Baker Institute for Animal Health in Ithaca, N.Y., have conducted intensive research on CPV. They re-examined about 1,000 blood samples stored in a "serum library" at the institute and found no evidence that CPV had existed before mid-1978. This indicates that the virus is truly a new pathogen for dogs.

Veterinary researchers at Baker Institute's Research Laboratory for Diseases of Dogs have since learned what causes this disease and thus how to control it.

Signs of infection. Dogs with parvoviral enteritis usually stop eating and act depressed 12 to 24 hours before they show other indications of disease. Vomiting often occurs next, followed by diarrhea, which may become bloody. Most dogs run a fever; a pup's temperature may exceed 105°F. (a dog's normal temperature is 101.5°F.). A blood count often, but not always, reveals leukopenia, or a very low number of white blood cells.

The severity of illness varies even within a litter. Some puppies have such a mild illness that CPV may not even be recognized. Others become ill and die in spite of receiving good nursing care and having body fluids replaced. Young animals are more often severely affected, but dogs of all ages may die of CPV.

There are many causes of vomiting and diarrhea in dogs. To ensure accurate diagnosis and proper treatment, it is important that you seek veterinary advice and care whenever your dog shows severe depression, vomiting, and diarrhea. Animals with severe parvoviral enteritis need lots of fluids; treatment with antibiotic, antiemetic, and antidiarrheal drugs; and skilled nursing.

The other form of CPV causes myocarditis, or inflammation of the heart, in puppies less than 3 months old. Pups with CPV myocarditis may act depressed, gasp for breath, and stop suckling or eating shortly before they collapse. Death follows within minutes. A puppy may appear normal and yet die within hours. Others in the litter may die at intervals during the next several days.

Myocarditis, unlike enteritis, is not accompanied by diarrhea. The virus multiplies rapidly in muscle cells of the growing heart, and the heart weakens and fails. There is no effective treatment. Puppies that survive may have permanently damaged hearts. They may die of heart failure weeks or even months after they have recovered from the initial infection.

Transmitting the disease. CPV virus is transmitted mainly through the feces of infected dogs. More than 1 billion infectious virions, or virus particles, may be found in a diarrheal stool. A susceptible dog can become infected by eating less than 1/1,000 gram of infected fecal material.

The CPV virus is extremely stable and can survive for as long as six months after being passed in the stool. Thus, it can be readily transported on the hair or feet of infected dogs, by contaminated cages, and by shoes and other objects worn by people.

Even animals that have mild or undetected cases of the disease can shed millions of infectious virions in their stools. Thus, dogs may be a source of contagion wherever they are brought together, as in boarding kennels or at dog shows. Viruses remain in the stool for up to two weeks.

Fortunately, dogs that recover are immune to reinfection. Human beings cannot be infected by CPV but can transport the virus — on their clothes, for example.

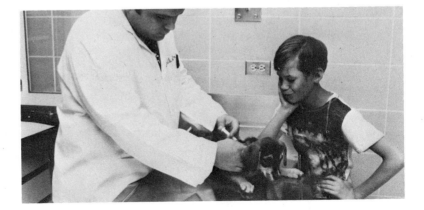

A veterinarian vaccinates a 2-month-old puppy against canine parvovirus, which can cause a fatal inflammation of either the heart or intestines.

Reducing the incidence. There are two basic procedures for the control of CPV. The first is scrupulous hygiene. Dogs should be housed in isolated kennels and those kennels should be cleaned thoroughly with large amounts of steaming hot water or chlorine solution. But even the best hygienic procedures are of limited value because CPV remains infectious for so long and is so highly concentrated in feces.

The second control measure is vaccination. Vaccines protect by stimulating the body to produce antibodies that fight the virus.

Researchers have developed four types of vaccine that fit into two categories — living vaccines and inactivated, or killed, vaccines. These are subdivided into the *heterologous* (immunologically related but not identical) and *homologous* (immunologically identical) types.

Examples of heterologous vaccination include cowpox virus, which protects people against smallpox; and measles virus, which protects puppies against distemper. A CPV heterologous vaccine is made from feline panleukopenia virus (FPV), a disease of cats. Homologous vaccination uses special strains of CPV itself.

Veterinary scientist Max J. J. Appel and his colleagues at Baker Institute demonstrated in October 1978 that FPV vaccines developed for cats can protect dogs against CPV. Although the feline virus is remarkably similar to CPV, there are subtle differences. The feline virus does not cause disease in dogs. Instead, antibodies form in response to the feline virus that neutralize CPV and protect dogs against infection.

Inactivated FPV was the first vaccine used to protect dogs against CPV. Because it had been used for many years to protect cats against feline distemper, it was readily available.

Chemically inactivated vaccines, both heterologous and homologous, now have been developed and licensed for the immunization of dogs against CPV. Both provide protection against CPV, but for an undetermined period. As with most killed vaccines, two injections are required. Periodic revaccinations, or booster shots, are necessary every six months.

Veterinary scientist Roy V. H. Pollock showed in laboratory studies that antibody levels that completely protect dogs from infection last for only a few weeks after a second injection of killed viral vaccine. Killed vaccines completely protect dogs only briefly, but the low levels of antibody that persist provide some protection against disease.

The period of protection varies. Blood tests can determine whether dogs require revaccination. In the absence of such tests, dogs should be revaccinated at least once every six months.

Another important fact about killed vaccines is that dogs inoculated with them and later exposed to CPV will transmit the infectious virions in their feces after a few weeks. Therefore, there is little prospect that killed vaccines could interrupt the spread of active virus in dense and rapidly changing dog populations, such as exist in breeding kennels.

Live heterologous vaccines. Live FPV vaccines confer longer-lasting immunity than do the killed types, provided they contain sufficient living virus. Dogs at the Baker Institute developed excellent immunity when inoculated with 1,000 times the amount of live FPV contained in many commercial vaccines produced for cats. Therefore, FPV vaccines licensed for dogs are now required to contain substantially more virus than are vaccines for cats.

Dogs become immune to CPV as early as five days after successful vaccination with live FPV, and most still have protective levels of antibody one year later.

Several commercial live-FPV vaccines for dogs have been licensed by the U.S. Department of Agriculture. Sometimes, FPV vaccine is combined with vaccine against canine distemper or hepatitis. Because not all dogs are successfully immunized with live-FPV vaccine after a single injection, two vaccinations should be given about three weeks apart. This procedure has a success rate of more than 80 per cent.

Live homologous vaccine. Researchers at the Baker Institute in 1980 developed a live-CPV vaccine. Its advantages over previous vaccines include a much smaller minimum immunizing dose than is required with live FPV; a greater number of antibodies created earlier; a more uniform response to vaccination; and longer immunity. Vaccinated dogs pass modified live CPV in their feces, but it can no longer cause disease.

Protecting puppies. There have been a number of reports of CPV occurring in vaccinated pups. Typi-

cally, the pups were vaccinated at 6, 8, and 10 weeks of age. Nevertheless, at 10 to 16 weeks of age, these pups get parvoviral enteritis, and some of them die from CPV infection. Vaccine failures of this kind result from the presence of antibodies to CPV in pups born to an immune mother. Such antibodies suppress the puppy's own response to vaccination or natural infection.

Unfortunately, there is no way to guarantee successful immunization of pups. However, we suggest that CPV vaccine be given at the same time as distemper shots — pups between the ages of 2 and 4 months should be vaccinated every two to three weeks.

Special precautions should be taken to avoid exposure of pups to virulent CPV during this critical period. In particular, kennel owners should be sure their older dogs are immunized with vaccines that interrupt the transmission of infectious virus.

Veterinary scientists have made rapid advances in dealing with a new virus, but many important aspects of CPV are not yet understood and improvements in control methods are needed. Researchers are continuing their efforts to subdue this serious threat to dogs. [Leland E. Carmichael]

Virus

Herpes viruses continued to occupy the spotlight in medical viral research in 1980 and 1981. Virologists estimate that more than 90 per cent of the population of the United States has been infected by some form of herpes virus by the age of 18.

The number of recognized cases of one such disease, genital herpes, has increased dramatically in recent years. The Centers for Dis-

ease Control in Atlanta, Ga., makes the conservative estimate that 300,000 new cases of this sexually transmitted disease occur each year in the United States. Other sources estimate the new cases to be in the millions. See Venereal Disease.

Identifying and tracking herpes viruses. At a meeting at Mount Sinai Medical Center in New York City in June 1981, researchers presented some of their findings on basic virus research to physicians in an effort to find practical applications for this research. Timothy Buchman of Johns Hopkins Hospital in Baltimore discussed a new method of determining the source of an infection of *herpes simplex,* the virus that causes cold sores and genital herpes.

This method can be useful in several situations. For example, if A gets a *herpes simplex* infection and B, who lives nearby, then gets a similar infection, how can we determine whether B got it from A? Or is there a third person who transmitted the disease to either A or B, or to both?

These questions are particularly difficult to answer about herpes viruses because these viruses can remain latent, or concealed and inactive, within tissues for a long time, then suddenly reappear as a seemingly new infection. So a herpes infection may be caused by a reactivated latent virus or it may be caught from another person. The answers to such questions are of more than academic significance. They can help researchers and epidemiologists understand and accurately trace the origin and spread of an outbreak.

The new method was developed in the laboratory of virologist Bernard Roizman, a herpes researcher at the University of Chicago. First, large numbers of *herpes simplex* viruses from A and B are raised, separately, in the laboratory. Then DNA, or genetic material, of these viruses, is isolated and treated with enzymes that break it into pieces. Finally, the DNA pieces derived from the two persons' viruses are put through a standard procedure that separates and concentrates the pieces into groups that form visible patterns.

If the patterns of the DNA pieces

from the viruses for A and B match, the viruses were genetically identical, and either one of the two persons transmitted the infection to the other or a third person transmitted it to both A and B. If the patterns are different, neither of these two situations is possible.

The new technique has turned up an interesting, but discouraging, fact about genital herpes: A person infected with one genetic type of *herpes simplex* can be infected simultaneously with a second genetic type. This is discouraging because it may make it impossible to create one effective vaccine against genital herpes.

Help for herpes victims. Rein Saral of Johns Hopkins University School of Medicine and his colleagues reported in July that a drug called acyclovir was effective against *herpes simplex* virus.

Few people realize that there have been only four drugs available in the United States to fight viruses, and their capabilities are quite limited. Methisazone fights smallpox virus; Amantadine fights influenza-A virus; Idoxuridene combats *herpes keratitis,* the leading cause of infectious blindness in young adults; and Ara-A fights herpes keratitis and encephalitis. Acyclovir promises to combat the herpes viruses that cause genital herpes, cold sores, chicken pox, and shingles.

Viruses damage the body by invading the cells and diverting their efforts and machinery from the processes that keep us alive and healthy to those that will help the viruses thrive. Thus they multiply, killing or damaging the cells they inhabit and occupying more cells until they are stopped by natural defenses or by a drug.

Acyclovir is inactive until it enters a cell infected by herpes viruses. There, a substance produced by

"You appear to have a touch of the flu—If you want a second opinion, I think you're pretty ugly."

children between 4 and 15 years old who have recently had a viral infection, such as flu or chicken pox. The disease damages the liver and makes the brain swell, sometimes causing brain damage. About 350 children in the United States have died of the disease since 1977, yet the cause of Reye's is unknown. Scientists have suspected that a virus is the culprit, but they cannot find one.

The researchers compared the medication used by 16 flu patients who recovered uneventfully with that used by seven flu patients who later developed Reye's syndrome. The study indicated that those who ultimately came down with Reye's syndrome used aspirin more frequently and in larger quantities than the other group. In addition, the more aspirin taken by those who later developed Reye's syndrome, the more severe the disease. The researchers ended their report with a caution against giving children aspirin when it was not absolutely necessary.

While the issue was still controversial in March 1981, the American Academy of Pediatrics magazine, *Pediatrics,* published a statement saying, "It should be emphasized that what has been demonstrated is an association only, and causation has not been established."

Also in March, a "Consensus Development Conference on the Diagnosis and Treatment of Reye's Syndrome" was held by the National Institutes of Health in Bethesda, Md. The conference concluded that all drugs have some bad effects and that caution is advisable when giving aspirin to children who have flu or chicken pox. But, the conference participants also suggested that further studies were advisable before changing therapy.   [Michael Reed]

the viruses themselves converts acyclovir to a monophosphate, a substance that inhibits the viruses' ability to make genetic material and so stops their reproduction.

However, acyclovir is promising only for control of herpes infections, not for their prevention or cure. The drug does not combat latent, or temporarily inactive, herpes viruses, which do not produce the substance that converts acyclovir to a monophosphate.

Aspirin and Reye's syndrome. Karen M. Starko of the Centers for Disease Control and several colleagues who worked with her in Arizona during a flu outbreak, reported on Dec. 6, 1980, that the use of aspirin was linked to a disease called Reye's syndrome. This report caused substantial furor, and the shock waves it generated are unlikely to subside for many months.

Reye's syndrome typically strikes

Scientists at the Eye Research Institute in Boston in 1980 produced three new instruments in which lasers — generators of narrow and intense beams of light — were used for diagnostic eye tests. Tatsuo Hirose developed an instrument that uses a weak laser beam to illuminate a tiny area of the retina — the part of the eye that transmits images to the optic nerve when stimulated by light — and take a precise measurement of that area's response to light. The new instrument enables ophthalmologists to diagnose many eye problems that affect only small parts of the retina.

The second instrument, the television ophthalmoscope, developed by Robert Webb, also uses a weak laser beam to scan the retina. The light reflected back is used to produce a television picture of a patient's retina. This image can be transmitted over telephone lines during consultations between ophthalmologists.

A third device developed at the Eye Research Institute — the Retinal Laser Doppler Velocimeter — accurately measures the speed of red blood cells moving through vessels in the retina. Because the eye is the one place in the body where blood circulation can be observed without performing surgery,

the instrument makes it possible to detect early signs of diabetes, hypertension, heart disease, and other disorders involving changes in blood circulation.

New contact lenses. Silcon, a new type of contact lens combining the advantages of hard and soft lenses, was introduced by Dow-Corning Corporation in 1981. The new lens is as durable as a soft lens, but holds its shape better. If a lens warps, an overnight stay in the small container with a heating unit that is provided with the lenses will restore its form.

Wearers of most hard lenses find that their eyes become irritated when they wear the lenses for long periods of time. This is because these lenses allow little oxygen to reach the cornea — the transparent outer covering of the eyeball — and the cornea begins to swell after 12 to 16 hours of wear. The Silcon lens permits oxygen to permeate to the cornea, reducing swelling and allowing the wearer to keep them in for a longer period.

Experimental eye surgery. The National Eye Institute is conducting a study of an experimental procedure to correct nearsightedness surgically. Nearsightedness results when the lens — the transparent structure that focuses light on the retina — is curved too much, or the eyeball is too long. Either condition focuses the light rays in front of the retina, rather than on it.

In the experimental procedure, known as radial keratotomy, the surgeon makes as many as 16 deep cuts in a wheelspoke pattern in the cornea. This flattens the cornea, so that it bends the light passing through the eye at a different angle. The flatter cornea compensates for the curvature of the lens or too long eyeball, to focus images on the retina. In the study, conducted

A radial keratotomy, an operation to correct nearsightedness, results in a number of spoke-like slits in the cornea. The experimental surgical procedure is a source of controversy among ophthalmologists.

at Emory University in Atlanta, Ga., physicians performed keratotomies on one eye on each of 400 patients. If no problems develop within a year, they will operate on the second eye.

One of the ophthalmologists performing the surgery, Peter Brazis of Central DuPage Hospital in Winfield, Ill., says keratotomies are undesirable for patients who can wear glasses or contact lenses, and the surgery may not eliminate the need to wear glasses for full vision. Although about 2,000 persons in the United States and 3,000 Russians have had keratotomies, long-term effects are as yet unknown, and the National Advisory Eye Council reported in 1981 that there is not enough scientific evidence to indicate whether the operation is safe and effective. See *Surgery*.

Gel protects eye cells. Ophthalmologists in 1980 announced that some eye surgery patients were seeing better thanks to a clear jelly from rooster combs. Surgeons at Harkness Eye Institute in New York City found that after cataract removal, lens implantation, and retinal surgery, the gel – sodium hyaluronate – can protect the 250,000 fragile, transparent endothelial cells that line the back of the cornea and supply it with nutrients.

The gel is injected behind the cornea through a hair-thin needle. It becomes the main component of the vitreous humor, which fills the interior cavity of the eyeball behind the lens and in front of the retina. Without the gel, half of the endothelial cells might be damaged during lens surgery. When the gel is injected during surgery, only 17 per cent of these cells are injured.   [Eleanor Dunn]

Weight Control

A report by Harvard Medical School researchers in late 1980 supports the claims of many overweight people that they cannot lose weight on normal reducing diets and that they gain weight even when they eat only moderately. According to the Harvard study, such people may be victims of a biochemical defect in the body mechanism that "burns" food to provide energy.

Central to the study is an enzyme called sodium-potassium-ATPase, or simply ATPase. This substance acts as a sort of chemical pump, adjusting the body's levels of sodium and potassium by moving them across the membrane – and, therefore, in and out – of every living cell.

In people of normal weight, ATPase works so hard that it consumes a full 20 to 50 per cent of daily food intake. The medical investigators believe that overweight people may not be expending as much energy as most people do through ATPase activity. The result, of course, is that less food is used up and, naturally, weight is gained.

In the study, the Harvard researchers compared the amounts of ATPase in the cells of 20 overweight people and 20 people of normal weight. The overweight group had markedly lower levels of ATPase in their cells. Perhaps even more telling, the heavier the person, the lower the level of ATPase in their cells.

The study may have important implications beyond understanding weight gain. Since ATPase and its activities are linked to other biological processes, further study along these lines may uncover important details about disorders such as heart disease, high blood pressure,

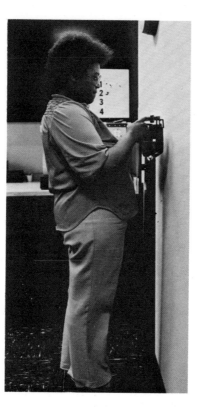

A woman checks her weight in the constant battle against extra pounds. In many people, obesity may not be due simply to overeating but to a complex biochemical defect.

and diabetes, which are particularly common among overweight people.

A no-fill pill? Scientists at the National Institutes of Health in Bethesda, Md., may have discovered a drug that will help dieters as much or more than drugs now available and without undesirable side effects. The drug, naloxone, was given to some young, specially bred, mice that normally become very fat. These mice and a similar group not getting the drug were then allowed to eat as much as they desired. After five weeks, the mice given naloxone had gained much less weight than those not getting the drug.

The tests were carried out because naloxone is known to block the effects of the natural body chemicals called endorphins. At least one of these endorphins can trigger overeating, evidently by stimulating the pancreas to secrete insulin. Insulin then does its normal job of lowering the amount of blood sugar, which signals the brain that more food is needed.

But will naloxone work on overweight humans? Richard L. Atkinson an endocrinologist at the University of Virginia is taking the first step to find the answer. He is treating overweight people with naloxone, then measuring their insulin levels. If their insulin levels go down, a pill that keeps people from overeating safely and, thus, controls weight may not be far off.

Weight and blood pressure. People who have high blood pressure and are overweight are commonly advised to lose weight and consume less salt. Many doctors believe that decreasing the amount of salt in the diet is more important than weight loss in reducing blood pressure. In April 1981, a team of researchers from the University of California, Los Angeles, and the Veterans Administration Medical Center in Sepulveda, Calif., reported an experiment that contradicts this assumption.

The scientists put 25 overweight people on strict 12-week reducing diets. Fifteen members of the group got normal amounts of salt, while 10 of them received only one-third as much. As expected, all 25 people lost weight, but two other interesting findings were not expected. First blood pressure dropped significantly equally well in both groups. Second, a 10- to 30-per cent reduction in body weight lowered blood pressure significantly. In fact, only 6 of the 25 overweight subjects reached ideal weight during the study, but all showed significant drops in blood pressure, including 12 persons who entered the study with high blood pressure levels and left the study with normal levels. [Michael Reed]

How Well Do You Know Your Body?

A Quiz for the Medically Curious

1. The body's largest organ is the: **(a)** liver, **(b)** stomach, **(c)** large intestine, **(d)** small intestine, **(e)** none of the above.

2. The color of a person's eyes is determined by: **(a)** the amount of brown pigment, **(b)** the amount of green pigment, **(c)** the amount of blue pigment, in the iris.

3. A cross section of a strand of naturally curly hair, when seen under a microscope, is: **(a)** flat, **(b)** round, **(c)** square.

4. The skin that is most sensitive to touch is that on the: **(a)** back of the neck, **(b)** navel, **(c)** fingertips.

5. Objects are often suspended in fluid to protect them from shocks. Which of the following body organs is contained in a biological shock absorption system? **(a)** the eye, **(b)** the brain and spinal cord, **(c)** the kneecap.

6. The total surface area of the lungs that is involved in exchanging gases is about the size of a: **(a)** city block, **(b)** football field, **(c)** tennis court.

7. The body replaces 2.5 million worn-out red blood cells each: **(a)** week, **(b)** day, **(c)** second.

8. The skin regulates body temperature by: **(a)** sweating, **(b)** flushing, **(c)** breaking out in goosebumps, **(d)** all of the above, **(e)** none of the above.

9. On the average, all of a person's permanent teeth will have formed in the jaw by the time he is **(a)** two, **(b)** four, **(c)** six, **(d)** eight, years old.

10. When people are having a good cry, tears stream down their cheeks. However, if the occasion only warrants moist eyes, the excess tears: **(a)** evaporate into the air, **(b)** drain into the nose, **(c)** are not produced in the first place.

11. Hunger strikers may appear to have sunken eyes because: **(a)** the muscles behind the eye have become wasted, drawing the eye back into the socket, **(b)** the facial bones protrude more in contrast, **(c)** the fat behind the eyeball is depleted.

12. The average man is taller than the average woman because: **(a)** men's digestive systems make better use of the minerals that form bones, **(b)** male hormones do not work as quickly as female hormones to stop bone growth, **(c)** the male chromosome carries a gene for longer bones.

13. Men and women have different distributions of body fat. Which is characteristic of men more than women? **(a)** an accumulation of fat above the belt, **(b)** fat on the upper thighs, **(c)** relatively little fat on the side of the abdomen.

14. In general, even when extended straight out, a woman's arm curves slightly in from the elbow, while a man's arm does not. This is so because: **(a)** the woman's pelvis is wider, and the greater angle at the elbow enables it to clear the body, **(b)** the muscles of a woman's arm are distributed differently, **(c)** the man's arm has proportionately larger bones that pull on the elbow, resulting in a straighter arm.

15. A man's voice is usually deeper than a woman's because: **(a)** the throat and mouth are wider to provide greater resonance, **(b)** the larynx or voice box is larger and farther forward in the man's neck, **(c)** women generally have smaller noses, giving their speech a higher-pitched nasal quality.

16. When a person dies his last breath will be: **(a)** inhaled, **(b)** exhaled, **(c)** gulped, **(d)** accompanied by a rattling noise.

Answers to quiz appear on page 250.

Family Health and Medical Records

This section of *Medical Update* is designed to give you a place for recording vital health information about each family member. At a glance, you can find the pediatrician's telephone number, see when every member of the family last had a dental checkup, and keep an organized tally of medical and dental costs that can be deducted from your income tax.

In addition, this year's *Medical Update* contains a special Family Health History section. We have included this because doctors are finding that many diseases have genetic links, that is, they tend to run in families. Therefore, it is important for you to know what disorders your relatives had.

The Health History section has two parts, one for each parent to fill out. When completed, this section will provide not only an easy reference for your own medical history, but will also be an invaluable guide for your children — and perhaps your grandchildren — in determining their genetic inheritance.

Items in this section include:

Visits to the Doctor and Dentist

Drugs Administered or Prescribed

Family X-Ray Records

Annual Family Health Appraisal and
Vital Information

Mother's and Father's Family Health History

Emergency Telephone Numbers and Addresses

239

Visits to the Doctor and Dentist

Family Member	Date	Specialist

Reason	Treatment	Cost

Drugs Administered
or Prescribed

Family Member	Date	Drug	Cost

Family X-Ray Records

Family Member	Body Part X-rayed	Reason	Date

Annual Family
Health Appraisal and
Vital Information

Family Member	Age	Height	Weight	Blood Pressure

Blood Type	Allergies	Eye Lens Prescription	Other

Mother's Family Health History

	Name	If Deceased Date	Age	Cause of Death
Mother				
Father				
Maternal Grandmother				
Maternal Grandfather				
Paternal Grandmother				
Paternal Grandfather				
Brothers				
Sisters				

Father's Family Health History

	Name	If Deceased Date	Age	Cause of Death
Mother				
Father				
Maternal Grandmother				
Maternal Grandfather				
Paternal Grandmother				
Paternal Grandfather				
Brothers				
Sisters				

Chronic Illnesses

Diabetes	Heart Disease	Cancer	Asthma or Allergies	Arthritis	Other

Chronic Illnesses

Diabetes	Heart Disease	Cancer	Asthma or Allergies	Arthritis	Other

Emergency Telephone
Numbers and Addresses

	Phone	Address
Family Doctor		
Other Specialists		
Dentist		
Optometrist		
Veterinarian		
Local Hospital		
Fire Department		
Police		
Local Ambulance Service		
Local Health Department		
Other Important Numbers		

Index

This index covers the contents of the 1982 edition of *Medical Update,* the *World Book* Family Health Annual.

An index entry that is the title of an article appearing in *Medical Update* is printed in boldface italic letters: ***Cancer.*** An entry that is not an article title, but a subject discussed in an article of some other title, is printed: **Herpes virus.**

The various "See" and "See also" cross references in the index are to other entries within the index:

> **Operation.** See ***Surgery.***

Clue words or phrases are used when two or more references to the same subject appear in *Medical Update* or when the entry needs further definition:

> **Ara-A (drug):** virus, 232

The indication "*il.*" means that the reference is to an illustration only:

> **Spirometer,** *il.,* 174

A

Answers to Quiz

1. (e) The skin is the largest organ. 2. (a) 3. (a) 4. (c) 5. (b) 6. (b)
7. (c) 8. (d) 9. (b) 10. (b) This accounts for the sniffles that often
accompany teary eyes. 11. (c) 12. (b) 13. (a) 14. (a) 15. (b) 16. (b)

251

Lung cancer: cigarette smoking, *Medical Report,* 94

Lupus: arthritis, *Medical Report,* 63

Lyme arthritis: arthritis, *Medical Report,* 69

Lymphocytes: multiple sclerosis, 208

Lymphoma: cancer, *Medical Report,* 122

M

Macrophage: multiple sclerosis, 210

Magnetrode: cancer, 187

Mammogram: cancer, *Medical Report,* 124

Mastectomy: second opinion, *Medical Report,* 109

Medical Costs, *chart,* 196

Medical Records, 239

Medroxyprogesterone acetate: sleep disorders, 218

Melanoma: cancer, *Medical Report,* 125

Meniscectomy: sports medicine, 219

Meniscus: sports medicine, 219

Menopause: headache, *Medical Report,* 161

Menstrual irregularity: sports medicine, 220

Menstruation: headache, *Medical Report,* 161

Mental Health, 206

Mesothelioma: cancer, *Medical Report,* 125

Metabolism: burns, *Medical Report,* 36

Methapyrilene: cancer, *Medical Report,* 124

Methisazone: virus, 232

Methylene chloride: cancer, *Medical Report,* 123

Methylphenidate: hyperactivity, 202

Midwives: childbirth, 189

Migraine: headache, *Medical Report,* 157

Minimal brain dysfunction: hyperactivity, 202

Monocyclic disease: arthritis, *Medical Report,* 63

Monocytes: multiple sclerosis, 210

Monophosphate: virus, 233

Montezuma's revenge: digestive disorders, 191

Mortality rates: cancer, *Medical Report,* 118; cigarette smoking, *Medical Report,* 95; high blood pressure, 201; hospices, *Medical Report,* 140

Mouthwash: gum disease, *Medical Report,* 77

Multiple Sclerosis (MS), 208

Muriatic acid: Beaumont, William, *Medical Report,* 134

Muscle tension: headache, *Medical Report,* 165

Mutagen: cancer, *Medical Report,* 122

Myelin: multiple sclerosis, 208

Myocardial infarction (MI): aspirin, *Medical Report,* 28

Myocarditis: veterinary medicine, 229

Myopia: surgery, 222

N

N'-nitrosonornicotine (NNN): cancer, 186

Naloxone: weight control, 236

National Hospice Organization (NHO): hospices, *Medical Report,* 141

National Migraine Foundation: headache, *Medical Report,* 169

Nearsightedness: vision, 234

Neonatal hydrocephalus: surgery, 224

Nervous system: multiple sclerosis, 208

Neurology, 211

Nicorette (gum): cigarette smoking, *Medical Report,* 101

Nicotine chewing gum: cigarette smoking, *Medical Report,* 101

Nifedipine: drugs, 193

Night splint: burns, *Medical Report,* 40; *il.,* 40

Nitrite: cancer, *Medical Report,* 124

257

Acknowledgments

The publishers of *Medical Update* gratefully acknowledge the courtesy of the following artists, photographers, publishers, institutions, agencies, and corporations for the illustrations in this volume. Credits should be read from top to bottom, left to right, on their respective pages. All entries marked with an asterisk (*) denote illustrations or photographs created exclusively for *Medical Update*.

2	*Medical Update* photo by Daniel D. Miller*
12	*Medical Update* photo; Mackinac Island State Park Commission; Snowdon, Camera Press from Photo Trends
14	John Senzer, *Medical World News*
17	American Diabetes Association (*Medical Update* photo)
18	Zorica Dabich*
20	American Diabetes Association (*Medical Update* photo)
21	Bio-Dynamics, Inc.; Bio-Dynamics, Inc.; Bio-Dynamics, Inc.; American Diabetes Association (*Medical Update* photo)
22	Miles Laboratories, Inc.; R. Philip Eaton, University of New Mexico
23	Damon Corporation
24-27	*Medical Update* photos
29	Zorica Dabich*
32	*Medical Update* photo
34	Terry Cockerham, University of Texas Health Science Center
37	Zorica Dabich*
39	Terry Cockerham, University of Texas Health Science Center; © Dan McCoy, Rainbow
40-42	Terry Cockerham, University of Texas Health Science Center
43	Terry Cockerham, University of Texas Health Science Center; © Dan McCoy, Black Star
44	Terry Cockerham, University of Texas Health Science Center
46	© Peter Simon, Picture Group
49	U.S. Drug Enforcement Agency; © Curt Gunther, Camera 5; U.S. Drug Enforcement Agency
50	Barbara Van Cleve, Atoz Images
52	© William C. Pierce, Rainbow
55-56	Patrick Chauvel, Sygma
58	Rehabilitation Institute of Chicago (Ovie Carter, *Chicago Tribune*)
60-61	Zorica Dabich*
62	Radiology Dept., University of Illinois Medical Center
63	Children's Memorial Hospital (Ovie Carter, *Chicago Tribune*)
64	Rehabilitation Institute of Chicago (Ovie Carter, *Chicago Tribune*)
66	Bettmann Archive, Inc.; Arthritis Foundation, Chicago; Arthritis Foundation, Chicago
67-70	*Medical Update* photos
73	Zorica Dabich*
74-92	*Medical Update* photos
96	Chicago Lung Association; *Medical Update* photo
97	American Cancer Society
98	*Medical Update* photo; *Medical Update* photo; *Medical Update* photo; *Medical Update* photo; American Cancer Society
100	Richard Manning, Sygma; *Medical Update* photo by Joseph A. Erhardt*; National Institute of Child Health and Human Development
101	*Medical Update* photo by Brent Jones*
103	American Cancer Society
104	*Medical Update* photos
112	© Bill Benoit, Atoz Images
113	*Medical Update* photo
116	*Medical Update* photo by Daniel D. Miller*
119	American Cancer Society
120	*Medical Update* photo
121	Dominick's Food Stores; Milt and Joan Mann; Robert H. Glaze, Artstreet
123	Al Henderson, Atoz Images; Robert H. Glaze, Artstreet
125	*Medical Update* photo by Joseph A. Erhardt*; Gerry Souter, Atoz Images
128	Mackinac Island State Park Commission

Cyclo-teacher® The easy-to-use learning system

Features hundreds of cycles from seven valuable learning areas

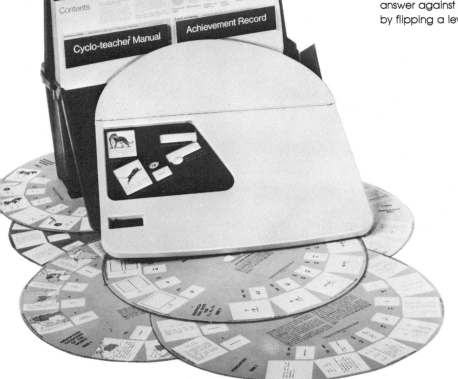

Silent Cycle

makes physical fitness surprisingly easy!

Now, you don't have to worry about inconveniences of bad weather or the time it takes to change and travel to your gym. With the Silent Cycle you can trim off inches and stay in good shape in the privacy and comfort of your own home,

Burn off hundreds of calories quickly and easily!

We all know how important it is to be in good shape. Exercise can help you look better and feel better. And doctors agree that a regular exercise program can burn off calories, curb appetite and strengthen the heart muscles —maybe even help prevent cardiovascular disease. Bicycling at only 5½ m.p.h. can use up more than 200 calories per hour!

Now you can exercise as often as you want, as long as you want. And because of its unique "Silent Features" you don't have to disturb others. Listen to music or even watch TV while cycling.

Silent...Safe...Comfortable

Exclusive automotive-type tension control featuring graphite pads. No thumping. Tension is applied directly to the pedal axle. NOT the front tire.

Patented elastomer drive belt. Quiet operation plus "lifetime" durability. Never needs adjusting. Belt is covered (not shown here) for rider protection.

Heavy-duty machined pedal crank assembly rides smoothly in self-lubricating industrial bearings.

Speedometer/odometer provides ongoing readout of speed and distance. Operates quietly.